Christopher Knowles, born in Essex, has spent much of his adult life abroad. He has taught English in France and Italy and led groups of tourists in many countries of the world from Albania to Zimbabwe. His enthusiasm for foreign places remains undiminished.

He has visited Shanghai literally scores of times and having been frustrated by the absence of effective guidebooks, he decided to write his own.

In 1985 he was one of the first westerners for 39 years to cross the frontier from Soviet Kazakstan into Chinese Turkestan.

When not leading tourist groups he is working on his next book which will cover travels in western Russia.

To my brother Simon

Acknowledgements

Many people have shown interest and kindness in the production of this book. My thanks to my wife Ming for her patience and calligraphy, to many friends with or formerly with Voyages Jules Verne especially Lescek, Sharon, John, Peter, Doug, Joshua and Elaine; to Cultural Tours for assistance in Hong Kong and Shanghai; to Roberta at Kuoni Travel for timely employment; to Johnson Yul and Shi Ting Liang and family of Shanghai; to the staff of the British Consulate in Shanghai for useful hints; to Ni Lian Sheng of Hangzhou; to Yvonne Messenger for helpful and patient editing; and to other friends and acquaintances who were sensible enough to show no interest whatsoever and take me to the pub instead.

A Request

Shanghai and China are undergoing tumultuous changes, and it is hard to keep up with them. Any observations and suggestions will be warmly welcomed by the publisher and author. Not only experiences of contemporary Shanghai are useful but also experiences of old Shanghai, either personal or those of friends or relatives, especially those which help to identify old buildings that are still standing. Please write to Christopher Knowles, c/o the publisher (address on the title page). A free copy of the new edition will be sent to those making a significant contribution.

Front Cover: *A view of the Bund and harbour showing the old Cathay Hotel (on the left) and the Bank of China building.*

SHANGHAI

REDISCOVERED

A guide to the city past and present

Christopher Knowles

Roger Lascelles, Cartographic and Travel Publisher
47 York Road, Brentford, Middlesex TW8 0QP.   Tel: 081 847 0935

Publication Data

Title	Shanghai Rediscovered
Typeface	Phototypeset in Compugraphic Times
Photographs	By the Author
Printing	Kelso Graphics, Kelso, Scotland.
ISBN	0 903909 75 8
Edition	First July 1990
Publisher	Roger Lascelles
	47 York Road, Brentford, Middlesex, TW8 0QP.
Copyright	Christopher Knowles

Distribution

Africa:	South Africa —	Faradawn, Box 17161, Hillbrow 2038
Americas:	Canada —	International Travel Maps & Books, P.O. Box 2290, Vancouver BC V6B 3W5
	U.S.A. —	Boerum Hill Books, P.O. Box 286, Times Plaza Station, Brooklyn, NY 11217, (718-624-4000).
Asia:	India —	English Book Store, 17-L Connaught Circus/P.O. Box 328, New Delhi 110 001
	Singapore —	Graham Brash Pte Ltd., 36-C Prinsep St
Australasia:	Australia —	Rex Publications, 413 Pacific Highway, Artarmon NSW 2064. 428 3566
Europe:	Belgium —	Brussels - Peuples et Continents
	Germany —	Available through major booksellers with good foreign travel sections
	GB/Ireland —	Available through all booksellers with good foreign travel sections
	Italy —	Libreria dell'Automobile, Milano
	Netherlands —	Nilsson & Lamm BV, Weesp
	Denmark —	Copenhagen - Arnold Busck, G.E.C. Gad, Boghallen, G.E.C. Gad
	Finland —	Helsinki — Akateeminen Kirjakauppa
	Norway —	Oslo - Arne Gimnes/J.G. Tanum
	Sweden —	Stockholm/Esselte, Akademi Bokhandel, Fritzes, Hedengrens Gothenburg/Gumperts, Esselte Lund/Gleerupska
	Switzerland —	Basel/Bider: Berne/Atlas; Geneve/Artou; Lausanne/Artou: Zurich/Travel Bookshop

Contents

Recent Events 8

Introducing Shanghai 9

Part 1: Preparation

1 Before you go
Group/individual travel 11 — Passports and
visas 13 — Advance reservations 15 — Prices 15
— Health and vaccinations 17 — Climate 18

2 Getting there
By air 21 — **Map - The Far East 23** — By rail
24 — By sea 25

3 What to take
Clothes 27 — Luggage 28 — Money 28 —
Photography 29 — Presents 32 — Food 33 —
Cigarettes and alcohol 33 — Books 34

Part 2: Practical information for visitors

4 Arrivals and departures
More forms to fill in 35 — Arrival by air 36 —
Arrival by rail 37 — Arrival by sea 38 —
Chinese currency 39 — Leaving Shanghai 40

5 Local transport
Taxis 43 — Car rental 44 — Buses and
trolleybuses 44 — Bicycles 45

6 Accommodation
What to expect 47 — Downtown 48 — Central
50 — Suburban 55 — Others 58 — Electricity
58

7 Eating out
Prices 59 — Banquets 60 — Chopsticks 62 —
Shanghai cuisine 62 — Some aspects of Chinese
cooking 63 — Drinks 65 — Where to eat 66 —
Snacks, dumplings and pastries 72 — Western
snacks 74

8 Etiquette
Tipping 75 — Clapping 77 — Speeches 77 —
Patience is a virtue 77 — Taboos 77

9 Entertainment and recreation
The Peace Hotel 79 — The circus 79 — Chinese
opera 80 — Concerts 82 — Cinemas 82 —
Discotheques 82 — Cafés and bars 84 — Sport
84 — Other diversions 86

10 Useful addresses
Airline offices 87 — Banks 87 — Boats, ships,
etc 88 — Business 88 — Churches and places of
worship 89 — Clubs 89 — Consulates 90 —
Dentists, doctors and hospitals 90 — Exhibition
centres 90 — Film studio 91 — Library 91 —
Police 91 — Post and communications 91 —
Railway station 91 — Taxis 91 — Travel 92 —
Universities 92

11 Shopping
Friendship stores 94 — Antiques 95 — Arts and
crafts 96 — Silk 98 — Tailoring 99 — Carpets
99 — Jade 101 — Other shops 101 — Sending
things home 103

Part 3: Shanghai: a background

12 A brief history
Humble beginnings 105 — The Foreign Devils
arrive 106 — Down to business 107 — Growing
up 108 — A model settlement 109 — The Devils
at their ease 110 — **Map - Shanghai before 1949**
118-119 — All good things ... 120 —
Revolutionary Shanghai 125 — Aftermath 133

13 Shanghai hands
The Soongs 137 — Pockmarked Huang and
Big-eared Du 141 — Several Sassoons and a
Hardoon 143 — Sir Robert Hart and the
Chinese Customs Service 148

14 Economy
Industry 153 — Commerce 154 — Finance and trade 154 — Silk production 155 — Agriculture 157 — The cultivation of rice 158

15 An aspect of Chinese life: acupuncture
The theory 161 — Diagnosis and treatment 163 — Moxibustion 163

Part 4: What to see

16 The former Concession areas
The Bund and environs 166 — Nanking Road 178 — The race course 182 — Along and around the Bubbling Well Road 184 — Shanghai Industrial Exhibition 188 — Jing An Temple 189 — The Children's Palace 191 — The vicinity of the Nanking Road 192 — The French Concession 198.

17 The old town and the Yu Garden
The Chinese Bund, a market, and the way to the old town 213 — The Temple of the City God 214 — The Yu Garden 217 — Out of the old town 219

18 Visits and excursions
The Jade Buddha Temple 221 — Parks 223 — Shanghai Zoo 226 — Museums 226 — Arts and Crafts Research Institute 228 — Touring the Huangpu River 228 — Pudong 229 — Ziccawei Catholic Cathedral 230

19 Farther afield
Jiading 231 — Jinshan 232 — Qingpu 232 — **Map - Shanghai region** 233 — Songjiang 234 — And beyond... 234 — Suzhou 235 — Wuxi 236 — Changzhou 236 — Nanking 237 — The Grand Canal 237 — Yangtse Cruise 238 — Hangzhou 238 — Ningbo 239

Index 241

Map - Shanghai after 1949   246

Recent events

Following the events of June 1989, both prices and timetabling, particularly of international flights, are subject to change. Thus most prices in this guidebook date from before June 1989 (although there has been a 20% reduction in costs at the moment) and some of the flights have been suspended (British Airways to Peking for example) but are included here in the expectation that things are likely to return to normal fairly soon.

Introducing Shanghai

The recent brutal suppression of the student protest movement has left a sour taste in foreign mouths. For a while events in Peking and in other cities, including Shanghai, seemed to presage another period of introspection. The Middle Kingdom seemed to be turning in on itself yet again. Fortunately the government has made it plain that China intends to pursue its 'open door' policy, and is once again encouraging foreign visitors. Analysis of what happened in 1989 and what is likely to happen can only be speculative in a country where tradition, secrecy and corruption are indivisibly bound together. China had developed a reputation for being the 'cuddly' country of Communism, all Pandas and paddy fields. The Tian An Men massacre has at least served the purpose of forcing visitors to look beneath the glossy surface of luxury hotels and slick, glib smiles.

In that superficial sense, life in China is returning to normal. Foreign newspapers, banned immediately after the government had re-established complete control, are back on sale. So great is the need for foreign currency that prices which had climbed to ridiculous proportions have come tumbling down. There will now be seats on trains and aeroplanes, and space to enjoy the Shanghai Bund and the Jade Buddha. For the visitor there can be no better time to visit China and Shanghai. These are interesting times.

The mention of a great city conjures up an image. Rome may bring to mind the Colosseum; New York, skyscrapers; Istanbul, a scarlet sunset behind the silhouette of a slender minaret. And Shanghai? Everything is in the name. To be shanghaied is to be 'drugged and shipped as a sailor when unconscious'. Shanghai evokes the underworld, mobsters and sleazy quay side bars. It is also glamour, fizz, style, the Orient — in short it has mystique. It became a legend in the space of a hundred years, until the Second World War and the coming of Mao gutted its personality. Yet over forty years later the name has still a certain resonance.

It is tempting to wonder whether the legend was nothing more than the figment of some Hollywood director's imagination. The cinema is not beyond allowing invention to masquerade as historical fact. Perhaps our imaginations have forever been caught by Marlene Dietrich in *'Shanghai Express'*. More recently the opening sequences of the film *'Indiana Jones and the Temple of Doom'* were set in Shanghai. Films of the genre have tended to linger on the ritzy side of old Shanghai and to ignore the grimmer aspects. This is not to say that the glamour was not really there. Shanghai was without doubt an outrageously exciting city, dependent, however, on a set of freak circumstances which are unlikely to combine again.

The history of Shanghai stretches back well before the coming of the Europeans, but it was their presence that transformed a moderately important port into a dazzling metropolis. Shanghai became part of the unique phenomenon of concession ports. The 19th century was an era of expansion for the major European powers but they had no wish to colonise China. They needed only to have the use of certain strategically placed ports like Shanghai. A weak Chinese government gave in and ceded areas of land to the foreigners where they most wanted them. Thus, the Concession came into being, and with it the notion of extraterritoriality. Shanghai was born again, to become a city of extraordinary contrasts, partly Chinese, partly European. It grew quickly, shone brightly and as quickly vanished.

Indeed part of the fascination of Shanghai lies in the recentness of its rise and fall; There was a way of life so out of the ordinary that it may just as well have been medieval, and yet it was all happening a mere forty years ago. Many people who were part of old Shanghai are still living.

The Shanghai of today cannot be compared with the Shanghai of before 1949. It is now wholly Chinese run; those peculiar circumstances no longer exist. Life is altogether more restrained. Yet, remarkably enough, almost all the present city dates back to before 1949. Everything you see is a legacy from those heady days. Most of the buildings have their own story, from mock-Tudor villa to bank headquarters to bar and brothel. If they now serve different purposes they remain as material associations of a lost era. They are Shanghai. Happily the policy of the local government is to preserve them, but without, fortunately, turning the city into a theme park. Despite some stumbles, Shanghai is being revitalised on its own terms but without sacrificing the aura and memory of its past. The character of modern China combines with a unique history in Shanghai to produce a singular city.

ONE

Before you go

Group/individual travel

Whether to travel in a group or not depends on your itinerary in China, your age and health, the time at your disposal, and the money you want to spend. Broadly speaking, there are three ways of visiting China — in a group with a fixed itinerary and provisions for guides, hotels and transportation; travelling alone, but with everything arranged in advance through a tour operator or through one of the Chinese travel services; or travelling alone armed only with visa, and ticket to first port of call. The first option is for those people who want to be able to visit a variety of places in a reasonable amount of time for a reasonable amount of money, with most of the problems eliminated; the second for those who want the same but who can afford the additional expense of travelling alone; and the third for those who need to travel as cheaply as possible, or who want their visit to China to bring them as close as possible to the way of life of the Chinese, and who perhaps have more time at their disposal.

Although it has become easier in recent years, extensive independent travel in China without the security of a pre-arranged itinerary is not for the faint-hearted. Aeroplane and train tickets are often hard to come by, hotels difficult to book in advance, and the standard of service somewhat variable. Many people travel about China this way, however, and find it highly rewarding, but fitness, determination and patience are vital prerequisites. If in doubt it is far better to go in a group or pay for a bespoke itinerary that is organised in advance.

Shanghai, however, is easy on all counts. Most package tours include it on their itineraries, and at the same time it is one of the Chinese cities that is comparatively easy to visit alone. It is, for example, ideal for someone visiting Hong Kong and who wants to sample a little of China, but who wants to go farther afield than

Canton. Visas can be easily obtained in Hong Kong, Shanghai is served by plane, train, and ship, there are any number of hotels where rooms can be reserved in advance by telex or by telephone, and it is a city that can be explored quite easily by oneself. What is more, although Shanghai is itself a fascinating city, it is also close to a number of other places just as enticing, such as Hangzhou, Suzhou, and Nanking.

Below, a list of companies offering packages to China which include Shanghai. Many of them are able to arrange itineraries (including hotels, guides, and transportation) tailored to individual requirements. Information for independent travellers is given in Chapter Two.

UK: London

— Cultural Tours, Morley House, 320 Regent Street, London W1R 5AB. Tel: 01-636 7906.

— Voyages Jules Verne, 10 Glentworth Street, London NW1. Tel: 01-486 8080.

— UK China Travel Service, 24 Cambridge Circus, London WC2 H8HD. Tel: 01-836 9911.

— SACU (Society for Anglo-Chinese Understanding), 152 Camden High Street, London NW1 0NE. Tel: 01-482 4292.

— Speedbird Holidays, Alta House, 152 King Street, London W6 0QU. Tel: 01-741 8041.

— Globepost Travel Services, 324 Kennington Park Road, London SE11 4PD. Tel: 01-587 0303.

— Abercrombie and Kent, Sloane Square House, Holbein Place, London SW1W 8NS. Tel: 01-730 9600.

— China Discovery, 22-23 Denman Street, London W1V 7RJ. Tel: 01-734 9476.

The China Tourist Office is at 4 Glentworth Street, London NW1. Tel: 01-935 9427.

UK: outside London

— Regent Holidays, 13 Small Street, Bristol BS1 1DE. Tel: (0272) 211711.

— Kuoni Travel, Kuoni House, Dorking, Surrey. Tel: (0306) 885044.

— Bales Tours, Bales House, Dorking, Surrey. Tel: (0306) 885991.

— Occidor Ltd, 10 Broomcroft Road, Bognor Regis, West Sussex PO22 7NJ. Tel. (024) 369 2178.

— SCT-China, Rose Crescent, Cambridge, CB2 2LL. Tel: (0223) 311103.

— Travelsphere, Dept. CTO, Coventry Road, Market Harborough, Leics LE16 9BZ. Tel: (0858) 66211.

Hong Kong

Some of the above have offices in Hong Kong, and their addresses are given here:
— Harvest Travel/Cultural Tours, Room 2003, Bank of Canton Building, 6 Des Voeux Road, Central, Hong Kong. Tel: 5-258195
— Voyages Jules Verne, Office 203, 2/F Arcade, Lee Gardens Hotel, Hysan Avenue, Hong Kong. Tel: 5-8953181.
— Abercrombie and Kent H.K. Ltd, 6th floor, Sutherland House, 3 Chater Road, Central, Hong Kong. Tel: 5-8657818.
There are many companies offering short packages to Shanghai. One is Harvest Travel/Cultural Tours whose address is given above.

Other countries

There are, of course, many other companies from other countries offering tours to Shanghai and China — to obtain information about them you may contact any of the following tourist offices of the People's Republic of China:
— China Tourist Office, 6F Hanchidai Hamamatsu Cho Bl., 1-27-13 Hamatsu-Cho, Minato-Ku, Tokyo, Japan. Tel: 433-1461.
— China Tourist Office, Lincoln Building 6OE, 42nd Street, Suite 465, New York, N.Y. 10165. Tel: (212) 867-0271.
— Office du Tourisme de Chine, 51 Rue Sainte-Anne, 75002 Paris. Tel: 2969548.
— China Tourist Office, Eschenheimer Anlage 28, D-6000 Frankfurt Am Main-1, W. Germany. Tel: 0611-555292.
— China Tourist Office, 33/336 Sussex Street, Sydney, New South Wales 2000, Australia. Tel: (02) 2679674.

Passports and visas

A valid passport with Chinese visa is required for a visit to Shanghai.

South African passport holders may not enter the People's Republic of China. Theoretically nor can Israeli passport holders, but it seems that in this case a substantial number of exceptions are made, so it may be worth trying. Israeli, South African, or Taiwanese stamps in any other passport do not affect eligibility for a Chinese visa.

Obtaining an individual visa in Great Britain has recently become easier. You may apply directly to the consular section of the Embassy of the People's Republic of China (address below) with a return air or train or boat ticket; or a receipt proving purchase of traveller's cheques to the value of at least £600 sterling from either the Bank of China (address below) or any other of the big banks. You will also need to provide your passport, a passport-sized photograph, completed visa application form, and visa fee (currently £20 for a British passport). Three working days are normally required to process the visa. Anyone wishing to apply for a visa by post will need to pay an extra £3 handling fee, although cheques cannot be accepted.

The whole thing becomes much easier if done through certain tour operators, who will charge a fee but who will waive the need for return tickets or proof of financial security — some addresses are given below.

Alternatively, visas may be obtained very simply in Hong Kong. There it normally takes three days (although it can be done in one if you pay more) and there are none of the aforementioned complications. The address of the relevant office is given below.

An ordinary tourist visa is valid for 3 months from the date of issue and covers all the principal tourist destinations of China, including Shanghai. A special stamp is required for certain areas, such as Tibet.

Once in Shanghai should you need or wish to extend the validity of your visa, or to obtain stamps for restricted areas, it is necessary to address your request to the Security Bureau, found at 210 Hankou Lu. Tel: 211997.

A Chinese stamp in your passport does not currently hinder entrance to any other country, including Taiwan.

Travelling in a group usually involves a 'group visa'. This is a single document which covers all the members of the party but which is valid only in conjunction with your passport. Check with the company organising the journey for precise details.

It is recommended that you take a photocopy of both your passport and your visa, as well as some spare photographs, keeping them separate from the originals.

Transit visas

If your visit to China will not exceeed ten days, it is possible to obtain a transit visa. The main disadvantage to this is that it cannot be changed or extended in China.

Visas for business purposes

Visitors intending to go to China for business purposes need to have an invitation given by their host organisation in China, and should apply directly to the visa section of the Chinese Embassy.

Addresses

— Embassy of the People's Republic of China (Visa section), 31 Portland Place, London W1N 3AG. Tel: 01-636 1835. Office Hours: 0900—1200 Monday to Friday.

— Bank of China, 107 Shaftesbury Avenue, London W1. Tel: 01-437 5975.

Tour operators providing visa service:

— Cultural Tours, Morley House, 320 Regent Street, London W1R 5AB. Tel: 01-636 7906.

— UK China Travel Service Ltd, 24 Cambridge Circus, London WC2 H8H. Tel: 01-836 9911.

For obtaining visas in Hong Kong:

— China International Travel Service (H.K.), CTS House, 4/F., 78-83 Connaught Road C., Hong Kong. Tel: 5-8533888.

Advance reservations

For the independent traveller not relying on the services of tour operators or travel agents, advance bookings in most areas are a difficulty. Domestic flights, for example, can be booked only upon arrival in China, and only from one city to the next. Hotels in many parts of China must either be booked through one of the Chinese travel services, or upon application at the hotel itself once you arrive.

Shanghai is less problematic. There is a variety of ways to reach it (see Chapter Two), and there are many hotels that allow you to reserve rooms in advance, either by telex or by telephone (see Chapter Four, 'Accommodation').

Prices

The intention here is not to give a list of approximate costs, but rather to prepare the visitor for the seemingly erratic nature of prices and the difficulties involved in assessing value for money, in Shanghai, as well as in the rest of China.

China's economy has undergone many changes in recent years. Until the end of the 1970s, almost every aspect of economic life was administered by the state — prices were more or less uniform and the standard of service uniformly appalling. The government began to experiment with a more mixed economy, devolving some of the burden of financial administration away from Peking to the provincial governments and encouraging a certain amount of enterprise. So far, the changes have been, on the whole, beneficial, but there remain many unsolved problems caused mainly by the fact that at the moment the economy is neither one thing nor the other. Prices are not fixed by the government, nor are they allowed to fix themselves according to market forces with the result that for the outsider there is no coherent pricing pattern to follow.

The paradox is at its most obvious in places frequented by foreigners, hotels for example. A new hotel in the suburbs of Shanghai, that would warrant a rating of three stars in the West, may charge at five star rates for one star service, whereas in one of the older, but more centrally located hotels, the prices may seem almost cheap.

It has to be remembered too, that the average wage in China is only about 100 yuan a month (about £18) — Chinese cannot be expected to pay the higher prices charged to foreigners for certain commodities (e.g. aeroplane tickets), and therefore pay less for the same thing. Foreigners tend to be charged at what are considered to be international rates. However, these differences apply only under certain circumstances. When it comes to the small local restaurants, for example, one may expect to be charged at local rates.

By the same token, because of the unsettled economy, what is true one day is not true the next. In China things have a habit of changing just as they seem to be taking root, and this is as true of prices as of anything else. Inflation is no longer kept at bay through government subsidies. Thus any prices quoted in this guide can be only approximate, and should be checked whenever possible.

Health and vaccinations

Unless you have passed through an area where yellow fever is endemic during the ten days prior to your arrival in Shanghai (or indeed anywhere in China), vaccinations are not currently a requirement. However, it would be as well to consult a doctor on the subject at least two weeks before departure — doctors should be aware of any changes and may have ideas of their own. They may, for example, advise a course of anti-malaria tablets (which usually must be started before arrival in the country), or, in view of the recent outbreak of the disease, a dose of hepatitis vaccine.

In London advice and on the spot vaccinations are available, for a fee at the following places:

— British Airways Passenger Immunisation, 75 Regent Street, London W1. Tel: 01-439 9584.

— Thomas Cook Medical Unit, 45 Berkeley Street, London W1. Tel: 01-499 4000.

— Trailfinders, 42-48 Earls Court Road, London W8 6EJ. Tel. 01-938 3444.

— Airport clinics at Heathrow Airport, London. Tel: 01-562 5453; Gatwick Airport, London. Tel: 01-668 4211.

In Hong Kong, most of the private doctors and clinics, of which there are many, are likely to be able to give advice and administer vaccines. They are listed in the 'Yellow Pages' section of the Hong Kong telephone directory. There are a number of government run hospitals, too, which should be rather cheaper.

Basic health care

Until the recent outbreak of hepatitis, it would have been true to say that you are unlikely to encounter any particular problems in Shanghai. The situation is normal once again but an inoculation is recommended (even if the vaccine is far from foolproof), and particular care should be taken in matters of personal hygiene. It may be sensible to take your own mug and cutlery/chopsticks, and to avoid eating shellfish. When there is an outbreak of something like hepatitis in China, the problem is exacerbated by the fact that diners around a table all serve themselves from the same plate, frequently using their own chopsticks. Still, all things considered, China is remarkably clean and healthy but the climate is wearing, and minor ailments can occur.

The following items could be useful:

● Electrolite powders to help prevent dehydration in the summer
● A course of antibiotics against chest infections
● Tablets against diarrhoea
● Insect repellant
● Aspirins
● Throat lozenges
● Plasters
● Suncream, sunglasses, and sun hat

- Salt tablets or better still ordinary table salt to add to your food (to replenish what is lost through sweating)
- Natural fibre clothes (much more comfortable in the sticky heat of the summer)
- Talcum powder (against prickly heat)
- Tampons
- A water bottle
- Umbrella (preferable to a raincoat in a humid climate)

If you have particular medical requirements, bring good supplies — when you run out you may not be able to replenish your stock.

Water

Tap water should be avoided. However, clean water is usually available, either boiled or boiling, in flasks in hotel rooms and is reliable. The Chinese habitually drink hot water (it is considered to be more healthy), so cold drinking water is harder to find (although mineral water is becoming more common). Generally speaking, any water you are offered will be safe to drink — the Chinese are very conscientious about this. The same is true of ice. However, if you are suspicious about any water you are given, or if you intend to travel further afield in more primitive conditions, do take water purifying tablets, which are available from chemists.

The word for water is 'shui', pronounced 'shway'; for boiling water 'kai (as in kite) shui'; for cooled boiled water 'liang kai shui'.

In the summer it is important to drink as much liquid as possible — remember that tea is just as good as water.

Climate

Shanghai has a climate that is usually described as sub-tropical, which basically means hot summers and cool winters. The average annual temperature is 58 degrees Fahrenheit (14 centigrade). In July the average daily temperature is 80 degrees (27), and the average minimum in January is 37 (3). There are roughly 45 inches of rain per annum (1140 mm), falling most heavily in June. The driest month is January — it is also the coldest, and snow does occasionally fall.

The best months for visiting Shanghai are April or early May, when a warm spring is well established, and the trees are in blossom, but before the rains and sticky heat of summer. The end of September or beginning of October are also comfortable; but in the

Rainfall and temperature chart

Month	TEMPERATURE						Precipitation	Days of Rain
	Average C°	F°	Maximum Average C°	F°	Minimum Average C°	F°		
January	3.5	38.3	7.6	45.7	0.3	32.5	44.0	9.0
February	4.6	40.3	8.7	47.7	1.4	34.5	62.6	10.6
March	8.3	46.9	12.6	54.7	4.9	40.8	78.1	13.1
April	14.0	57.2	18.5	65.3	10.4	50.7	106.7	13.4
May	18.8	65.8	23.2	73.8	15.3	59.5	122.9	14.5
June	23.2	73.9	27.3	81.1	20.1	68.2	158.9	13.7
July	27.8	82.0	31.8	89.2	24.7	76.5	134.2	11.5
August	27.7	81.9	31.6	88.9	24.7	76.5	126.0	9.9
September	23.6	74.4	27.4	81.3	20.5	68.9	150.5	12.0
October	18.0	64.4	22.4	72.3	14.3	57.7	50.1	8.3
November	12.3	54.1	16.8	62.2	8.6	47.5	48.8	7.9
December	6.2	43.2	10.7	51.3	2.7	36.9	40.9	7.9

wake of China's modernisation programme, air conditioning systems are a common feature, rendering even the summer tolerable. November and early December are usually chilly, but not prohibitively so, and a visit at those times could be pleasantly bracing. However, although the average January temperature is 3.3 centigrade, minus 12 is not unknown. Yet homes in the area south of the Yangtse are not centrally heated — it is not considered cold enough. Hotels are of course heated.

Shanghai is on the typhoon belt. A gale of force 8-11 is a

typhoon, and anything above force 12 is considered to be a strong typhoon (the word typhoon is from the Cantonese *Ta Fung* meaning 'big wind'). The southeast coast is vulnerable to typhoons between the months of May and December, but the vast majority strike between July and September, and it is usually the provinces of Fujian and Guandong, to the south of Shanghai, that take the greater share.

Since only a small minority are sufficiently powerful to cause any damage, typhoons sometimes come as a great relief in the humid summer months.

Fish out of water, their captors in it — the eel market on the Old French Bund in the rain.

TWO

Getting there

By air

Shanghai is already comparatively well served by international flights, and there are plans for more

From Europe
Alitalia is the only airline to provide a direct service to Shanghai. It leaves from Rome, once a week on a Friday.

From London there is a wide choice of indirect flights. The *ABC World Airways Guide* has several suggestions for the quickest route:
- Via Narita (Japan) on Japanese Airlines (JAL) linking with a CAAC (Civil Airline Administration of China, the national carrier of the People's Republic of China) flight to Shanghai. Total journey time: 21 hours.
- Via Helsinki on Finnair, changing to another Finnair flight to Narita and then to Shanghai on CAAC. Journey time: 23 hours.

Via Hong Kong
Most people, however, are likely to combine a visit to Shanghai with one to Hong Kong, from where there are daily flights, not only to Shanghai but to plenty of other cities in China (see below 'From Hong Kong').

Three airlines offer direct daily flights to Hong Kong from London (Cathay Pacific, British Caledonian, and British Airways), but cheaper fares can be obtained by using other airlines if you are prepared to change planes. For example, you can go on Singapore Airlines, changing at Singapore, or Philippine Airlines, changing at Manila. The journey becomes several hours longer, but the price difference may make it worthwhile.

From Hong Kong, Shanghai is served by two airlines — Cathay Pacific, and CAAC. An advantage of flying to Hong Kong on Cathay Pacific is that the whole ticket to Shanghai can be purchased in advance in London, since the airline operates four flights a week between Hong Kong and Shanghai on a Tuesday, a Thursday, a Saturday, and a Sunday. CAAC run at least one flight a day. The cost one way is about £75.

Via Peking

Another possibility is to enter through Peking. The capital is served by many of the world's major airlines, and from London there are direct flights on British Airways and CAAC. Again, it is possible to find cheaper fares using other airlines, but there are likely to be long stopovers as well as changes of plane. JAT (Yugoslavian Airlines) via Belgrade, Aeroflot via Moscow, Tarom via Bucharest, and Pakistan International Airlines via Islamabad or Karachi are possibilities here. However, if you want to book onward domestic flights to Shanghai, or any other city in China, in advance, you must fly to Peking on CAAC, and then ensure that the ticket is reconfirmed as soon as you arrive. Even using CAAC for the flight to Peking it is possible to book only one onward domestic flight in advance. Otherwise, all domestic tickets can be purchased only upon arrival in China.

From Japan

There are regular direct flights to Shanghai from the cities of Nagasaki (every Saturday with JAL and on a Monday and Friday with CAAC), Osaka (at least one a day on either JAL or CAAC) and Tokyo (Monday, Saturday, and Sunday on JAL, at least one a day on CAAC, and one every Saturday on Northwest Orient).

From Canada

There is a flight every Sunday on CAAC. Canadian Pacific fly Shanghai-Vancouver every Thursday.

From the USA

There are two flights a week from New York on CAAC (on a Wednesday, and on a Saturday); one from Los Angeles (on a Friday with CAAC); four flights a week from San Francisco (on a Monday, Thursday, Friday and Sunday, with CAAC), and from Seattle on a Friday with Northwest Orient.

From Singapore

There is one flight a week on a Wednesday with Singapore Airlines.

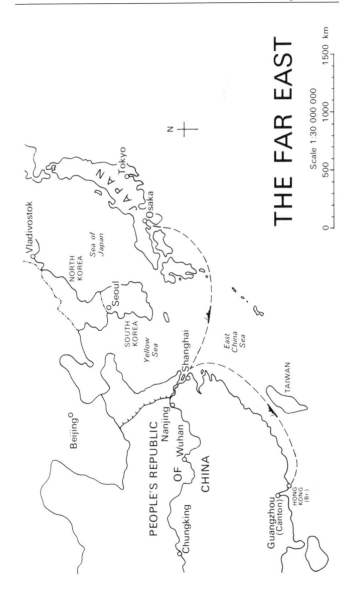

THE FAR EAST

By rail

From Hong Kong

There is not yet a direct rail service to Shanghai from Hong Kong. At the moment it is necessary to change trains at Canton, which would mean an overnight stop. However, it is still cheaper than flying and is certainly much the most interesting method — the journey through Guandong province is beautiful. The line follows the Bei Jiang River and winds around terraced hillsides for several hours after leaving Canton. Journey time from Canton is 33 hours, on the express service.

On Chinese trains there are two classes — soft and hard, very approximately first and second. Even in soft, there are four berths to each compartment (privacy is not a feature of Chinese life), but, whilst far from luxurious, they are decent enough in the cooler months. Towels are not provided. Each compartment has a flask of boiling water which can be refilled by the carriage attendant. Each compartment is cooled by an electric fan. A dining car is attached to the train, but bring your own drinks, as supplies are erratic. The same is true for lavatory paper.

Hard class looks worse than it is. There are no compartments, only doorless alcoves, six bunks to each. The main disparities between the two classes are questions of privacy and of the thickness of the upholstery; and soft class looks nicer.

The Hong Kong—Canton express train takes two and three quarter hours, and all the carriages are air conditioned.

London to Shanghai

An unusual possibility is to make the whole journey from London by train, one of the longest train rides in the world. Carriages of Soviet Railways link up with ferry services at Ostend and the Hook of Holland, and the journey to Moscow takes about forty hours. From Moscow there is a once-weekly service to Peking, via Irkutsk and Ulan Bator (a journey of about six days). Peking-Shanghai takes twelve hours. Transit visas for Poland, the USSR and the Mongolian People's Republic must be obtained in advance; a transit visa for East Germany may be purchased at its border. For China, see Chapter One 'Passports and visas'. Tickets to Moscow may be purchased through British Rail, and from Moscow to Peking through 'Intourist' in London.

By sea

If the idea of going by train does not appeal, then go by ship from Hong Kong. It is not particularly expensive (in April 1989 the cost of a berth in a good, spacious second class cabin with bath, sharing with one other, all meals included, was about $HK 900), and it is surprisingly comfortable; and as the ship enters the mouth of the Yangtse, breaking off to cruise amidst the ships that line the banks of the Huangpu, it provides a magnificent introduction to Shanghai as the grandiose esplanade that is the Bund comes into view. Journeytime is about 60-65 hours.

The ship referred to here is the *M.V. Jin Jiang,* among the best in the fleet. It is 171.8 metres in length, and weighs 21,000 tons. There are six decks, with 193 cabins capable of accommodating 406 passengers. Among the facilities are a swimming pool, a tennis court, a mini-golf course, a lounge, a discotheque, a bar, coffee shop, and Japanese restaurant (as well as the main restaurant where the included meals are served). There is also a duty-free shop. Cabins cheaper than the one mentioned are available. Payment for anything aboard may be made with Hong Kong dollars.

There is a service in either direction every five days, either by the *Jin Jiang* or one of its smaller sister ships. Tickets are obtainable from the following:

— Jin Jiang Travel (HK) Ltd., Room 1806, Wing On House, 71 Des Voeux Road, Central, Hong Kong. Tel: 5-265651, 5-8680633
— China Travel Service, Alpha House,1/F, 27-33 Nathan Road, Kowloon, Hong Kong. Tel:3-7211331. Tx:40536 CTSKL HX.
— China Foreign Shipping Agency Co., Shanghai Branch, Room 301, 12 Zhongshan Dong 2-Lu, Shanghai. Tel:264357, 280010.
— U.K. China Travel Service, 24 Cambridge Circus, London WC2H 8HD. Tel: 01-836 9911. Tx: 263492 UKCTS G.

There are ships (the *S.S.Shanghai* and the *M.V.Haixing)* run by another Chinese shipping organisation doing the same run at similar prices and offering a similar service. Passages on these ships may be booked at:
— China Merchants Shipping & Enterprises Co. Ltd, 1/F, 152-155 Connaught Road C., Hong Kong. Tel: 5-8151006.
— International Liner Booking Office, 1/F, 1 Jinling Dong Lu, Shanghai. Tel: 261261.

The point of embarkation in Hong Kong for all the mentioned services is usually Tai Kok Tsui Ferry Pier, Kowloon. However, it isn't always so do check with the company concerned.

The Huangpu. Shanghai harbour is one of the busiest in the world, but Chinese ships in the old style are few and far between.

THREE

What to take

Clothes

Comfort is everything. Formality counts for very little anywhere in China, so is unlikely to be a requirement unless it is a personal preference or unless it is an indispensable part of your business life.

What you take depends on the time of year you go (see below), but how much you take need hardly vary — take as little as possible and less than you think you need. It is futile to take many clothes as the laundry service is usually good (although it is not a good idea to entrust delicate or fine items to it), and reasonably priced. If you prefer to wash your own clothes, powder is not hard to find.

Shorts, T-shirts, and sandals are quite acceptable, both for men and for women, even in temples. However, anything brief may not go down too well — nobody is likely to pass comment, but older people will regard it as rather offensive.

Business
Whilst it is true that informality is the rule rather than the exception, greater exposure to foreigners, and the gradual discarding of Mao suit austerity, has meant that many members of the business community have taken to wearing Western style suits, and therefore expect foreigners to do the same. In the humid summer a safari suit is admissible.

What to take in summer
You will need lightweight, natural fibre clothes, a sun hat and sunglasses. Sandals are cool but not comfortable for walking so well ventilated lightweight shoes are preferable. Take a pullover, cardigan, or jacket against fierce air conditioning or sea air, and an umbrella. You'll need a towel should you be travelling by train and its best to take your own supply of toiletries — the choice available in the shops is either small or expensive.

What to take in winter

Although the winters are not extreme, they are cold enough to warrant an overcoat and a pullover; and thick underwear for those particularly sensitive to the cold. A hat, scarf and stout walking shoes could all be useful. It is worth taking an umbrella just in case; and, once again, take your own supply of toiletries.

Luggage

The main considerations are weight and durability. Weight if it is you doing the carrying, and durability because if you are not, the porters in China are extremely careless.

A rucksack is the best on both counts, but if you prefer something more elegant, or something less reminiscent of country hikes, either use an old case to which a few extra scars won't make any difference, or take one of the Samsonite type — the soft variety seems to be best, but others swear by the hard shell ones.

At any event, you should be able to lock your case because, although China is still a very safe country compared with most, theft does occur; and also because if by any chance you will be travelling by train, and intend to put your luggage in the luggage van, China Railways will not accept it unless it is locked. CAAC may well introduce the same rule for flights.

An extra nylon strap is suggested in case of damage to your luggage; and do ensure that your name and contact address are securely affixed to any bags. An address inside the case is a reasonable precaution. **Electricity** in China is 220v; sockets are mostly two or three round pin. You are advised to buy a universal adaptor.

Money

China'a unique dual currency system is explained under 'Practical Information'.

Chinese money (yuan) can be purchased only in China. Since yuan is easily changed back upon leaving the country and since they obtain a higher rate of exchange, travellers cheques are both secure and practical — in Shanghai there is no shortage of places where they can be exchanged. Any major currency is acceptable (£,$,DM,Swiss francs,yen,etc.), but when it comes to names, go for the big ones, such as American Express, Thomas Cook.

Cash

Take a good supply of cash as well. It is convenient if you want to change only a small amount of money, and it is now sometimes possible to pay directly with foreign currency.

You may encounter problems with the pound coin — single dollar notes are better.

Credit cards

Credit cards cannot be used as a matter of course, particularly in local shops, but are usually accepted in establishments aimed at foreign clients. However, don't depend on it. Visa, Access/Master Card, American Express are the most widely favoured. The aforementioned cards may be used to obtain cash (Foreign Exchange Certificates only) at the Bank of China and some of its branches, and sub-branches (i.e. some hotels). In the case of American Express, the card may only be used to obtain cash against a personal cheque. The maximum amount of cash drawable on credit cards not only varies according to the card in question, but also, it seems, according to the branch. The maximum figure quoted was 1500 yuan. A passport will be perhaps required as proof of identity.

Thefts

For a foreigner Shanghai is a pretty safe place — most crime takes place amongst the Chinese population. Still, it would be foolish to become complacent. The average hotel, for example, does not have safe-deposit boxes. If you leave anything remotely valuable in the hotel room, ensure that it is at least locked in your case, have two supplies of money in case you get relieved of one of them, and photocopy all your important documents, keeping the copies separate from the originals.

A money-belt is sensible if it makes you feel more secure, but you are less likely to be robbed on the streets of Shanghai than in London. In Shanghai, should disaster befall you, certain countries are represented by consulates such as U.S.A., United Kingdom, Canada, Italy, Poland, France, Japan, West Germany, Australia, Belgium, and the Soviet Union. See 'useful addresses.'

Photography

There is plenty to photograph in Shanghai, from life on the waterfront to people making dumplings at the street side. What is more, since the Chinese are themselves keen photographers, foreigners wielding cameras are not regarded with any suspicion. There are quite a number of photographic shops these days, but they are not evenly distributed about the city and their stock is unpredictably variable.

Film and batteries

The main thing is to take more film than you think you will need. Most types of 'Fuji' and 'Kodak' colour film can be found, but not always when and where you want it. Certainly there are a considerable number of shops selling film these days, but black and white film is unavailable and print film is far more common than slide, although slide film is now beginning to make regular appearances in the shops. The Chinese are now producing 35mm film, but the quality is an unknown factor. Cassette and disc film and video or cine are rarities.

The cost of imported film is about the same as in Britain — it is cheaper in Hong Kong. Wherever it is bought, check the expiry date and, for slide film, whether processing is included.

It is advisable to take some film with a high ASA rating, for use inside where the lighting is poor, or where using flash is either inappropriate or forbidden.

It is wiser to bring your own batteries, as there is no guarantee of finding replacements.

Repairs

There are so many shops dealing in photographic equipment that it shouldn't be too difficult finding one willing to undertake repairs if necessary. The address of a centrally located one that advertises itself as being equipped to do repairs is given under 'useful addresses'.

Polaroid

The 'instant' picture is both a joy and a nuisance. A joy because it has the power to make people very happy very quickly, and a nuisance because a lot of proud mothers are under the illusion that all cameras are able to provide a fast portrait service for their children. If you use a Polaroid, be prepared to give away a lot of photographs, and if you don't, you may well be asked to send copies. If that is the case, please oblige — a small gesture, but a powerful one.

You are advised to bring a good supply of film — it may be very hard to find supplies.

Video and cine

Cine cameras should be no larger than 8mm (although in practice nobody knows the difference). As for video cameras, there does not appear to be any rule on the subject but objections are not raised. One thing is sure though — cine film makes only occasional appearances in the shops, and video film is very hard to find (although there is plenty of tape available for video recorders).

Filters

Haze is the photographers' enemy in China. An ultra-violet filter is essential. Some filters are sold in the larger photographic shops.

Regulations

A little research would reveal that, strictly speaking, the usual 'strategically important' areas (airports, railway stations, bridges etc.) are forbidden to photographers. In practice, the Chinese are sensible enough not to enforce such outdated rules. Still, you never know — if you are the only person using a camera at the airport, and there are uniformed airport personnel in the vicinity, it is better to ask. Certainly refrain from photographing anything of a military nature, or from taking pictures of individual soldiers without their permission.

It is not permitted to take photographs in certain places of historic interest, for instance the Jade Buddhas in the Jade Buddha temple. Flouting these rules can have unpleasant consequences (confiscation of film etc.); and, no matter how stealthy you are, the chances are your actions will not go undetected. Most of these sites sell postcards or slides.

In some cases photography is allowed without a flash (for fear of causing damage), which is where fast film becomes useful. Fast film (1000—1600 ASA) is quite effective, but produces a very grainy finish.

Photography is allowed in theatres, even with flash. This means that acrobats, even at the pinnacle of their act, are subjected to a continuous son et lumière that has all the subtlety of an air raid. The Chinese are blessed with enormous powers of concentration, and don't appear remotely nonplussed by all the activity; but for many members of the audience, it is an irritating distraction. If your camera cannot take fast film, or its lens is inadequate, be discreet and choose your moment.

In general, with the observance of the aforementioned rules, taking photographs in Shanghai presents no particular problem — in fact it is only too easy to consume your supply of film. In most cases people do not object to being photographed, but if you are focusing very obviously on an individual, it is only polite to ask their permission.

Developing film locally

Film can be developed in Shanghai at new laboratories built to deal with imported varieties, and using methods approved by the companies concerned. Please see 'useful addresses' section.

X-rays

The x-ray machines at Shanghai airport are 'micro-dose', and advertise themselves as film-safe. Up to a point they are — film passed a couple of times through the machines will come to no harm, but since the effect is cumulative, regular exposure may do some damage. If you are worried, ask for your hand-luggage to be hand searched.

The machines at Hong Kong airport used to advertise themselves as not film safe but apparently new ones which have recently been installed are as safe as any other.

Presents

Tipping has become something of a problem in China and the dilemma is explained elsewhere (see 'Etiquette'). It is, nevertheless, worthwhile having a reserve of small gifts, as they are sometimes more appropriate than giving money. Even if you don't smoke, buy some duty-free cigarettes to give to porters, drivers etc. — '555' used to be particularly desirable for some reason (perhaps the Chinese infatuation with symbolic numbers), but now 'Kent' and 'Marlboro' are more sought after. If you don't want to buy a whole carton, individual packets of foreign made cigarettes (they must be foreign made, otherwise the whole point is lost), are for sale in some places (hotels, Friendship store etc.) at prices lower than in Britain; and there is no shortage of touts in the streets.

Since the Chinese have become sophisticated beyond the point of pens (especially the Shanghaiese), what to take that is portable and reasonably priced? Amusing T-shirts or pop/classical cassettes of the Woolworths variety are quite satisfactory. Life is far from frivolous in modern China, so anything that lightens the atmosphere is welcome. For more formal occasions, Pitkin Pictorial Guides (e.g. The Queen's visit to China and Hong Kong) which specialise in aspects of Britain might be suitable.

Food

Details of local cooking and restaurants are given elsewhere. Here, the intention is to suggest one or two items that you may like to take with you. Some of them are obtainable, not only in the shops aimed at foreigners but also in some of the local grocery stores. However, supplies are irregular and prices tend to be higher.

● Instant coffee or coffee bags. Imported instant coffee is becoming widely available, for a price, in Shanghai, where it is fashionable. Coffee bars sell coffee by the cup, but it is rarely very good except in the major hotels.
● Milk powder (can also be found in some local shops).
● Sugar.
● Salt.
● Tea, surprisingly — in Shanghai, the local tea is the green variety, very leafy and pungent, and not to everyone's taste. Black tea (or red tea as it is called by the Chinese, from the colour of the liquid rather than the colour of the leaf) will not necessarily be served in restaurants or hotels. Local shops sell 'red' Chinese tea, but if you are attached to the flavour of English breakfast tea, or any speciality, bring your own.
● Cheese. No cheese is eaten in tropical China (think of the climate, and lack of grazing land and refrigeration).
● Chocolate. Although it is manufactured in China, most of it is not of a very high standard and is cloyingly sweet.

Cigarettes and alcohol

Most Chinese cigarettes are not to Western taste. American and British brands are for sale (and more cheaply than in Britain), but still the invariable problem of uncertain supplies. Bring your own.

There is no shortage of alcohol, both local and imported. Chinese beer is good, and there are local brands of gin, brandy, whisky, etc, as well as international brands which tend to be rather expensive. The Chinese produce an assortment of liquors, many of which are an acquired taste, as well as their own wine.

Duty free
Strictly speaking you are allowed to import 400 cigarettes and two bottles of liquor, each of ¾ litre. However, the customs officials are not strict.

Books

Shanghai is distinct from most other cities of China in coming to prominence during the past one hundred years and in having a history that is as much European as Chinese, as if the plot of *Private Lives* was enacted on the set of a Chinese opera. A great many books have been published over the years on the unique phenomonen that was pre-war Shanghai, but many are now out of print. The following make fascinating advance reading if you can find them in second hand book shops, or in libraries:

● *The Sassoons* by Stanley Jackson (London: Heinemann 1968)
● *Shanghai Saga* by John Pal (London: Jarrolds 1963)
● *Shanghai Episode:* the end of Western commerce in Shanghai by Lucian Taire (Hong Kong: Rainbow Press 1958)
● *Shanghai, Paradise of Adventurers* by G.E. Miller (New York: Orsay Publishing House 1937)
● *Shanghai: Revolution and development in an Asian metropolis* edited by Christopher Howe (Cambridge: Cambridge University Press 1981). This contains an extremely scholarly and detailed analysis of Shanghai's development since 1949.

From books in print:
● *China to me* by Emily Hahn (London: Virago Press 1987)
● *The Soong Dynasty* by Sterling Seagrave (London: New English Library 1986)
● *Life and Death in Shanghai* by Nien Cheng (London: Grafton Books 1987)
● *Shanghai, Crucible of modern China* by Betty Peh-Ti Wei (Oxford University Press 1987)
● *Empire of the Sun* by J.G. Ballard (London: Grafton Books 1985)

And books to take:
● *In search of old Shanghai* By Pan Ling (Hong Kong: Joint Publishing 1983)
● *All about Shanghai* (Oxford: Oxford University Press 1986), which is a reprint of a 1935 guidebook.
● *Shanghai* (a novel) by Christopher New (Futura 1985)

Maps

A good city map would be worth buying in advance. There is a reasonably good one produced by 'Falk Plan' which is combined with maps of Eastern China and Peking and Canton. However, bookshops in Shanghai sell streetplans with the main thoroughfares and landmarks mapped out, and the Cathay Pacific office in the Jin Jiang Hotel carry their own version.

FOUR

Arrivals and departures

More forms to fill in

If you enter China through Shanghai, there will be several forms to fill in — they should be given you on the boat or plane before you arrive, but sometimes they are unavailable, in which case it will be necessary to fill them in upon arrival. It will save you time and nervous energy if you know how to deal with them. Arriving with individual visas probably will mean three forms, i.e. an immigration card, a health declaration form, and a currency and valuables declaration form.

- The immigration card is straightforward enough, but it helps if you have the following information written down beforehand: number, and date and place of issue of passport, and number and date of issue of visa. If there is a question 'type of visa', the answer is 'tourist'. Travelling on a group visa exempts you from filling in this form.

- The health declaration form requires you to list the countries visited in the two weeks prior to your arrival in China, and whether you are suffering from any of a list of symptoms — unless you are chronically ill, it is wiser to say no. Often the question 'host organisation in China?' comes up. If you are travelling on business the answer is the Chinese company with whom you intend to do business; if you are travelling in a tourist group, the answer is the Chinese tourist organisation (for example CITS) dealing with your group, not the foreign company through whom you booked the tour; and if you are not in a group, the answer is, strictly speaking, 'independent', although to avoid unneccessary questioning it might be better to write CITS.

- The currency and valuables declaration form is two sheets, one of which is a carbon copy. This form asks you to write down the quantity and type of camera, cassette recorder, radio, and so on, that you are bringing into the country, and to list the quantities of different currencies you are carrying (both travellers cheques and cash). It is worthwhile to have totted up these figures before arriving, and it is also a good idea to have items like cameras to hand, so that they can be quickly produced if the customs officer wishes to inspect them.

Arrival by air

The volume of air traffic has increased in China in a way that would have seemed impossible fifteen, or even ten years ago. The national airline, CAAC, and the airports at its disposal, were hoplessly disorganised and ill-equipped to deal with the new strain on their resources — too few aircraft, an ineffective booking system, and airports thirty to forty years out of date. All these problems have been lessened, but not yet solved.

Shanghai airport is an international airport, as well as one of the busiest domestic airports in the country. New terminals have been added and facilities improved, but passengers still have to expect occasional moments of disorganisation in the form of unexplained delays and sudden changes of procedure. The main consolation has to be that things run more smoothly than they did, and that CAAC (now split up into regional airlines for domestic services — the one serving Shanghai is called 'East China Airlines') expects to operate a computerised booking system in the near future.

Customs and immigration

Generally speaking the entry procedures are slightly chaotic, but not particularly difficult if you remain calm. Events will probably take place in the following way:

- First you will be required to hand in the health declaration form, from where you pass on to the passport inspection booths.
- Hand in your passport with the immigration card. If you are travelling on a group visa the group leader will hand it in, after which each member of the party will file through according to the sequence of names on the visa (although sometimes all the passports are collected and handed in for inspection together). If you want a stamp in your passport, then you need to ask, although these days the immigration officers are usually reluctant to provide it.

● Then collect your suitcase and head towards the exit, where you must hand in the currency and valuables declaration form. Both copies will be stamped and one of them handed back to you, which you must keep and give up upon leaving the country. You are highly unlikely to have your luggage searched but may be asked to produce items declared on the form.

There is a bank where you may change money, but failing that there is another located in the Airport Hotel which is just to the left of the Terminal as you exit. Porters are likely to be thin on the ground, but trolleys may be available (possibly for a small fee).

The air terminal

Once you emerge into the arrivals area, which is rather small, you will find lavatories and telephones on your left, and beyond them a desk offering taxis and hotel reservations (it may not be manned), and, again to your left, a restaurant/bar and a left-luggage office. There is also a drinking fountain in the vicinity. There is an information desk on your right. The exit is straight ahead of you.

Getting to the centre from the airport

The airport is 30-40 minutes from the city centre. When you exit from the terminal building you will find another booth on your left offering taxi services. This one should be manned and is the official one, run as a government service. If possible get a taxi here, as the government taxis are cheaper, safer, and more honest. If you cannot secure one, then try asking any driver in a car marked 'taxi'. Many of these are private, and are likely to prove more expensive. The going rate should be around the 25 yuan mark.

There is a shuttle bus service too. These buses are marked F.T. and appear to emanate from the downtown offices of CAAC. If in doubt ask at the information desk located in the terminal.

Arriving by rail

Shanghai is now the proud possessor of one of the largest and newest railway stations in China, replacing the smaller one just up the road that was rather charming, but totally inadequate for a city of 12 million people. When you arrive, follow the crowds downstairs. You will emerge from underneath the platforms, and will probably be asked to produce your ticket.

Outside the station there is a vast concourse. You may find a taxi if you are lucky, but you are more likely to have to depend on a bus of one sort or another. Bus number 113 could deposit you on the Nanking Xi Lu (Nanking Road West) near Shimen Lu, and the 64 (crossing the Nanking Road at Jiangxi Road) on the Bund near the old town. Bus 110 also goes to Nanjing Lu.

The station is in the north of Shanghai, in the Hongkou district. There are shuttle minibuses that connect the railway station with the major bus stations. The number 3 runs between the railway station and the West Bus Station, which is in the southwest of the city, and therefore must pass through the centre at some point. You may have to pay the full fare (just over one yuan), but the driver will probably drop you off somewhere on his route. The route varies from driver to driver.

Arrival by sea

The ship will dock at the International Passenger Terminal which is located to the north-east of Suzhou Creek and is within walking distance (about 15 minutes) of the Bund. Normally your luggage will be unloaded from the ship and delivered to the customs area. Since some ships charge more for this service, it would be as well to check with the purser well before you arrive.

A bus may be provided to transport passengers to the custom's shed in the event of the ship having to dock some distance away.

The formalities are very simple. You will be asked to present passport and declaration form after you have claimed your luggage, and sometimes to submit declared goods for inspection.

Walking out of the custom's area will bring you onto Danming Lu. You may find a taxi; failing that, there are two buses that can take you to the Bund. The 27 travels the Bund as far as Nanking Road, which it takes as far as the Jing An Temple. The 28 terminates on the Bund just after the junction with the Nanking Road. The stops for both these buses are are found on Chang Yan Lu, the road to the north of Danming Lu. However, in view of the crowded conditions on the buses, you are advised to walk to the nearest hotel (Shanghai Mansions), which will take no more than 10/15 minutes, from where a taxi can be hired. To get there, walk south-west along Danming Lu until you reach the hotel, a large brick building overlooking Suzhou Creek to the north of Waibaidou Bridge.

Chinese currency

China retains a unique dual currency system. In other words, there is one currency for the local Chinese (Renmimbi or RMB), and one for holders of foreign currency (Foreign Exchange Certificates or FECs). They both have the same nominal value but the term RMB is generally used to cover both types. Theoretically, foreigners are supposed to use only FECs, and when you change money, those are what you are given. FECs are distinguishable from RMB by the writing in English on the back of each note, and the pictures of Chinese scenery rather than pictures of tractors. Each time you change money, you will fill in and be given a copy of a form. Keep them, as without them it is impossible to change money back when you leave the country.

At present there are about six and a half yuan to the pound (£1 = 1.7 American dollars). The yuan is sub-divided into 10 jiao, each of which is worth 10 fen. There are, therefore, 100 fen to each yuan. The nomenclature is complicated by the fact that the Chinese rarely use the words 'yuan' or 'jiao' — these are merely titular. In everyday speech, people say 'kwai' (which can be roughly translated as 'unit of money') for yuan, and 'mao' for jiao. So, if you wish to say, for example, '3 yuan and 2 jiao (or 20 fen)', you have to say 'san kwai er mao'.

On any one day the official exchange rate should be the same everywhere, since all places authorised to change money, including hotels, are branches of the Bank of China.

Contradictions

There are further complications. Although you may use FECs everywhere, if you are given RMB in your change you might have difficulty in spending it, especially in those places which are geared to foreign patronage, and where the staff have been told to accept only FECs. Yet the same establishment may well try to palm you off with RMB in the change. If the amount in question is only small, there is no point in making a fuss, but for a large amount it may be worth your while to insist on being given FECs. This is good only in hotels and shops frequented by foreigners; in local shops there may well be no FECs available, so try to avoid buying small items with large denomination notes. If, when you come to leave China, you still have some RMB, you should be able to change small quantities back into foreign currency, along with all your FECs, provided you can produce the requisite bank receipts. This can be done only in banks at your point of exit from China, whether railway station, airport, or port. RMB may not be exported, but FECs may, although they cannot be spent or exchanged outside China — therefore they are only good as souvenirs.

Black market

Despite the intricacies of the Chinese money system, there is a black market. The marketeers are prepared to exchange RMB in excess of the nominal value of your FECs, but bear in mind that this is illegal, and there is the problem of spending the RMB, something which is more difficult in large cities where even the local shops are used to dealing with foreigners. However, perseverence in small shops and in that area of restaurants not reserved for foreigners may win the day.

Leaving Shanghai

By air

If you are leaving Shanghai for another country, remember that you will need the customs declaration form you were given upon entering the country, your passport, and 15 RMB, payable only in Foreign Exchange Certificates, for airport tax.

To get to the airport, either take a taxi, which will cost 25/30 yuan from downtown, or the shuttle bus from in front of the CAAC building on Yanan Zhong Lu. Journey time is about forty minutes. At the terminal there are two areas — domestic and international.

Domestic flights In the domestic area, you check in as normal (there is no internal airport tax, and bear in mind that Chinese airlines seem to be on the point of demanding that all check-in luggage be locked). Following check-in, you may have to go through a security check, which may include X-rays, and where you will have to produce your boarding pass. You may also have to produce your passport and visa. Once through to the departure lounge, there are lavatories and small shops, where drinks and snacks are available.

International flights Although several doors theoretically lead into the international area, usually only one is open, which tends to create a bottleneck. Once inside you will find that there is a restaurant/bar, an information desk, a left luggage room, toilets, and telephones. Unfortunately, it is not always possible to check in immediately, since passengers are frequently asked to wait until their flight is called. This often means more queues. Once the flight is called, you may proceed to the check-in desk, handing in the declaration form (do not forget to fill in the exit column and that you may be asked to produce items mentioned on it — have them to hand in your hand luggage), and passing an X-ray machine where you may be asked to submit your suitcases to a check. Check in as normal. Airport tax is payable afterwards at another desk. You then proceed to passport control (if travelling on an individual visa, you will need to fill in a departure form), then to another security check for hand luggage, and thence into the departure area. Here you will find a desk for changing Chinese money back into foreign currency, for which you will need receipts given you when buying Chinese currency.

There is a large duty-free shopping area and a restaurant. The prices in the shops are marked in Hong Kong and American dollars (sample prices: 200 Marlboro = US$13. One litre of Johnny Walker Black Label = US$24.), and there is a wide range of goods available including jewellery, leather handbags, books, tea and perfumes, as well as arts and crafts. Credit cards are acceptable. There are telephones and a post office (not always open). In the gate area is a little snack-bar.

By sea
The International Passenger Terminal is off Danming Lu, not far from Shanghai Mansions Hotel. A taxi will cost very little.

Remember to fill in the exit column of the declaration form, and to have items declared on it available in your hand luggage. There are facilities for changing Chinese money into foreign currency, provided you have the requisite 'bank exchange memos' (receipts from the banks where you bought Chinese currency).

By rail
On the whole, by rail is the best way of travelling in China. The new railway station is north of Suzhou Creek, on Jiaotong Lu. It is massive, but well designed for coping with thousands of passengers. Tickets must be bought from the ticket office outside the main building, to the right as you look at it. Remember that return tickets cannot be purchased and that foreigners are expected to pay a higher price, although it is sometimes possible to pay with RMB. However, the competition is so fierce that it may be worth paying the full price to let CITS deal with the hassles. The tickets, even at foreign prices, cannot be considered expensive.

Then you must show the ticket to enter the station. The platforms all radiate from a central corridor, the train numbers clearly indicated. Remember that drinking water will not be available (except in boiling form), so it's a good idea to take along some mineral water. The quality of the food in the dining cars is variable, as is the range and quality of available drinks. There are very few air conditioned carriages, but check because they are gradually being introduced. For example there is usually one on the express service to Nanking, and on certain sleepers to Peking.

When you arrive at your destination, the carriage attendant will return your ticket to you, if she has retained it during the journey. Keep it, as you will be expected to produce it on leaving the station.

Customs
Chinese Customs are usually fairly straightforward. You are likely to be asked only to produce the items that were mentioned on your declaration form. It is illegal, it should be noted, to attempt to export antiques without the red seal that proves them to be no older than 150 years.

Great Britain has particularly strict customs restrictions. Goods of a value of up to £32 are exempt from duty, but anything of greater value should be declared. Normally duty amounts to some 30 per cent of the items' value, but in the case of some goods from China (carpets for example), the import tax is waived. You thus pay only the 15 per cent VAT.

Double Happiness. Someone in the house is getting married and such symbols should bring good luck.

FIVE

Local transport

How you move around Shanghai obviously depends on the location of your hotel, how much money you want to spend, and how much time you have at your disposal. It is an ideal city for exploring on foot, since a lot of the fascination lies in wandering the streets whilst taking in the relics of old Shanghai and seeing the Chinese going about their daily lives. If you prefer not to walk, or if you intend to visit places dotted all over town, there are other means at your disposal:

Taxis

Although there are many more taxis than in the recent past, it is still difficult to hail one in the street. The reason for this is not clear, but one driver explained that the municipal authorities do not wish to add to the already congested roads by allowing cabs to load and unload passengers. Be that as it may, some drivers will stop which means that it is always worth trying to flag them down.

Otherwise taxis are obtainable only at certain points, usually the major hotels. The system varies slightly from hotel to hotel, but generally speaking there is a taxi desk manned by someone to whom you give your destination, and who will obtain a cab as soon as possible. Sometimes it is the doorman who does the job.

There are two types of taxi in Shanghai. Most are attached to companies run by the Municipal Government, and hotels normally deal with this type. They are safe and nearly always honest, even if most of the taxis are not metered. The second type is private. They are usually to be found around hotels (and other places) too, but you must approach the drivers directly, and negotiate the price in advance if they are willing to take you to the place you want. They tend to be more expensive and less honest. They are less skilled in the art of driving, and should be avoided if possible. After a while it becomes easy to distinguish them from the others — the vehicles are usually in far from immaculate condition.

It is sometimes very easy to obtain a taxi in the hotels, but at other times you may have to wait for up to an hour. It is worth ordering one sometime in advance if at all possible, and if you are going to somewhere where there are unlikely to be taxis available for the return journey, think about keeping the same one. In this case it is essential to make the arrangement in advance, and to discuss the price. On the whole, taxis are not expensive, particularly the municipal ones.

It is customary for the driver to give a receipt. In the unlikely event that you meet a dishonest driver (among the municipal ones anyway), demand one, and take a note of the car registration number.

Tips are not expected, although this is beginning to change. A packet of cigarettes may be acceptable and may encourage reluctant drivers.

Car rental

Self-drive car hire does not yet exist in China, although the idea of introducing it has been mooted. When it comes, foreign drivers will need to have their wits about them, not because of high speed recklessness but, on the contrary, because of the infuriatingly slow tempo of the traffic and the arrogance or carelessness of some pedestrians and cyclists.

However, it is possible to hire a car with driver. This can be arranged through CITS, at their information desk in the Peace Hotel, or directly at the hotel taxi desks. Prices are likely to be negotiable.

Buses and trolleybuses

Buses are an extremely cheap means of transport, and the network is extensive, although route maps are very difficult to find. Because of the language barrier, they may seem difficult to use, but once you have the routes sorted out, and if you have your destination written down in Chinese to show the conductor everything becomes easier. Although you will almost never need to wait more than a few minutes for a bus the main disadvantage, in the absence of a metro system, is that the buses are severely crowded, and very often a great deal of pushing and shoving is required to get on. Do not baulk at getting on buses that seem impossibly full — push with everyone else. Once aboard pay the conductor, who will have a seat by the window. Within the city limits the fare is not likely to be more than 10 fen.

Travelling in buses shows the Chinese at their rudest. Although you need often to push in order to get aboard, never be aggressive, even if you feel that others are. At any one time you are likely to be the only foreigner on the bus and your behaviour will be very obvious.

Bicycles

It is well known that the principal means of transport for the Chinese is the bicycle; private cars remain a comparitive rarity. Riding a bicycle is the best way to cover large areas in a leisurely manner. Unfortunately there are no official outlets for hiring them

in Shanghai because of the concern by the authorities that foreigners will not be able to cope with the admittedly idiosyncratic traffic conditions.

What you do obviously depends on the length of your stay, but if it is to be for a reasonable length of time, and especially if you are considering visits to other cities in the area, it might be worth buying a bicycle. A new one can be purchased for about 200 yuan. They have been seen for sale in the Jinjiang branch of the Friendship Store, but local shops sell them too, of course. There is a large shop around the corner from where Xizang Zhong Lu meets Yanan Dong Lu. Bicycles can be bought second hand as well, and occasionally impromptu markets are arranged in the street. For news of this sort of thing you need to speak to someone in the student community — students eager to practise their language skills are legion, and if you stand still long enough almost anywhere, but especially on the Bund, someone is sure to approach you. He may know of someone wishing to sell a bicycle, or even of someone willing to lease one out.

Shanghai and the surrounding area is flat, and therefore ideal for cycling. There are plenty of bicycle lanes in the city, but it must be borne in mind that the streets are crowded and that many people have little or no idea of the highway code. However, many foreigners cope perfectly well so, remembering to stay particularly alert, there is no reason not to take it on.

When you buy a bicycle, do make sure that the brakes work, that the saddle is secure, and the tyres firm. If you intend travelling any distance, bring your own repair kit from home, although there are many pavement repair shops, who will do a good job at reasonable cost. It might also be as well to attach a distinctive piece of material to the bike, in order to quickly distinguish it from the millions of others. In some areas of the city there are bike-parks, attended by elderly people bearing red arm-bands, to whom you may entrust your bike for a few fen.

SIX

Accommodation

Shanghai has a profusion of hotels, but none that fall into the pension class. Nor is there very much for the traveller on a very tight budget who is looking for dormitory accommodation. On the other hand it is possible to stay in some glorious old hotels for comparatively little. The lawns are still impeccable, the shrubberies manicured, the kitchen gardens doing well, and the stained glass still in place. These are the places to stay if at all possible.

What to expect

Broadly speaking, hotels in Shanghai can be placed into three categories.
- Older hotels, referred to above, built mostly by foreigners in the Concession years either as hotels, service flats or as private mansions and which have the best locations. Their faded opulence is highly appealing, and still comfortable. Some of them have been modernised without sacrificing their charm.
- Hotels built by the Chinese to cope with the newest foreign invasion. These are highly variable in quality, price, and location.
- New foreign built or joint venture hotels, comfortable in the way of international chain hotels, but expensive.

Until recently it was a problem to make a booking directly with a particular hotel: one made a request through the state tourist organisation or arrived on the doorstep and hoped for the best. This aspect has improved immeasurably and most desirable hotels claim to accept direct individual bookings from abroad either by telephone or by telex.

The Chinese refer to some of their hotels as 'guest houses'. These are not small, family run hotels, but large hotels, often used to accommodate VIPs as well as foreign tourists.

The following guide is as comprehensive as possible in a city changing as quickly as Shanghai. Where certain, information about dormitory accommodation and advance booking is given. Prices, where quoted, are for one night; meals are not normally included in the price.

Most hotels are built along the axis between the airport and the Bund, a not inconsiderable distance. For that reason the hotels are listed according to location — 'downtown', meaning on or near the Bund or the Nanking Road; 'central', meaning well within the city limits and in an interesting area but not within casual walking distance of the downtown area; and suburban, meaning at the edge of or outside the city proper, which may nevertheless include hotels of a high standard.

Downtown

Peace Hotel (Heping Binguan 和平饭店) 20 Nanjing Dong Lu. Tel.211244/218050. Cable: 3266 Shanghai. The Peace Hotel, which is a combination of the former Cathay Hotel (Sassoon House) on the north side and the former Palace Hotel on the south side, overlooks the harbour from the junction of the Nanking Road and the Bund. Despite neglect and disregard for the elegance of its interior, it is a fine example of art-deco, and a glimpse into Shanghai's past. It could be considered as shabby first class. Best location, and still only eleven miles from the airport (40 minutes) and two miles from the railway station. It is essential to stay in the north wing. Amenities: airconditioning, phone, colour T.V., private shower/bath, bar with live music (the famous Peace Hotel Jazz Band), hairdressers, massage, shops (including bookshop), money exchange, post office. Western and Chinese food. Advance booking is certainly possible through travel agents in Hong Kong but it may be harder to do it oneself.

Shanghai Mansions (Da Sha Fandian 上海大厦) 20 Suzhou Lu. Tel.246260. Telex 33007 BTHSH. Cable: 1111 Shanghai. Formerly 'Broadway Mansions', this early sky-scraper (1934) has another very good location, just across the bridge from the Bund, overlooking Suzhou Creek. Recently refurbished, it used to be a residential hotel for the rich. Part of it also housed the American Military Advisory Group before 1943. It is not quite as evocative of old Shanghai as the Peace Hotel, but is comfortable and offers a wide range of facilities. No.of rooms:254, including suites in Chinese, American,

English, French, Japanese, and Arabic styles. Amenities: airconditioning, phone, private bath/shower, colour T.V., ballroom, banquet hall, bar, billiards room, live music/disco, hairdresser, massage service, shop (well stocked), bookstore, money exchange, post office and telex room. Yangzhou and Cantonese style Chinese food; Western food includes some French and Russian dishes that have metamorphosed over the years. Direct bookings are acceptable. Cost: Cheapest double room: 138 yuan.

Park Hotel/International Hotel (Guo Ji Fandian 国际饭店). 170 Nanjing Lu. Tel. 225225. Cable: 1445 Shanghai. Another thirties skyscraper (until quite recently the tallest building in China and at the time of its construction the tallest outside the Americas) and yet another splendid location in the heart of the shopping district, opposite the old racecourse that is now the People's Park. It is noted for the excellence of its Chinese food, but offers only moderate comfort and service. The main plusses are the location and the view from its upper floors. No.of rooms: 150. Amenities: air-conditioning, phone, colour T.V., private bath/shower, ball-room, bar/coffee shop (poor), shop, money exchange. Peking style Chinese food; pseudo-French cooking in the Western restaurant. Booking through CITS only. Cost of cheapest double room: 120 yuan.

Seventh Heaven Hotel (Qichong Tian Binguan 七重天宾馆) 627 Nanjing Dong Lu. Tel.220777. Tx.33907 BTHQC. This hotel has yet another fine location half-way between the Park Hotel and the Bund, and is to be found in a rather oddly shaped pre-liberation skyscraper next to the refurbished No.10 Department store, and in front of an interesting maze of old narrow streets. It had the same name before 1949. The hotel occupies only one part of the building, and you must take a lift to the lobby. There is a small shop, a bar, and a restaurant. All rooms have private facilities and air conditioning. There are regular 'dance parties'. For the visitor who needs to be in the heart of the city, this is a good place to stay, but the presence of a telex does not apparently guarantee advance reservations.

Overseas Chinese Hotel (Huaqiao Hotel 华桥饭店) 104 Nanjing Xi Lu. Tel.226226. Tx: 33909 BTHHF Cable:4321 Shanghai. This is a sixty year old building in Italianate style that was originally an insurance company with appartments for its employees. Once again the location is excellent (close to the Park Hotel). As you might expect, this hotel is mostly patronised by Chinese from abroad, but other foreigners are welcome. The rooms are comfortable, if not in the first rank, but the staff seem friendly and willing. Amenities: airconditioning, phone, colour T.V., private bath/shower, ballroom (dance party every night: 12 FECs entrance including drink), bar, barber, shop, money exchange, post office, ticketing service, telex room. Chinese food in the Fujian, Cantonese, and Chaozhou idioms. Western food available. No.of rooms: 120. Advance bookings may be made direct. Cost of cheapest double rooms: 90-130 yuan.

Pujiang Hotel (浦江饭店) 17 Huangpu Lu. Tel.246388. Formerly the luxurious Astor Hotel, the Pujiang is now a budget hotel, and seemingly the only one offering dormitory accommodation. It has a good location (on the banks of the Huangpu across the road from the Shanghai Mansions hotel and the Soviet Consulate), two restaurants and a shop. A double room, of which there are only ten, will cost 97 yuan and dormitory accommodation 20.

Seagull Hotel (Hai'ou Fandian 海鸥饭店) 60 Huangpu Lu. Tel. 251043. Tx.33603 SISC. Cable: 2114. This was built as an extension to the Seaman's Club in 1984, and is now a hotel open to all. Yet another good location, next to the Soviet Consulate, and with a fine view along the Bund and over the harbour. No. of rooms: 105. Amenities: airconditioning, private facilities, phones, bars (including one in an annex with a view across the harbour, open until 24.00), shops, small business centre. There are three restaurants including a banqueting hall on the 12th floor, a Chinese food restaurant on the second floor, and a western one on the first floor. Cost of cheapest double room: 121 yuan.

Youth Association Guesthouse (Qingnian Hui Binguan 青年会宾馆) 123 Xizang Nan Lu. Tel: 261040. A budget hotel and by all accounts worth trying. Expect to pay about 130 yuan for a double room.

Central

Jinjiang Hotel (锦江饭店) 50 Maoming NanLu. Tel. 582582. Tx. 33380 GRJJH. Cable: 7777 Shanghai. Built in what used to be the French Concession, in 1931, it was originally a private residential hotel. In 1951 it reopened as a general hotel, and it was here that Zhou En-lai and President Nixon signed the Shanghai Communique in February 1972. Opposite is the Jinjiang Club, the old 'Cercle Sportif Français', currently being converted into a hotel. The Jinjiang has a wide array of facilities, and in some ways could claim to be a luxurious hotel — there are rooms that are not only immaculate, but which have retained perfectly their period charm. However, the service is patchy, and new additions jar with the style of the original buildings. The Jinjiang is several original buildings, one newer building, and a new skyscraper awaiting completion. They stand in spacious gardens. Although the location is not strictly 'downtown', it stands in an interesting part of the former French Concession, close to a number of historically important sites and one of Shangai's main shopping streets, Huaihai Lu. Amenities: airconditioning, phone, colour T.V., private bath/shower, ballroom, bar (in the style of the Bull and Bear pub in Hong Kong), billiards room, health club, bowling alley, massage room, indoor swimming pool, large shopping arcade with a branch of the Friendship Store, jewellers, boutiques, supermarket, porcelain shop, bookstore, film developers, and travel agent, money exchange, post office, hairdresser, coffee shop. There are several restaurants — those serving Chinese food specialise in Sichuan and Cantonese styles; there is a Japanese restaurant, and a new French one, the 'Café de Rêve', which claims to be Shanghai's only 'International Class Restaurant Lounge'. In the middle building you will find a Japanese Karaoke bar, and what is supposed to be the best discotheque in Shanghai, the 'Club d'Elegance'. The entrance fee is 35 yuan (including two drinks) and has a good laser show. No. of rooms: 720. Advance reservations can be made directly with the hotel. Cost of cheapest double room: 136 yuan.

Jingan Guest House (靖安饭店) 370 Huashan Lu. Tel.551888. Tx: 30022 BTHJA. Cable: 3304 Shanghai. The Jingan Guesthouse is one of three hotels clustered together in what was a residential part of the old French Concession, the others being the Hilton and the Shanghai. Its old name was 'Haig Appartments', and it now has two wings of which the western one is new, and lacks the period charm of the other. Comfortable in a quiet way, this is a hotel worth considering. Amenities: airconditioning, phone, colour T.V., private bath/shower, bar, beauty salon, massage room, shop, money exchange, post office, bakery, business centre (photocopying, telex, fax). Chinese cooking: Sichuan and Yangzhou styles — these restaurants have a good reputation. There is a

Western style restaurant too. No. of rooms: 217. Advance reservations can be made directly. The cheapest double room costs 115 yuan.

Shanghai Hilton (上海希尔顿) 250 Huashan Road. Tel. 563343. Tx.33612 HILTL CN. Cable: Hiltels Shanghai. This massive construction, completed in 1987, is the tallest building in the city, with a good location in the heart of the former French Concession. It offers a wide range of amenities, and service as good as you are likely to find in Shanghai. Amenities: airconditioning, phone, refrigerators, television, videos, swimming pool, health club with sauna, outdoor tennis court, recreation room (billiards,table-tennis, darts), underground car park, executive business centre (including secretarial services, interpreters, photocopying, telex/cable and facsimile services, mail facilities and packaging services), shops including airline office and florist, Western café, rooftop bar, entertainment lounge, patisserie/bakery. There are three Chinese restaurants and a Western/Japanese restaurant. No. of rooms: 800 on 40 floors. Advance bookings may be made direct. The cost of the cheapest double room is 417 yuan.

Shanghai Hotel (上海宾馆) 505 Ulumuqi Bei Lu. Tel.312312. Tx.33295. Cable: 0244 Shanghai. Next to the Hilton, this was one of the earlier home grown efforts (1983), and apart from being the tallest building in Shanghai when it opened, succeeding the Park Hotel, seemed fairly promising. At one time it could have been considered one of the better hotels in the city, but it has worn very badly, and the service is poor. These days, with the wide variety of hotels to choose from, it is very unlikely that you will need to make use of this one. Amenities: airconditioning, phone, colour T.V., private bath/shower, ballroom, bar, shop, bookstore, beauty salon, massage room, post office. Chinese cooking: Sichuan and Cantonese. Western: French. Cost: approximately 120 yuan a night. Advance bookings can only be made through CITS.

Ruijin Guest House (瑞金饭店) 118 Ruijin Lu. Tel.372653. Tx.33003 BTHRJ CN. Cable:2870 Shanghai. A country hotel in the middle of Shanghai, made up of four villas. A delightful evocation of old Shanghai. Amenities: airconditioning, phone, refrigerators, colour T.V., central music system, private bath/shower, massage service, beauty salon, shop, money exchange, post office. Chinese cooking: Cantonese and Sichuan. Western: French. Cost: about 200 yuan.

DongHu Guest House (东湖饭店) 167 Xinle Lu. Tel. 370050/550758. Tx:33453 BTHDH Cable: 4605. This hotel consists of one large main building, and a few other smaller villas. One of them, currently being refurbished, used to belong to one of the most infamous characters of old Shanghai, Du Yue Sheng. This is building number seven. The other villas used to belong to wealthy foreigners. This is a very pleasant place to stay, and is located in the old French Concession, not far from Huaihai Lu, the main shopping street in the area. Amenities: airconditioning, private shower/bath, phone, refrigerators, colour T.V., central music system, bar, beauty salon, swimming pool, tennis courts, shop, money exchange, massage service. There are four Chinese restaurants. No. of rooms: 140. Advance reservations can be made direct. Cost of the cheapest double rooms: 170-200 yuan.

Hengshan Guest House (衡山饭店) 534 Hengshan Lu.Tel. 377050. Tx. 33009 BTHHS CN. Cable: 5295 Shanghai. The Hengshan, another old block of flats that used to be known as Picardie Mansions, lies in the southwestern part of the city, a little to the south of Huaihai Lu, in a quiet part of the old residential part of the former French Concession. It has been modernised and is comfortable. Amenities: airconditioning, colour T.V., private bath/shower, bar, hairdressers, massage room, shop, money exchange, post office. Chinese cooking: Sichuan, Cantonese, Shanghai. Western: French, American and Russian. No. of rooms: 220. Advance reservations can be made direct. The cost of the cheapest double room is 155 yuan.

Dahua Guest House (达华宾馆) 914 Yan'an Xi Lu. Tel. 512512. Tx: 30029. Cable: 1208 Shanghai. This is another converted block of flats (built 1937) and until recently was one of the cheaper hotels in the city. Now, following a reconversion to service flats, it is among the most expensive, the cheapest room available for 350 yuan. It is probably aimed at the long term business visitor. It has an air of what in another age would have been called 'discretion'. Certainly it is in a comparatively secluded corner of Shanghai, towards the western boundary of the city, built around a courtyard. There is one Western restaurant and one Chinese, a bar, shop, conference room, billiards room and business centre.

Huating Sheraton Hotel (华亭宾馆) 1200 Caoxi Bei Lu. Tel.386000. TX.33589 SHHTH CN. Cable: 0703. This massive 'S'-shaped hotel, with its marble halls, is one of the most comfortable hotels in the city, but expensive and on the south-west boundary, close to Shanghai Stadium. It is an integral part of the Sheraton chain, and is currently foreign managed. Amenities: airconditioning, phone, mini-bar, colour T.V., central music system, refrigerator, videos, ballroom, 'Nicole's Disco', bar, café, four lane bowling alley, health club, indoor swimming pool, sauna and massage, tennis courts, beauty salon, barber shop, photo studio, shopping arcade, bank, post office, billiards, international conference hall with simultaneous translation facilities, roof garden, indoor garage, shuttle buses to the airport and to the downtown area. Chinese cooking: various. Western: English and French. No. of rooms: 1000. Advance bookings may be made direct. Cost of cheapest double room: around 100 U.S. dollars (payable in FECs at the exchange rate of the day).

The White House. Said to be favoured by Mao when he was in town, it is now part of the Xing Guo Guest House.

Hua Ting Guest House (华亭二号楼), 2525 Zhong Shan Xi Lu. Tel: 391818. Tx:30192 HTGHS. Cable: 9985. This new hotel stands next to the Sheraton in the southwest corner of the city. It is a home grown effort and seems comfortable and reasonably well run, although the dining room is small and stuffy. Residents may use the facilities of the Sheraton. Amenities: airconditioning, phone, colour T.V. with in-house movies, refrigerator and mini-bar. The restaurant offers Cantonese, Sichuan, and Shanghai cooking. No. of rooms: 216. Advance bookings may be made direct. Cost of cheapest double room is 200 yuan.

Xinguo Guest House (兴国旅社) 72 Xinguo Lu. Tel.374503. Tx.33016 BTHXG. Cable: 6222. This is one of the most exquisite hotels in Shanghai. It is located in the western part of the city, in what used to be a residential part of the French Concession. If you want to have some idea of how the very rich used to live before 1949, this is the place to stay. The hotel consists of about ten former villas of varying degrees of grandeur, set in grounds of 15 hectares. When you enter the grounds it is hard to believe not only that you are in the unendingly noisy city of Shanghai, but that you are in the Shanghai of the late twentieth century. The lawns are immaculately cared for, teams of gardeners tend the flowerbeds, and birds with long, bluish tails glide about the trees. The no.1 building is the proudest of all — this was built in 1932 by a British businessman, and in later years was used by Chairman Mao when he was in town. The staff appear very helpful. This is not, perhaps, the hotel for the business person, but apart from a shop and a variety of restaurants, other facilities include a team of taxis, post office, photocopying, medical treatment, film developing, hairdresser, and massage. The cheapest double room costs 130 yuan, and the average cost is 180.

Suburban

Jin Sha Hotel (金沙饭店) 801 Jin Sha Jiang Lu. Tel: 546000. Tx: 33454 BTHJD. Cable: 4650. This brand new hotel looks to be a reasonable effort, but is not very well located for the downtown areas, though fine for the airport, which is only five kilometres away. It is situated in the northwest part of the city overlooking Changfeng Park. Amenities: airconditioning, colour T.V., telephone, two bars, 24-hour coffee shop, discotheque, business centre (secretarial services, business information, cable, telex), gym and billiards facilities, shuttle bus. Chinese cooking: various. Western: various. No. of rooms: 300. Advance bookings may be made direct. The cheapest double room costs about 150 yuan.

Western Suburbs Guest House (Xijiao Guest House 西郊宾馆) 1921 Hongqiao Lu, Changning District. Tel.379643. Tx.33004 BTHHQ CN. Cable: 9919 Shanghai. Like the Xinguo mentioned above, this is a hotel, set in a beautiful 80-hectare garden, that transports you away from the hurly-burly of modern Shanghai. The main building is approached by a long drive that winds through vast expanses of lawn and rockery. Lakes, lotus pools and bridges bring Chinese flavour to a landscape that owes something to Kew Gardens. Facilities are extensive and good. The only disadvantage is the location, which is good for the airport but less so for the city centre. Amenities: airconditioning, phone, colour T.V., central music system, refrigerator, ballroom, bar, billiards, massage room, beauty salon, shop, money exchange, post office. Chinese cooking: Sichuan, Cantonese, Huaiyang. Western: French. No. of rooms: 150. Advance bookings may be made directly with the hotel. Cost of cheapest double room: 200 yuan.

Xijiao Dongyuan Guest Hotel (西郊宾馆东院) 1591 Hongqiao Lu, Changning District. Tel.372170. Tx.33004 BTHHQ CN. Cable: 9919 Shanghai. This is the other of the older hotels in this area, again set in gardens, and in fact under the same management as the Western Suburbs Guest House. It consists of four villas built in the 1950s and it is believed that they were used exclusively by Lin Biao. Amenities: airconditioning, phone, refrigerator, colour T.V., swimming pool, shop, money exchange. Chinese cooking: various.

Cypress Hotel (Longbai Fandian 龙柏饭店) 2419 Hongqiao Lu. Tel.329388 Tx.33288 CYH CN. Cable: 9921 Shanghai. Another hotel in a garden setting, it opened in 1982, one of the first of the new hotels to cater for foreign visitors. It remains one of the pleasantest hotels in Shanghai, convenient for the airport (five minutes drive), with helpful staff and management. The villa next door used to belong to Sir Victor Sassoon, and is now part of the hotel, serving as a garden bar and guest house. The main building is modern in style but sits very well in the landscaped gardens. For long term foreign residents of Shanghai, the hotel manages 69 self-contained modern villas, built in Western and Japanese styles. It offers a wide range of facilities, including an enormous entertainment centre that will soon be completed. This will house two swimming pools, an area for practising golf, tennis courts, squash courts, bowling alleys, and a fishing river. Amenities: airconditioning, phone, colour T.V., ballroom, bar, billiards, sauna, massage room, money exchange, post office, clinic, business centre, shuttle bus to city centre. Chinese cooking: Sichuan and Huaiyang. Western: French. No. of rooms: 161 plus villas. Advance bookings may be made direct. Cost of cheapest double room: U.S.$50 or local equivalent. After a certain number of nights the price is reduced.

Hotel Nikko Longbai (上海日航龙柏饭店) 2451 Hongqiao Road. Tel:593636 (598888 for reservations). Tx: 30138 NHISH. Cable: Nikkohtl 9923. This is a brand new Japanese-built hotel next to the Cypress Hotel, and therefore marginally closer to the airport. It is aimed at the business person on a hefty expense account, and boasts a considerable array of facilities. Amenities: individual climate control in all the rooms, plus radio, in-house movies, phone, refrigerator/mini-bar; banquet and conference facilities, outdoor swimming pool, tennis courts (with night lighting), fitness centre including sauna, massage and gym, business centre, newsstand, gift shops, hairdresser, florist, delicatessen, car parking, shuttle bus. No. of rooms: 387 + 32 suites. Advance bookings may be made direct. Cost of cheapest double room: 394 yuan.

Chengqiao Hotel (程桥宾馆) 2266 Hongqiao Lu. Tel.329641. Some of the newer hotels are rather sloppily built and run. This is one of them, and although it has reasonable facilities, the visitor will do better elsewhere. It is also badly located. Amenities: airconditioning, phone, colour T.V., central music system, beauty salon, shops, money exchange, post office. Chinese cooking: Cantonese. Western: French.

Cherry Holiday Villa (Yinghua Dujia Cun 樱花渡假村) 77 Nonggong Lu. Tel. 328350 Cable: 89960 Shanghai. This is another newer hotel similar to the Chengqiao, above. Amenities: airconditioning, phone, colour T.V., ballroom, bar, beauty salon, shop, money exchange, post office. Chinese cooking: Cantonese and Pekinese.

New Garden Hotel (新园饭店) 1900 Hongqiao Lu. Tel.329900. Cable: 9027 Shanghai. This hotel is also new but an improvement on the Chengqiao and Cherry Holiday Villa, above. However, long walks are required to get to some of the rooms and the service in the restaurants is appalling. Amenities: airconditioning, phone, colour T.V., bar, beauty salon, shop, money exchange, post office. Chinese cooking: Peking and Sichuan. Western: French.

Others

Here are two hotels that should be completed by the time you read this book.

Huashan Hotel (华山饭店) 2004 Nanjing Xi Lu. Tel: 513040, 523080. For the budget traveller. Rooms from about 80 yuan.

Xinya Hotel (New Asia Hotel 新雅旅社) 422 Tian Tong Lu. Tel: 242210. This is a promising hotel in a newly restored period building a little to the north of Suzhou Creek, within walking distance of the Bund. All rooms are airconditioned; the cost is about 120 yuan.

Signs of life in Shanghai.

SEVEN

Eating out

Eating out in Shanghai, as in the rest of China, is an unpredictable business. First, since there is no rating system, and since 'free enterprise' is still a novelty, the concept of producing good food for all-comers, no matter how much or little they spend, has not made much headway. A good restaurant one day becomes poor or indifferent the next. There is, as yet, no idea of establishing a reputation. Second, eating singly or in a pair makes it harder to obtain good food in a country where the idea of feasting is a banquet around a large table for at least eight people. Third, many restaurants are divided in two — a downstairs area, cheaper and scruffier, and an upstairs banqueting area, probably air-conditioned and more expensive, to where eager proprietors will try to propel foreigners. There is unlikely to be any difference in the quality of the food at its simplest, but more complicated dishes are likely to be served only upstairs. If all you want is a bowl of noodles, some vegetables, and soup, then insist on eating downstairs (unless you want airconditioning and cleaner surroundings). If you are after more gourmet food, then you will probably have to go upstairs.

Remember that in China it is customary to eat in the early evening. With the exception of some hotels, it will be difficult to eat after 8.00 pm.

Prices

In the downstairs part of restaurants, prices should be in line with Chinese incomes (low), and even as a foreigner there is no reason to pay foreign prices. You may also be able to pay with RMB. Upstairs the prices are likely to increase somewhat, and may seem excessive but up to a point that is to be expected — the Chinese attitude to pricing is rather unnerving, but you get used to it. However, it has been noted that some restaurateurs have become a little over-confident in their approach to this matter, charging outrageous prices. It is as well to settle the price beforehand; and then if you still feel aggrieved at the quantities, complain. If restaurants try to pull a fast one, they are usually honest enough to tacitly admit as much by producing more food.

Banquets

Unless you are lucky, you are unlikely to taste the best of Shanghai cooking without paying for a banquet. This is not quite as alarming as it sounds — it simply means enough diners to sit around a table, in the Chinese fashion, thus producing the best conditions for the cooking of Chinese food. It is sensible to book a table and negotiate the price in advance, ordering local delicacies according to how much you want to pay.

The word banquet is used lightly here, simply to convey the fact that in China you can usually only begin to experience the best in Chinese cooking by eating in a party (although there is still no guarantee of quality!). The minimum one should expect is four cold plates, four hot dishes, soup (which normally comes at the end), and rice. A banquet, in the sense that a foreigner would understand the word, might consist of four cold plates, eight main dishes, two showpiece dishes (a whole fish, for example), as well as soup, rice, pastries, and fruit.

Traditionally, main dishes are placed in the middle of the table, from which each guest helps himself, whilst only the rice is served in individual portions. Sometimes, especially in Cantonese restaurants, it is customary for the waitress to serve the food to the diner.

Banquet etiquette

A true banquet is one given by a host for a guest. In modern China the host is likely to be the representative of a Chinese business corporation, and the guest a foreign business-person. In this case the seating arrangements are likely to be those shown in the diagram opposite.

Under these circumstances the host will herald the arrival of each dish by serving the principal guest. It is quite possible that, lavish though each might be, the formality of the occasion will demand that the diners have only one bite from every dish. One of the reasons for this is that toasts and speeches are a vital part of the

Seating at a Chinese banquet

1. First host.   2. Main guest
3. Wife of main guest, or second most important guest.
4. Second host.   5, 6. Second most important guests.
7. Interpreter.   8, 9, 10. Others.

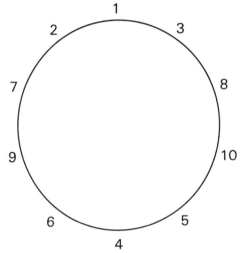

banquet (in fact it may be considered impolite to drink liquor without offering a toast), and after the host has made his opening toast, usually with 'Mao Tai', or a local equivalent, the main guest answers, followed by everyone else at the table, throughout the course of the meal. The Chinese equivalent of 'cheers!' is 'gan bei!', which means 'empty your glass' or 'bottoms up'.

Tea is almost never drunk during a meal — only before or after, although in a less formal atmosphere, nobody minds, and it should be readily available in restaurants.

Do not be surprised when your fellow eaters raise their rice bowls to their mouths, and shovel the rice in with their chopsticks — this is normal and acceptable, even at a banquet.

You will know when a banquet is over because the host will probably make a little farewell speech, there will be a great flurry of shaking hands, and the host and his friends or associates will melt away.

Chopsticks

Like skiing or riding a bicycle, using chopsticks is one of those things that look impossible to the uninitiated, but after the art is acquired seem ridiculously easy. Most chopsticks ('kwaizi') are made of bamboo, wood, or plastic, but they can be made of lacquer, jade, ivory, aluminium, silver, or gold. Their use is at least 3000 years old, and if there is one good reason for their retention, it is that they encourage smaller mouthfuls and therefore better digestion.

How someone manipulates chopsticks is an entirely personal matter, a question of comfort and ease. However the basic idea is to rest the thick end of the sticks, one on top of the other, in the cleft between the thumb and forefinger, and to allow them to point out across the other fingers, like a pistol. The bottom stick should rest on one finger, whichever you find most comfortable, and remain stationary. The uppermost stick is the one that needs to be manipulated to pick up food, and can be moved using the thumb and the next one or two fingers. The closer the hands to the top of the chopsticks, the better the leverage.

Forks can usually be provided on request. Serving spoons or chopsticks are not always provided, but in these days of hepatitis it is worth insisting on them.

Shanghai cuisine

The range of Chinese cooking is limitless, but experts seem to agree that broadly speaking there are four styles of Chinese cooking — Shandong, Sichuan, Cantonese, and Yangzhou. These are names of towns or provinces, but for different reasons their influence has extended beyond their original limits. The cuisine of Peking, for example, is considered to be in the Shandong style, although Peking is not in that province, and has its own dishes.

Shanghai cuisine comes into the category of Yangzhou cooking, the representative school of Eastern China. Located in the fertile Yangtze River Valley, the 'land of fish and rice', and on the Grand Canal, and therefore open to influences from both north and south, the city of Yangzhou developed its own style of cooking as it prospered in the days when it was an important commercial centre.

Yangzhou dishes are characterised by the use of heavy and highly flavoured sauce, and are frequently cooked in deep fat and soy sauce. Shanghai, in particular, is noted for stir-frying, simmering, deep-frying, pan-frying, and braising in red sauce. Famous dishes include crab roe dumplings, steamed Mandarin fish, lion's head meatballs flavoured with crab roe, fried whitebait, boiled shreds of pressed beancurd, Songjiang perch, Chongming crab and Dianshan lake crab, Sheshan orchid bamboo shoots, Shanghai fermented beancurd, spiced beans, and assorted styles of dumplings.

Some aspects of Chinese cooking

Soup

Westerners tend to regard soups as a sort of savoury aperitif. In China, soup might accompany a meal at home, providing much of the liquid intake, but for any meal approaching banquet proportions, soup is always (with the exception of Cantonese cooking) served at the end. It is supposed to ease digestion, and since the soup is frequently poured into the same bowl as the rice, it ensures that all the rice is eaten. Often the soup will seem rather watery but will be usually more palatable than it appears — it may consist, for example, of the broth from boiled chicken and duck bones and skin, or pork bones, or shrimp shells. On the other hand, a Chinese soup can be a magnificent spectacle. Winter melon soup is a whole winter melon partially hollowed out and filled with stock and a variety of other ingredients. The top is replaced and the whole melon cooked in a steamer. After, the cooked melon is presented on the table and the broth is ladled from inside.

Beancurd

Beancurd ('doufu' in Chinese) is a universal part of all Chinese cooking, and has been eaten for at least 1500 years. It is made from milled soya beans to which water is added, producing soya milk (a popular drink in its own right), followed by calcium salt to act as a coagulate. Then the water is gradually removed according to the consistency required. It is highly regarded in China for its healthy properties, being high in protein and calcium, and low in fat.

It may appear at the table in a variety of guises — vegetarian chefs, for example use it to cook mock fish or duck, or indeed any type of meat. It can be eaten raw, but at the table it is more likely to be served hot, covered with a spicy sauce, or mixed with pieces of pork, bamboo or mushroom. Its consistency, colour and shape are highly variable, depending on how it was made — for the uninitiated, it can be hard to distinguish from meat or vegetables. It may be soft and spongy, or yellow corrugated shreds, and can be preserved through pressing, drying, or smoking. Preserved spiced beancurd is not unlike a spicy cheese.

Blandness

Some of the dishes served are likely to seem rather bland. Many chefs do this intentionally as a counterbalance to the other more delectable dishes. Thus bread is steamed rather than baked, and retains a certain doughiness that is supposed to ease digestion. Chinese never add soy sauce to their rice (except sometimes for children) as it would spoil its purity and neutrality, which it needs to bring out the best in the other dishes. You will always find a bottle of soy and a bottle of vinegar on the table, to be used as you like, but particularly for dumplings and soup. They are used instead of salt and pepper which are almost never found at table.

Thousand-year-old eggs

The name is a fine example of the Chinese penchant for colourful nomenclature. These duck eggs are in fact only six months old, and are created by covering the raw egg in potash and storing them in a sealed earthen jar for about six months. The yolk becomes the greenish colour of pond water, and the white becomes a brown, diaphanous jelly. It usually appears as one of the cold dishes, and is an acquired taste.

Puddings

Sweet things do not feature much in a Chinese meal and, if at all, are most unlikely to appear at the end, since it is thought that it is healthier to eat sweet things before savoury. Thus the occasional pudding, or sweet gelatinous soup, or toffee-covered sweet potatoes, can be served at any time deemed by the chef to be appropriate. The main ingredients are small translucent fungus, walnuts, lotus seeds, dates, almonds, sesame, Ginko nuts, and red bean paste.

A famous pudding, eaten in Shanghai traditionally on Chinese New Year, is the one known as 'eight-precious rice'. This is a

Opposite: *The harbour and the Bund.*

mound of steamed glutinous rice, its surface decorated with 'eight precious' varieties of candied fruit, and the inside stuffed with sweet red bean paste, chestnuts or taro. Sometimes the paste is served alone with the addition of lotus seeds and covered with a honey sauce. It is delicious, but extremely heavy. A glass of Shaoxing wine, or a cup of tea would help to wash it down.

Comparisons

You cannot expect the food in China to be necessarily the same as you are used to at home. The vast majority of Chinese restaurants abroad are Cantonese, and not a few dishes have been adulterated to suit Western taste. A little adjustment is required, therefore, in Shanghai, in order to fully appreciate the food, apart from the fact that the standard can vary from poor to marvellous.

It is easy to be put off by some of the ingredients, but usually the name is more horrifying than the thing itself. For example, 'silver ears' are nothing more than a species of mushroom. In the case of items that are as described, for example snake or sea-cucumber (sometimes known as sea-slug) — which is classed as an animal, not an insect — do try them, because they are far better than you might imagine.

Drinks

Chinese beer is mostly good, and easy to buy (despite occasional newspaper reports complaining that demand outstrips production). The local brew is called 'Shanghai beer', accurate if unimaginative. Just over 300 miles to the north of Shanghai, on the coast, is the city of Tsingdao, home of China's most renowned beer — 'Tsingdao' beer. Like Shanghai, Tsingdao was a treaty port, in the German sphere of influence, and the Germans built a brewery, which they have recently helped the Chinese to modernise. The beer is supposed to derive its special flavour, however, from the purity of the local mineral water, 'Laoshan', which is used in its manufacture.

Opposite: *View from the tea house, Yu Garden. On hot summer days this is the place to languish.*

China's most famous spirit is 'Mao Tai' (nothing to do with the former Chairman, and not to be confused with the cocktail 'Mai Tai'). The Chinese refer to all their most lethal alcoholic concoctions as 'wines', but don't be taken in — no grape was ever anywhere near them. 'Mao Tai' is the gourmet among many similar spirits distilled from sorghum and rice, and its all too special flavour is worth sampling. Like every other national drink, outlandish claims are made that its purity becomes a great healer the following day, should you get carried away the night before; but don't bank on it. Such is the fame of 'Mao Tai', that it has become expensive and scarce. In that case try Qi Bao or Zao Lo, which are practically the same thing.

Both red and white grape wines are produced in China. Dry red wines are rather vinegary, the others are very sweet but have good flavour, reminiscent of port. There are some white wines that have been produced with the help of the French — 'Dynasty' and 'Great Wall' are lightweight but not bad.

The most famous of all the 'yellow' wines made from fermented glutinous rice, is produced in Shaoxing, not far to the south of Shanghai, in the province of Zhejiang. It is often drunk warm.

China also produces gin, vodka, whisky, and brandy at low prices, among which the vodka is all right with a mixer, and the brandy is considered to be reasonable.

Foreign made drinks are available, either by the bottle in places like the Friendship store, or by the glass in hotel bars. The prices are rather high.

There are plenty of soft drinks available, of good quality in hotels and in some restaurants. The standard soft drink, available in most restaurants and the average shop, is a rather grim fizzy orange drink. Shops aimed at foreigners sell a variety of international soft drinks, and restaurants are unlikely to protest if you bring in drinks bought outside.

Where to eat

There are plenty of restaurants in Shanghai, many of which have been, or are in the process of being, refurbished. Nor is there any shortage of snack food, since the Shanghai area is well known for things like dumplings. To give a comprehensive list of reliable restaurants is not yet possible. What follows is a list of well known establishments, or restaurants recommended by local people. Bear in mind that it is often advisable to book in advance, especially at night, since wedding parties, extravagant in China, often take up the available space.

Don't assume that the cooking in the hotels will necessarily be of a lower standard than in the restaurants outside. At least they will be used to serving individuals.

Most restaurants are in the central area around the Nanjing Dong Lu (Nanking Road East), and therefore in the following list only one division is made. 'Central' refers to that area eastwards from the Bund, either side of Nanjing Dong Lu, as far as the People's Park and the Park Hotel at 170, Nanjing Xi Lu (Nanking Road West). 'Others' refers to any other restaurant outside this area.

A stroll along the Bund is sure to attract the attention of locals wanting to practise their English — they should also be able to furnish you with the latest information about restaurants and entertainment.

Central

Dongfeng Hotel (东风饭店) 3 Zhongshan Dong Yi Lu (the Bund). Tel: 218060 Yangzhou/Cantonese style. Famous dishes: Dongfeng chicken legs (东风鸡腿), yellow croaker (黄鱼), fried shrimps (油爆虾仁), bean-curd stuffed with ham (火腿豆腐), duck with pinenuts (松子鸭). Formerly the Shanghai Club, that bastion of English male exclusiveness, the 'Long Bar' is still there.

Peace Hotel (和平饭店) 20 Nanjing Dong Lu. Tel: 211244. Mixed styles. Western food also available. Three main restaurants — the Dragon-Phoenix, the Crane of Longevity, and the Peace Hall. The last mentioned is a magnificent piece of old Shanghai.

Shanghai Mansions (上海大厦) 20 Suzhou Bei Lu. Tel: 246260. Most types of food are available here but the main attraction is the view across the Creek from the restaurants on the upper floors.

Yangzhou Fandian (杨州饭店) 308 Nanjing Dong Lu. Tel: 222779. Yangzhou style. This restaurant does have something of a reputation, so it is important to book in advance. Famous dishes: boiled beancurd shreds (烧豆腐丝), boned big fish head (鱼头浓汤), cured pork in jelly (酱肉冻), butterfly shaped sea cucumbers (蝴蝶海参).

Tong Tai Xiang Cai Guan (同泰祥菜馆) 497 Xizang Zhong Lu. Tel:221058. Shanghai style.

Yongjiang Zhuangyuan Lou (甬江状元楼) 162 Xizang Zhong Lu. Tel: 225280. Yangzhou/Shanghai/Ningbo styles. Specialises in seafood.

Wang Bao He Jiu Jia (王宝和酒家) 603 Fuzhou Lu. Tel:223673. This is a good place for sampling Chinese liquors.

Da Hong Yun (大鸿运) 556 Fuzhou Lu Tel: 223475. Yangzhou/Suzhuo style. Famous dishes: stuffed crab (大闸蟹), steamed mandarin fish (清蒸桂鱼), fried shrimps with green beans (碗豆虾仁), fried eel (炒黄鳝), chrysanthemum fire pot (菊花火锅).

Xinghualou (杏花楼) 343 Fuzhou Lu. Tel: 263492. Cantonese style. This old restaurant (nineteenth century) has an interesting list of specialities: stewed snake meat with shredded delicacies (炖蛇肉), stewed snake with wild cat and chicken (蛇猫鸡三味), fried snake with ham (火腿炒蛇肉), stewed boned chicken in oyster sauce (蚝油鸡肉), fish balls fried in bean juice (炸鱼丸). If you don't like the sound of some of these dishes, there are plenty of others to choose from, and a good snack shop downstairs.

Meiweishi (美味思) 600, Fuzhou Lu. Tel: 221705. Yangzhou/Suzhou/Wuxi styles.

Lao Ban Zhai Jiu Lou (老半斋酒家) 596 Hankou Lu. Tel: 222809,223668 Yangzhou style.

Da Hua Chao Zhou Cai Guan (大华潮洲菜馆) 403 Yanan Dong Lu. Tel:282845. Cantonese style.

Lao Zheng Xing Cai Guan (老正兴菜馆) 330 Shandong Zhong Lu. Tel:222624,229480. Shanghai style.

Qingzhen Fandian (清真饭店) 710 Fuzhou Lu. Tel: 224787. This Moslem restaurant specialises in beefsteaks (牛排), mutton and lamb (羊肉), and toffee-apples (or 'apple coated in thick syrup' in the Chinese translation 拔丝苹果).

Sichuan Fandian (四川饭店) 457 Nanjing Dong Lu. Tel: 222264. Sichuan style. Famous dishes: camphor tea duck (樟茶鸭子), pan-fried shredded beef (炒牛肉丝), sliced sichuan-style 'chicken of a wonderful taste' (noted in some guidebooks as 'chicken of a peculiar
taste': 四川怪味鸡).

Minjiang Fandian (闽江饭店) 679 Nanjing Dong Lu. Tel: 241009. Fujianese style (related to Cantonese).

Xinya (新稚粤菜馆) 719 Nanjing Dong Lu. Tel: 223636. Cantonese style. Famous dishes: beef in oyster sauce (蚝油牛肉), sweet and sour pork (古老肉), soup in white gourd (冬瓜盅), smoked pomfret, crispy roast suckling pig (烤乳猪).

Yan Yun Lou (燕云楼) 755 Nanjing Dong Lu. Tel: 223293. Shandong/Peking style. Famous dishes: Peking duck (北京烤鸭), bear's paw with four delicacies (四鲜熊掌), fried fish slices cooked in wine (酒香鱼片), fried tripe (炒牛肚).

Meilongzhen Jiujia (梅龙镇酒家) 22, Nanjing Xi Lu and 1081 Long (Lane) Tel: 532561. Sichuan style. One of the most famous restaurants in Shanghai. Famous dishes: savoury crisp chicken (香酥鸡), imperial concubine's chicken (贵妃鸡).

Overseas Chinese Hotel (Huaqiao Fandian 华侨饭店), 104 Nanjing Xi Lu. Tel: 226226. Cantonese and Western styles.

Park Hotel (国际饭店) 170 Nanjing Xi Lu. Tel: 225225. A variety of restaurants, both Chinese and Western — the Chinese ones have a good reputation, and those on the upper floor offer one of the best views of the Shanghai skyline (especially, apparently, from the ladies' lavatory).

Others

Yueyanglou Fandian (岳阳楼饭店) 28 Xizang Nan Lu. Tel: 282672 Hunan style (a cross between Sichuan and Cantonese styles). Famous dishes: Dongan chicken (东安鸡) spicy and slightly sour in taste, one chicken in three different flavours (三味鸡).

Renmin Fandian (人民饭店) 226 Nanjing Xi Lu. Tel: 537531. Yangzhou/Shanghai style. Famous dishes: semi-boned duck in superior soy sauce (酱鸭), shrimps in crust of fried rice (锅巴虾仁), fried black carp (炸黑鲤鱼), mandarin fish with pine nuts (松子桂鱼).

Lu Yang Cun (绿阳村) 763 Nanjing Xi Lu. Tel:537221. Yangzhou/Shanghai and Sichuan styles. Built in 1931, when Shanghai was at its most cosmopolitan, this restaurant has a reputation for cooking with traditional medicinal herbs. Famous dishes: black carp pieces in hot sauce (辣子黑鲤鱼), sour and peppery squid (酸辣鱿鱼), peanuts with pungently flavoured chicken (生仁辣子鸡), meat balls wth crab roe (蟹子肉丸), silver carp with lotus flavour (荷香白鲢).

Youyi Jiujia (友谊酒家) Friendship Restaurant on the roof of the Industrial Exhibition Centre), 1000 Yan'an Zhong Lu. Tel: 534078,581959. Cantonese style. Very popular.

Meixin Jiujia (美心酒家) 314 Shaanxi Nan Lu. Tel: 373919. Cantonese style. Famous dishes: chicken in spicy sauce (辣味鸡), Meixin crisp chicken (美心香酥鸡), crisp duck with lotus flavour (荷香酥鸭).

Da Tong Jiu Jia (大同酒家) 725 Huaihai Zhong Lu. Tel:378317. Cantonese style.

Chengdu Fandian (成都饭店) 795 Huaihai Zhong Lu. Tel: 376412. Sichuan style. Famous dishes: chicken in cellophane (赛璐鸡), cane-beaten chicken (棒锤鸡), beancurd with minced meat in chilli sauce (麻婆豆腐), braised sliced pork Sichuan style (鱼香肉丝), sour and peppery soup (酸辣汤).

Jie Mien Jing Chuan Cai Guan (街面景川菜馆) 47 Nanchang Lu (not far from Fuxing Park). Tel:288574. Sichuan style.

Lao Fandian (老饭店) 242 Fuyou Lu. Tel: 282782. One of the older resaurants of Shanghai, it sits in the old Chinese Town. Yangzhou/Shanghai style. Famous dishes: pig's trotters pickled with maize (玉米蹄筋), salted meat and fish soup (咸肉鱼汤), duck stuffed with choice ingredients (八宝鸭), fried shrimps (油爆虾仁), soft-shelled turtle stewed in soy (红烧甲鱼).

Huating Sheraton (华亭喜来顿) 1200 Caoxi Bei Lu. Tel: 386000. Cantonese, Sichuan, Yangzhou/Shanghai styles. Chinese food is served in the palatial roof-top restaurant, Guanyetai.

Jing'an Guesthouse (静安宾馆) 370 Huashan Lu. Tel: 563050. Yangzhou and Sichuan styles, in the Restaurant of the Bright Garden, in the West Building.

Hilton (静安希尔顿) 250 Huashan Lu. Tel:563343. Three Chinese restaurants (Sichuan, Cantonese Dim Sum, and Mixed); one restaurant serving Western and Japanese food.

Jinjiang Hotel (锦江饭店) 59 Maoming Nan Lu. Tel: 582582. Cantonese and Sichuan styles, in the opulent surroundings of the Friendship Restaurant. The 'Jinli', in the new South Building, is open 24 hours a day.

Vegetarian restaurants

In any restaurant serving Chinese food it is possible to order dishes of vegetables, but if you want more variety there are a couple of establishments catering specifically for vegetarians.

Gongdelin Vegetarian Restaurant (功德林素馆) 43 Huanghe Lu. Tel: 531313. Famous dishes in this restaurant that is found behind the Park Hotel are: mock fried crab meat (赛蟹羹), mock fried prawns (素虾), mock fried fish slices (素鱼丝), roasted bran dough (烤麸).

Vegetarian Restaurant of the Jade Buddha Temple (玉佛寺素菜馆) 170 Anyuan Lu. Tel: 535745. Famous dishes: bamboo shoots (春笋), beancurd (豆腐), green vegetable balls (青菜心), vegetarian mock ham (素火腿), fried mock eel shreds (炸素鳝丝). Open only at lunchtime.

Jing An Temple Vegetarian Restaurant (静安素菜馆) 1686 Nanjing Xi Lu. Tel: 583335. This restaurant is open between 1100 and 1300.

Longhua Temple Vegetarian Restaurant (龙华素菜馆) 2853 Longhua Lu. Tel:388104.

A couple of shops specialise in vegetarian food: **'Hongkouqu'**, at 10 Bei Jaining Lu, and the **Sanjiaodi Vegetable Market** at 150 Tanggu Lu, in the Hongkou district.

Western restaurants

If you start to hanker after Western food, then Shanghai is probably the best place to be. Although most Westerners had left by the mid-1950s, a tradition of foreign cooking has persisted until today in some of the old hotels, and in a couple of restaurants. Opinions of the quality of the cooking in these establishments vary. In the new international hotels the standards are likely to be higher (with supplies imported from Hong Kong), but more expensive.

The Peace, Park, and Jinjiang hotels probably offer the best hope of reasonable Western food in the old hotels, with the Jinjiang noted for excellent breakfasts. A new restaurant has recently been added to the Jinjiang — the Café de Rêve, which styles itself as the 'only International Restaurant lounge in the city'. Both the Sheraton and the Hilton serve Western food of international standard.

Hong Fanzi (The Red House) 37 Shaanxi Nan Lu Tel:565748. This must be the most well-known. Among its specialities: baked clam chowder, onion soup, beefsteak with mustard, chicken piccata, baked ice cream, souffle grand marnier. This pre-Liberation establishment used to be known as Chez Louis.

Tian Er Ge Xi Cai She (Swan Pavilion 天鹅阁西菜社) 1074 Huaihai Zhong Lu. Tel:374286

Deda Xicaishe (德大西菜社) at 359 Sichuan Zhong Lu, just to the north of the Peace Hotel. Of German origin, this restaurant also serves Sukiyaki during the winter.

Snacks: dumplings and pastries

Shanghai has always specialised in flavoursome dainties and snacks, sweet and savoury, Western and Chinese. Many of the Chinese variety, which are truly delicious, are to be found in the vicinity of the Old Chinese City and the Yu Yuan Garden. The Western style cakes and pastries found in the areas of the Nanking and Huaihai roads, again a legacy from foreign domination before 1949, are not quite as good as their counterparts abroad, but certainly worth sampling. Some of the specialities of Shanghai are:

- Nanxiang steamed dumplings (南翔小笼包): A traditional delicacy from Nanxiang, on the outskirts of Shanghai. They have thin, translucent pastry filled with meat, and are cooked in a small bamboo steamer. Dipped in vinegar they make excellent eating.
- Pigeon egg dumplings or Ningbo dumplings (宁波汤糰): The shape of pigeon eggs, they are made of glutinous rice paste and filled with sugar, osmanthus, and mint.
- Dumplings coated in mashed beans (糰子): Mashed red beans are the covering, and the filling may be of red beans too, or pork, or sesame seeds, or a combination.
- Crab-brown baked cake (蟹黄酥): A savoury cake filled with green onions and oil, or pork, crabmeat, shrimps, sugar, roses, mashed beans, or jujube paste.
- Gaoqiao Shortcake (高桥松饼): Main ingredients are wheatflour, lard, sugar, red beans, and osmanthus.

Some of the best outlets serving these or similar snacks are:

Yu Yuan Garden/Chinese Town area
Opposite the main entrance to the Garden, behind the Huxinting

Teahouse, the **Lubolang** at 131 Yu Yuan Lu, Tel: 280602, serves a variety of pastries, noodles, and dumplings. The **Nanxiang Steamed Dumpling Shop** next door to Lubolang specialises in the famous Nanxiang Dumplings. Opposite this is a button shop and around the corner from that a restaurant specialising in the delicious Ningbo dumplings.

These three are all on or near Yu Yuan Lu. Normally you pay the cashier first, and then take the receipt to the waitress.

There are a number of other snack shops in the area of the Yu Yuan and the surrounding bazaar. By wandering around you are sure to pass them. Some attract customers because the cooks — shaping and moulding the dumplings with great dexterity — are visible from the street as they work.

Nanjing Dong Lu area

Donghai Fandian (东海饭店), formerly Chez Sullivan, is at 145 Nanjing Dong Lu, whilst the **Xinjian Wineshop,** selling cold dishes and wines by the glass, and crabs in season, is at 547 Nanjing Dong Lu.

Wufangzhai (五芳斋), off Shanxi Road, specialises in sweet lotus root with osmanthus (桂花甜藕) and sweet taro with meat dumplings soup (肉汤甜芋). **Shendacheng** (沈大昌) is at 634 Nanjing Dong Lu not far from the junction with Zhejiang Lu, and specialises in glutinous rice dumplings for the lantern festival, and glutinous rice balls with green herbs.

Making dumplings. Cheap, delicious and nutritious, dumplings are one of the joys of eating in Shanghai.

Nanjing Xi Lu
The Wangjiasha Snackbar (王家沙) at 805 Nanjing Xi Lu, off Shimen Lu, serves chicken (鸡肉), shrimp in soup (虾汤), sweet and savoury glutinous dumplings (糯米糕糰).

Fuzhou Lu
The downstairs part of **Xinghualou** (杏花楼) at 343 Fuzhou Lu serves snacks, cakes, and refreshments.

Huaihai Zhong Lu area (formerly Avenue Joffre)
Canglangting (沧浪亭) at 10 Chongqing Nan Lu serves glutinous rice cakes and Suzhou dumplings (苏州汤元) whilst the **Tianshan Moslem Foodstore** at 671 Huaihai Lu sells sweets and cakes. The Gaoqiao Bakery on the corner of Ruijin Lu and Huaihai Lu specialises in Gaoqiao shortbread, and the **Tianjin** at 1029 Huaihai Lu serves Tianjin dumplings (天津包子).

Western snacks

Nanjing Dong Lu
The **Peace Hotel** bars on the ground floor of both wings serve cakes and pastries, as do the **Dong Hai** at 143 and the **Deda** on the corner of Sichuan Lu and Nanjing Dong Lu.

Nanjing Xi Lu
The **Park Hotel** downstairs coffee bar serves cakes and pastries whilst the **Kaige Coffee Shop** (凯歌咖啡馆) at 1001 Nanjing Xi Lu is a cafe and bakery. **Xilailin** (喜来临) at 569 Nanjing Xi Lu used to be the celebrated Kiesling and Bader coffee shop and still sells cream cakes. At 1442 Nanjing Xi Lu, near the Exhibition Hall, is the **Shanghai Coffee Bar** selling cakes and refreshments.

Huaihai Zhong Lu area
The **Laodacheng Bakery** and Confectionery (老大昌面包房) at 875 Huaihai Zhong Lu sells ice-cream, meringues and macaroons, whilst the **Shanghai Bakery** (上海面包房) at 979 Huaihai Zhong Lu sells baguettes and cream cakes. The **Shanghai Dairy** (上海牛奶棚) at 1568 Huaihai Zhong Lu sells dairy products. Both the **Sheraton** and the **Hilton** have coffee shops serving a large variety of gateaux, cakes, and pastries, and there is a bakery very close to the Shanghai Guest House.

EIGHT

Etiquette

A fundamental rule for a visit to Shanghai, or anywhere in China, is 'never take anything for granted'. Because the country is changing it is difficult, sometimes, to know what is acceptable, and what is not. One of the most contentious issues of late has been the desirability, or not, of tipping.

Tipping

The official line is that tipping, with money, is not allowed, and that China is respected around the world for it. Many people in the West, inured to the disgusted taxi driver and to the grumpy waiter, might agree wholeheartedly with this policy, but suffice it to say that the strictness of the rule throws up some unpleasant difficulties. When foreigners first were allowed again into China, a word of thanks or a small gift were satisfactory, but as the volume of visitors has increased, and the Chinese who deal with them have become more sophisticated, these are no longer enough. Many are happy to accept money, whilst others expect to be given cash whether they have provided an adequate service or not. This sort of thing arises because many Chinese are understandably frustrated at not being able to better their lot, and because there is no sense, yet, of value for money in the service industries. The problem is further compounded by those who steadfastly refuse to accept money under any circumstances, as a matter of honour. In short it is difficult to know what to do.

The problem arises only under certain circumstances — the average taxi driver, or waiter, does not expect any tip, and if they do, will probably make it very plain. You are more likely to meet the difficulty with a guide, or someone who has given service over a period of days. At the end of your time with them, and if you feel so inclined, the best solution is to simply place the sum (in FECs) in an envelope, and find a moment when it can be discreetly handed over. If it is refused there is nothing to be gained by remonstrating — the person concerned will have his reasons.

If you baulk at giving money, then a gift is nearly always acceptable, but it would be politic to give something imaginative, or useful, rather than ball-point pens. For smokers, foreign made cigarettes are ideal.

The Lady Pastor outside the Muen Church on Xizang Road.
Three services on a Sunday; total congregation of 3,000.

Clapping

Clapping is not in China, as in the West, exclusively a measure of gratitude or pleasure. It is also a sign of welcome. You may find, for example, that even if you are with a group of tourists who are visiting a kindergarten, you will be greeted by lines of clapping infants. One should clap back.

At the theatre, however, don't expect the audience to clap in the rather formal way found in the theatres of London or New York. People are more vocal, and tend to clap only when their enthusiasm brims over.

Speeches

The Chinese can be very formal on occasion. Banquets tend to demand speeches of thanks, future cooperation and so on. Your host will make the first one — you follow a couple of courses later.

Patience is a virtue

There may be occasions when your patience is sorely tried. It is worthwhile resisting the luxury of losing your temper under these circumstances — anger is a sign of weakness in China, and is more likely to produce laughter than action. Gentle insistence is much the better way, and should that fail, graceful resignation to the inevitable is called for. Anger may sometimes achieve something in the short term, but enemies will be made, and that counts for a lot in China.

Taboos

Certain subjects that are taken for granted in the West as being butts for humour would produce only looks of dismay at a gathering in China. Jokes about sex and politics are taboo with most Chinese, and jokes about the inadequacies of life in China may produce a polite smile, but are more likely to be interpreted as an attack on their country by a patronising foreigner. It needn't be thought, however, that Chinese do not have a sense of humour. On the contrary, they possess an excellent one, but feel unable to relax with foreigners until they know them well.

You will find that Chinese smile a lot, but the smile in China is not always what it seems. Often it is a cheery, jovial sign of welcome, but frequently it is used as a mask to conceal other emotions, and can vanish very quickly.

Preparing for the opera. Chinese opera is a great spectacle, but the melodies are hard on western ears.

NINE

Entertainment and recreation

As you might expect, Shanghai is no longer the city of endless nocturnal entertainment, as it was in before 1949. Most of the raciness has long disappeared. However, it probably remains the entertainment centre of China, although these days more wholesome pursuits are on offer, and you can expect to be in bed long before midnight. To check what's on, refer to the local newspapers, for example the *Wenhuibao*.

The Peace Hotel

The nearest thing to a live version of old Shanghai is to be found in the downstairs bar, every night between 8 and 11 o'clock. Here, the Peace Hotel Jazz Band thumps out its versions of Glenn Miller tunes and others of that era. Certain members of the band apparently date back to the 1940s, and although their playing is not exactly sophisticated, it is certainly infectious. The bar is packed every night, and not a few of the patrons, whether they are old enough to be nostalgic, or young enough simply to enjoy the beat, are coaxed onto the dance floor. The bar has something of the right atmosphere, too, with a cocktail menu and willing service from waiters who are able to memorise (usually correctly) any order. This is also a good place for meeting other foreigners.

There is a cover charge of a few yuan which is added on to your drinks bill.

Across the road is the Peace Café, with live music of a more contemporary nature. There is a cover charge here too.

The Circus

Circuses in China are rarely like their counterparts in Europe. In China the emphasis is on acrobats, and the most famous troupe of all is found in Shanghai. Nevertheless, although the acrobats remain the single most important feature, animal acts have also been introduced, among which Wei Wei the performing panda is the star. She doesn't do much, happily, apart from look beautiful. The real stars remain the acrobats, however, and there is no question of their extraordinary skills, presented with humour and panache — you will really gasp with pleasure and astonishment! Like everywhere else in the world, acrobats in China have had the status of gypsies, but since 1949 their art has been elevated in rank. Some of the acts are surely the same ones performed since time immemorial, and display the Chinese infatuation with taming the elements, or at least coming to terms with them. Don't be surprised at seeing a magic act included on the bill — one is often presented about half way through.

There are performances most of the time in the specially constructed building on Nanjing Xi Lu, about 10 minutes walk west of the Park Hotel. Tickets can be obtained through CITS, at a higher price, or directly from the theatre, where you should pay the standard price. Touts are often found on the street outside the theatre.

If there are no performances there, persevere — they are sometimes given elsewhere, for example the Youth Palace or the Pujiang Hotel.

Chinese opera

There are about one hundred types of opera, or drama, in China, each one employing the dialect of a particular area. The basic ingredients are otherwise very similar one to another. It resembles only very little the grand-opera of Italy and Germany — Chinese opera combines singing, dancing, and spoken parts in one single drama. There is traditionally almost no scenery, and particular gestures come to represent a certain location, or activity. The characters are heavily painted, and wear extravagant costumes, a certain style of make-up or dress describing the status or role of the character in question.

Chinese opera started as street theatre. Thus the make-up and costumes are bright, the gestures formal, and the singing and the music shrill and loud. In the past the female roles were all played by men (women were permitted rarely to leave home) although nowadays of course women do appear in the professional theatre.

Many operas have their origins in fairy tales, legends, or stories from classical literature, although there are leitmotifs that tend to occur time and time again. The struggle between good and evil is the principal theme, summed up according to two categories, 'wenxi' (civil themes), and 'wuxi' (martial themes).

The music and style of singing bear no resemblance at all to western opera. The music is loud, and like a commentary on the physical implications of all of the movements made by the various characters. The main stringed instruments are the 'jing hu' and the 'er hu', which are types of fiddles, and the 'pi pa' and the 'xian zi', which are types of lute. Percussion instruments have a major role to play and include a variety of gongs and drums. The singing is hard to describe. It is shrill and melodramatic, the melodies being an acquired taste. Yet it is for the arias that the true aficionado patronises the opera.

The roles can be described broadly in the following way. All female roles are known as 'dan', which are then sub-divided into 'qing yi' (quiet and gentle), 'hua dan' (vivacious or even dissolute), 'wu dan' (women with martial skills), 'dao ma dan' (women warriors), and 'lao dan' (old women). All male roles are are called 'sheng', divided into 'lao sheng', 'xiao sheng', and 'wu sheng', old man, young man, and warrior, respectively. Another role type is 'jing' which means painted face; depending on the style of make-up one can distinguish those who are honest from those who are not. Finally, there are the 'chou', the clowns, who are there as a foil to the more pompous characters. Strictly speaking, these definitions refer to Peking opera, but extend to all local operas.

It is worth going to a Chinese opera at least once. It is a fabulous spectacle, even if the singing and music are hard to identify with at first. It is heavily stylised, but there are good reasons for this, as evinced in this definition of the essence of Chinese opera:

- The essence of life — not life as it is, but life as extracted, concentrated and typified.
- The essence of movements — not the movement of daily life, but movement given new life by heightened dramatic effect.
- The use of lyrical language.
- Decor, not to imitate life but again to extract nothing more than the essential from one of life's episodes.

Opera of different types can be enjoyed in the theatres of Shanghai. One which is a little easier on the western ear is 'yue', which originated from Zhejiang, the province to the south of Shanghai.

The performances can be up to three to four hours long, but since a visit to the opera in China is an entirely informal affair, it is quite permissible to leave to wander in and out as you like.

Major theatres are:

Changjiang Theatre 21 Huanghe Lu. Tel: 539531

People's Theatre 663 Jiujiang Lu. Tel: 224473

Shanghai Arts Theatre 57 Maoming Lu. Tel: 530788 (this is the Lyceum Theatre of old)

Workers Theatre 701 Fuzhou Lu. Tel: 226270

Xianle Theatre 444 Nanjing Xi Lu. Tel: 533544

Concerts

Despite the fact that the Shanghai Conservatory had the best reputation of any in China, of course it suffered heavily during the Cultural Revolution. Such were the strictures imposed upon it that the heads of department were nothing more than Party ciphers, and the music was subject to such rigid censorship that even pieces that were sufficiently revolutionary in the 1950s were cast out if a single passage bore any similarity to music considered to be counter-revolutionary by the Gang of Four.

Now the Conservatory is thriving once again, and in the early 1980s one of its pupils, Jin Li, was turned into an international star with the help of Yehudi Menuhin. Concerts are given at the Conservatory (20 Fenyang Lu, Tel: 370137) on Sunday nights. Tickets need to be booked through CITS though, as usual, if you show up on the night, you are unlikely to meet any problems.

The principal concert hall is at 523 Yan'an Dong Lu. Shanghai boasts several orchestras, including one specialising in Chinese traditional music. Consult the papers for times and venues.

Cinemas

Shanghai has always been the Hollywood of China and, like its counterpart in the United States, produces the greatest volume of film, but not always the greatest quality. More thoughtful films are generally made elsewhere — Bernardo Bertolucci, director of *The Last Emperor* was evidently impressed by what he saw in the Xian Studio, for example. Yet, again like the real Hollywood, it is Shanghai that is associated with the essence of film-making that is larger than life, with the stars and the glamour. Not so long ago it was a second-rate actress from Shanghai, Jiang Qing, who was at least in part responsible for the Cultural Revolution, as the wife of Mao Zedong and one of the Gang of Four.

The Shanghai Film Studio at Xujiahui can sometimes be visited by applying through CITS. The address of the studio is: 595, Caoxi Bei Lu. Tel:388100.

There are plenty of cinemas in Shanghai. These days all sorts of films are shown, including foreign films (usually dubbed), and a visit to the cinema is a worthwhile experience. Censorship laws are strict, at least in relation to sexual matters, although they are ambivalent in other respects — *Rambo, First Blood* was a great success in China. Tickets are very cheap. Addresses of some cinemas:

Daguangming Cinema 216 Nanjing Xi Lu. Tel: 534260
Xinhua Cinema 742 Nanjing Xi Lu. Tel: 538050
Da Shanghai Cinema 500 Xizang Zhong Lu. Tel: 226624
Huaihai Cinema 555 Huaihai Zhong Lu. Tel: 285205
Guotai Cinema 870 Huaihai Zhong Lu. Tel: 372549
Cultural Cinema 234 Fuyou Lu (near old town) Tel:288433
Ping An Cinema 1193 Nanjing Xi Lu. Tel: 537898

Discotheques

Young Chinese are keen dancers, and discotheques have become popular, although most of them are confined to tourist hotels. When foreigners first began to reappear in Shanghai, some of the hotels advertised 'dance parties' which would take place in a hastily transformed restaurant, chairs around the walls in village-hall style, and a lone ghetto-blaster playing Western disco music to a gaggle of giggling hotel employees waiting expectantly for foreigners, of any age, to demonstrate the latest dance steps.

Charming though this was, it ultimately proved rather an embarrassment for all concerned and what discotheques there are have by now become more worldly. However, some hotels continue to advertise 'dance parties' which really means discotheque, perhaps with live music, open to Chinese as well as foreigners. These are to be found in the Overseas Chinese Hotel, the Park Hotel, the Seventh Heaven Hotel, the Seaman's Club (sometimes), the Huaqiao Hotel, and the Youth Association Hotel. A reasonable cover charge is payable.

Some of the above are quite sophisticated enough, but there are others, known as discotheques rather then dance parties, which are generally reckoned to be the real thing. Some of these are aimed exclusively at foreigners, although Chinese who can afford it do go. They are:

'Club D'Elegance' at the Jin Jiang Hotel. Laser show etc. Expect to pay 35 yuan to enter (includes two drinks).

'Nicoles' at the Sheraton. Conventional disco, entrance about 30 yuan.

Others can be found at the Dinxiang Garden at 849 Huashan Lu; the Shanghai Hotel; Cypress Hotel; and the Union Building on Yanan Lu.

Cafés and bars

Cafés, informal and with a relaxing, friendly atmosphere, are thin on the ground everywhere in China, but Shanghai is better off than most cities. With the new government encouragement of 'private' enterprise, café/bars are beginning to appear in increasing numbers. The best way to find them is to stroll the major shopping streets until you find one that suits. Otherwise, you will have to stick to the hotels. Of the private ones, three have been mentioned in passing in the section on the 'Concessions': Jam's Bar, 506 Wulumuqi Bei Lu; Smiling Bar, 449 Wulumuqi Bei Lu; and the bar with green facade and striped awnings just to the east of the Industrial Exhibition on the Nanjing Xi Lu.

Others in the hotels are: The Pub in the north building of the Jin Jiang Hotel; the bar of the Dong Feng Hotel on the Bund; the Peace Hotel Bar and the Peace Café; bar/café of the annexe of the Seagull Hotel; bars and cafés of the Hilton and Sheraton.

Sport

Shanghai has one very good stadium in the Shanghai Gymnasium, which seats 18,000, and which has been host to world championships of various kinds. See the papers for details.

There are swimming pools and gyms in certain of the hotels, e.g. the Sheraton and the Hilton. There are municipal swimming pools too, e.g. at 1 Lane 45 Handan Lu, and at 444 Jiangwan Dong Lu.

Above: *New Shanghai. Private cafés and bars are making a reappearance.* **Below:** *A man in a tricycle. A little piece of Old Shanghai.*

Other diversions

Local and visiting troupes will frequently give performances of other kinds, e.g. ballet, puppetry, traditional song and dance, and even rock music. Again it is necessary to refer to the newspapers for details, but remember that you may also find information from English speakers on the Bund.

Over the years public parks have been the sites for so-called 'English Corners', where people wishing to practise their knowledge of the language gather to chat, usually on a Sunday. Any foreigner able to help is welcome.

Wrought iron window. Like the stained glass, details of a European heritage are to be found everywhere in Shanghai.

TEN

Useful addresses

Airline offices

— Alitalia, Room 58660, 6th Floor, Building 4, Jin Jiang Club, 191 Chang Le Lu. Tel: 582582 Ext:58660,58662
— C.A.A.C. (Civil Aviation Administration of China) 789, Yanan Zhong Lu. Tel: 532255 (International), 535953 (Domestic).
— Canadian Pacific Airlines, Room 109, North Building, Jin Jiang Hotel. Tel: 376422
— Cathay Pacific Airways, Room 123, North Building, Jin Jiang Hotel.Tel: 312089
— Japan Airlines, Room 201, Ruijin Building. Tel: 378198
— Northwest Orient Airlines, Room 127, North Building, Jin Jiang Hotel. Tel: 377387
— Singapore Airlines, Room 110, North Building, Jin Jiang Hotel. Tel: 315939
— United Airlines, Jing An Guesthouse. Tel: 530210,530559
— Hongqiao Airport. Flight inquiries Tel: 537664 or 329434.

Banks

If you want only to change money, then you are as well off in a hotel as in a bank, since the exchange offices in the hotels are in fact sub-branches of the Bank of China. The following addresses will be useful for business, or for transactions that do not fall within the normal routine of sub-branches of the Bank of China.
— Bank of China (Shanghai branch) 23, Zhongshan Dong Lu. Tel: 215666 Tx: 33062/63
— Bank of America, Room 1802, Union Building, 100 Yanan Dong Lu. Tel: 201297
— Banque Indosuez, Room 1110, 205 Maoming Nan Lu. Tel: 311753 Tx: 33130

— Bank of Tokyo, Room 2301, 205 Maoming Nan Lu. Tel: 374657
— Fuji Bank, Room 1101, 205, Maoming Nan Lu. Tel: 375665
— Hong Kong and Shanghai Banking Corporation (Shanghai branch), 185, Yuanmingyuan Lu. Tel: 210811
— Société Generale, Room 58136, Jinjiang Club, 58 Maoming Nan Lu. Tel: 377838
— Standard Chartered Bank, 9th floor, Union Building, 100 Yana Dong Lu. Tel: 264820, 284022
— Banca Commerciale, Room 1410, Union Building, 100, Yanan Lu.

Boats, ships etc.

— Huangpu River Sightseeing Excursions Terminal, Beijing Dong Lu Wharf. Tel: 211098/99. Just north of the Peace Hotel, on the Bund.
— Shanghai Harbour Passenger Transport Terminal, 1, Jinling Dong Lu. Tel: 260050. Booking office at 230 Beijing Dong Lu. Tel: 261261. For ships to Hong Kong, Japan, and coastal cities of China.
— Shanghai Jin Jiang Shipping Co. 58, Maoming Nan Lu. Tel: 582582
— 218, Renmin Lu. For ships up the Yangtze to Wuhan, Chonqing, and the Gorges

Business

— International Club, see 'Clubs'.
— Service Centre for Overseas Traders (S.C.O.T.), Jinjiang Club, 58 Maoming Nan Lu. Tel: 375334. This is a business centre for visiting foreign businessmen. It offers trade consultancy services, business introductions, and translation, secretarial and guide services. Telex and photocopying facilities are available. It is open from 0830 until 1800 every day except Sunday.
— Huating Sheraton business centre, 1200 Caoxi Bei Lu. Tel: 386000. Tx:33589.
— China Council for the Promotion of International Trade (CCPIT) 27 Zhongshan Dong Lu. Tel: 214244
— China National Import and Export Corporations, Shanghai branches: Animal By-products, 23 Zhongshan Dong Lu Tel: 215630;

Arts and Crafts, 16 Zhongshan Dong Lu. Tel: 212100; Cereals and Oils, 11 Hankou Lu. Tel: 219760; Chemicals, 27 Zhongshan Dong Lu. Tel: 211540; Foodstuffs, 26 Zhongshan Dong Lu. Tel: 216233; Foreign Trade Transportation Corporation, 74 Dianchi Lu Tel: 213103; Light Industrial Products, 128 Huqin Lu. Tel: 216858; Machinery Imports and Exports, 27 Zhongshan Dong Lu. Tel: 215066; Metals and Minerals, 27 Zhongshan Dong Lu. Tel: 211220; Textiles (garments), 27 Zhongshan Dong Lu. Tel:218500; Textiles (silks), 17 Zhongshan Dong Lu. Tel:215770
— Shanghai Centre of International Studies, 33 The Bund. (Old British Consulate).
— Shanghai Stock Exchange, 1806 Nanjing Xi Lu.
— Shanghai Trust and Investment Corporation, 3rd Floor, Union Building, 100 Yanan Dong Lu. Tel: 284120. This organisation was founded in 1981 in order to funnel foreign finance and trade to Shanghai.

Churches and places of worship (active).

Apparently there are 23 Protestant and 26 Catholic functioning churches in Shanghai at the moment. Here are some of them.
— Community Church (Protestant), 53 Hengshan Lu. Tel: 376576
— Jin Ling Protestant Church, 135 Kunshan Lu. Tel: 243021
— Xujiahui Cathedral (St Ignatius Cathedral—Catholic), 201 Caoxi Bei Lu. Tel: 371328
— Zhabei Church (Protestant), 8 Baotung Lu. Tel: 629409
— Xiao Taoyuan Mosque, 52 Xiao Taoyuan Lu. Tel: 775442
— Fu You Lu Mosque, 378 Fuyou Lu. Tel: 282135
— Muen Interdenominational Church, 316 Xizang Zhong Lu. Tel: 225069

There are no functioning synagogues at present. The Shanghai Buddhist Association is at 160 Anyuan Lu. Tel: 537083. The Shanghai Taoist Association is at Lane 8, 100 Xilinhou Lu Tel: 775402

Cinemas See Chapter 9.

Clubs

— International Club, 63-65 Yanan Xi Lu. Tel: 538455,537040.

Consulates

— Australia. 17 Fuxing Xi Lu. Tel: 374580. Tx:33312
— Belgium. Rooms 305-307, Jingan Guesthouse, 370 Huashan Lu.
Tel: 563050 Ext.305
— Canada. Union Building, 100 Yanan Dong Lu. Tel: 202822.
Visas available only in Peking.
— Federal Republic of Germany. 181 Yongfu Lu. Tel: 379953
Tx:33140
— France. 1339 Huaihai Zhong Lu. Tel: 377414. Tx:33081
— German Democratic Republic. Room 806, Dahua Hotel.
Tel:525069
— Great Britain. 244 Yongfu Lu. Tel: 330508. Tx:33476. Visas
available only in Peking.
— Italy. 127 Wuyi Lu. Tel: 524374
— Japan. 1517 Huaihai Zhong Lu. Tel: 372073. Tx:33061
— Poland. 618 Jianguo Xi Lu. Tel: 370952
— USA 149 Huaihai Zhong Lu. Tel: 379880. Tx:33383
— USSR 20 Huangpu Lu. Tel: 242682

Dentists, doctors and hospitals

— Shanghai No.1 Hospital, 190 Suzhou Bei Lu. Tel: 240100,
240825. Outpatients departments: 410 Suzhou Bei Lu. Tel: 240100,
240825.
— Huadong Yiyuan (East China Hospital), 257 Yanan Xi Lu.
Tel: 523125. This has a department with English-speaking doctors
and dentists. Charges for simple treatment (consultation and
Chinese medicine) is quite cheap; treatment involving a stay in a
hospital, or Western drugs, becomes more expensive. Care for
foreigners is rather good, and if anything, errs on the side of
hypochondria.
— Shanghai Red Cross Society, 233 Hankou Lu. Tel: 210120

Exhibition centres

— Shanghai Agricultural Exhibition Centre, 2270 Hongqiao Lu.
Tel: 329535
— Shanghai Exhibition Centre, 1000 Yanan Zhong Lu. Tel: 563037

Film studio

— Shanghai Film Studio, 595 Caoxi Bei Lu. Tel: 388100.

Library

— Shanghai Library, 325 Nanjing Xi Lu. Tel: 563176

Police

— Public Security Bureau (Foreigners section), 210 Hankou Lu. Tel: 211997. This is where you go for changing or extending your visa. The attitude of the staff is variable, but remember that persistence, patience and politeness are more effective than ranting and raving. An ordinary local police station is to be found at 931 Yanan Zhong Lu. Tel: 379100.

Post and communications

— Shanghai Central Post Office, 359 Tiantong Lu.
— Shanghai Long Distance Telephone Bureau, 1761 Sichuan Bei Lu. Tel: 661221
— Shanghai Post Office (International Express Mail section), 276 Suzhou Bei Lu. Tel: 240395
— Shanghai Telegraph Office (Main branch), 30 Nanjing Dong Lu. Tel: 211130. Tx: 33006.

Railway station

— Shanghai New Railway Station, Tianmu Lu. Tel: 253030

Taxis

— Shanghai Tourist Taxi Co., 16 Wu Zhong Lu. Tel: 383420
— Friendship Taxi Company, 400 Changle Lu. Tel: 536363,584584
— Shanghai Taxi Corporation, 816 Beijing Dong Lu. Tel: 222999

Travel

— CITS (China International Travel Service), Shanghai branch. 33 Zhongshan Dongyi Lu. Tel: 214960. Telephone for independant travellers: 217200. Tx: 33277 SCITS CN. Also at 66 Nanjing Dong Lu.
— Information Service: Peace Hotel, 20 Nanjing Dong Lu. Tel: 211244
— China Youth Travel Service, Shanghai branch, 2, Hengshan Lu. Tel: 551349
— China Travel Service (CTS), 104, Nanjing Xi Lu (Overseas Chinese Hotel) Tel: 226226.
Until recently, arrangements for travel within China have been in the hands of CITS or CTS. Now, however, there are plenty of smaller operations who may well have the welfare of the traveller more at heart. Two are the following:
— China Comfort Travel, Room 5324, Jinjiang Hotel. Tel: 582582 Ext.5324.
— Shanghai Travel Service, 739 Fuzhou Lu. Tel: 221469, 221572.

Universities

— Fudan University, 220 Handan Lu. Tel: 484906. Tx: 33317
— Jiaotong University, 1954 Huashan Lu. Tel: 310310. Tx: 33262
— Shanghai Foreign Language Institute, 119 Ti Yu Hai Xi Lu Tel: 420900.

This list is far from comprehensive for the reason that it is no longer possible in a publication of this kind — Shanghai is changing too fast. As mentioned elsewhere, the solution is to buy the 'Shanghai Chinese-English Edition Telephone Directory', available in shops selling foreign language publications.

ELEVEN

Shopping

Shanghai is traditionally the emporium of China. Amongst the Chinese it has a reputation as a leader in things fashionable, and for being the place to shop. Even during the Cultural Revolution travelling interrogators and inquisitioners checking on the orthodoxy of political views would ensure visits to Shanghai in order to do a little shopping. From the international point of view, shopping has only recently once again become worthwhile, as the flow of foreign money and a modified economic policy have encouraged a new attitude to trade. For the Chinese, even if the name Shanghai is still synonymous with style, the city is rivalled for choice by Peking and Canton. Shanghai, it is true, does have many more shops than other cities and, being a port, will be among the first to be exposed to anything new, but China's distribution system is sufficiently sophisticated to ensure that the major cities are not far behind.

On the other hand, for the foreign visitor Shanghai is unquestionably the major shopping centre of China. It has to be remembered that, economic reforms notwithstanding, the best general shopping is mostly confined to stores aimed at the carrier of foreign currency (as manifested in Foreign Exchange Certificates), of which there are several in Shanghai. Not long ago one could have said with certainty that the average local shop was worth a visit only from the point of view of curiosity, with the exception of some specialist shops that deserved a look. One can no longer afford to be so glib — China is changing fast, and the enterpreneurial instinct is strong. The average local shop still does not offer an abundance of bargains, but the quality is improving, and so is the choice.

The pricing structure is a problem, as explained in the section 'Before you go', under 'Prices'. There is no solution to this, unless you have the time to make comparisons. One cannot say, for example, that prices are lower in factories than elsewhere.

Sometimes they might be, but not always. These days, however, the ideas of 'discount' and 'sales' are catching on, and although it is generally true that bargaining is possible only in street markets and a few independent shops, there is never any harm in trying anywhere if you are spending a lot of money — some managers, even of Friendship Stores, are becoming quite canny when it comes to the art of salesmanship. In other words, you have to play it by ear. Nor can you be sure that the prices are lower on the mainland than in Hong Kong — however, they are usually pretty similar. Overall, prices have gone up in recent years, but some things remain comparitively cheap, e.g. silk, handicrafts, some antiques, teas.

You are advised to keep the receipts from your purchases, especially antiques.

The following list is far from complete, but gives an idea of what is available. The section on 'What to see', under the heading of 'The Concessions' mentions some individual shops that are not mentioned here, although this list covers most types.

Friendship Stores

When China first opened its doors to the West, these were almost the only retail outlets for arts and crafts, souvenirs, and so on. The name caught on, and despite changes, many foreign visitors persist in thinking either that all shops of this type are entitled Friendship Stores, or that the Friendship Store is the only shop worth visiting. Neither is any longer the case.

Friendship Stores ('Youyi Shangdian') are government owned and are general clearing houses for sales to foreigners. In many towns, even now, they remain the only outlet for sales to foreigners, and if not the only outlet are frequently the largest. Large cities are sometimes peppered with branches located in hotels and other haunts of foreigners. Generally speaking, prices are fixed. It would be a mistake to dismiss them as expensive monopolies. Despite a restrictive economic system, the Chinese are nothing if not natural business people, and a great deal of the best merchandise finds its way into these stores.

The **Shanghai Friendship Store** (40 Beijing Dong Lu. Tel: 234600. Opening hours: 0900-2200) was originally housed in a building in the grounds of the old British Consulate before the construction of this purpose built block just behind the Peace Hotel. It is one of the largest, if not the largest, in China. There are facilities for changing money, and for depositing bags; there is a desk from where taxis may be ordered, there are snackbars on the top floor, and all the major credit cards are acceptable.

Ground floor: Some of the items here (refrigerators, washing machines etc.) are aimed at the overseas Chinese visitor who wants to purchase luxury items for relatives on the mainland. There is a supermarket, a counter selling traditional Chinese medicines, another selling confectonery and foods both Chinese and foreign, luggageware, teas, and Chinese wines and spirits.

First floor: A good range of antiques (ceramics, jewellery, clocks and watches, carvings, old embroidery), calligraphy tools, furniture and paintings.

Second floor: Silk and wool carpets, arts and crafts (jewellery, lacquerware, cloisonné, porcelain etc.), furniture, and embroidery.

Third floor: Silk material (excellent selection), clothes (cashmere sweaters, silk blouses, furs, padded jackets, leather), embroidered items (table cloths etc.), furs, and shoes and hats. In the past the main objection to buying clothes has been the lack of flair in their design, but this deficiency is slowly being rectified. It is possible to have clothes made to measure, for which you will need at least two days.

Fourth floor: Snackbars/restaurants.

Antiques

In Shanghai there is plenty of choice — the source seems limitless. Whether they are any cheaper here than in, for example, London street markets, is a moot point. Some say no, but this is the opinion of people whose expertise allows them to sniff out bargains in Europe. Amateur enthusiasts have also said, on the other hand, that some items, like old fob watches and old silk embroidery, are definitely cheaper. Anyway, there is a great deal to choose from, so find what you like and decide whether you can afford the cost. You may never see its like again, or if you do, it may be in worse condition, or more expensive.

Antiques may be exported from China provided they are stamped with a red wax seal at the point of purchase. This indicates that the item is a genuine antique, and also that it is no older than approximately 150 years. Anything older may not be taken out of the country, although rumour has it that this may change. It is occasionally possible to find items that date back further but still bear the seal — even the Chinese make mistakes!

There are older antiques to be found on the streets, but they will not have the red seal, and there is no guarantee of their authenticity; and to export them is, of course, illegal. It is also worth bearing in mind that the Chinese are expert in the manufacture of art reproduction. For the most part these are sold as such in museums and shops, but if offered on the street, it can be very hard to distinguish them from the genuine article. 'Genuine reproductions' do, in fact, have the appropriate characters printed on them, so it is worthwhile learning to recognize them. Shops dealing in antiques are:

— Shanghai Friendship Store, 40 Beijing Dong Lu.
— Shanghai Friendship Store, Antiques and Curios Branch, 694 Nanjing Xi Lu. Tel:530975 (Half a mile west of the Park Hotel).
— Shanghai Antiques and Curios Store, 218-226 Guandong Lu. Tel:212864
— Shaanxi Old Wares Store, 557 Yanan Zhong Lu. Tel:565489
— Chongshin Old Wares Shop, 1297 Huaihai Lu. Tel:372559

There is a small antiques section at the Arts and Crafts Trade Fair in the Industrial Exhibition Centre. As mentioned in the section on the 'Concessions', there are a few second-hand furniture shops around now, selling pretty ordinary stuff on the whole, but with the occasional surprise. The problem with such places is that they do not ship.

Arts and crafts

There are a great number of products in this field that can prove irresistible. There are two contradictory truths to bear in mind when shopping for them — one, that first impressions can be deceptive; and two, that if you like something buy it, because it may not crop up again. In the first case the problem is that Chinese wares are very appealing, and the tendency is to buy on sight. If you can, take the time to browse and get used to what is available. In the second case, the problem is that articles are sometimes manufactured in small numbers, or are not repeated; and there is no means of ordering items according to serial numbers. So, if after careful consideration you like a particular item, it is as well to buy it there and then.

The range of goods is extraordinary. Here are a few of the major categories:

Cloisonné
Although we use a French word (meaning 'cloistered'), the art is Chinese. In simple terms, it is coloured enamel ware. A copper

mould is covered with a network of metal strips, and the little enclosures (cloisters) so formed are filled, layer upon layer, with mineral colours. The articles are then fired and polished to produce a finish something like enamel. Some of it is on the garish side, but much of it is rather attractive. It tends to be pitted with pinprick holes, so try and find examples with as smooth a finish as possible.

Lacquerware

This tends to be thought of as a sort of varnishing effect, but it can be much more than that. The original process consists of spreading coating after coating of tree sap mixed with mineral colours on a wooden base that has been covered with layers of silk, after which it may be cut or carved. It is mostly red, and is nowadays often done on metal.

Painting and calligraphy

Painting in China is the art of brush and ink. Ink is traditionally considered to perform the function of colour, and shading is a technique alien to Chinese painting. So is realism — the art consists in reproducing the essence of the subject, its intrinsic quality and energy. Nevertheless, at different times exact reproductions of nature, notably birds and insects, have become fashionable, although the aim was not so much biological as to involve the viewer in a general scene of nature. Tradition was everything, and although there was room for the individual to make his mark, it was essential that he did so within the confines of those traditions. Many of the paintings you will see are modern versions of old themes or reproductions of old classics.

Calligraphy is at its simplest the ornate script of the Chinese language, and at best an art form in its own right. There are calligraphers as well known as opera singers and film stars. The calligrapher needs four vital tools — paper, ink (in the form of a solid stick inlaid with gold lettering and pictures), ink-stones (black slabs with hollowed out surface for mixing water with ink stick according to the required consistency), and brushes. These are known as the 'four treasures of the study'. How the calligrapher works is an expression of his own personality. The great calligrapher is a person able to turn an ordinary calligraphic character into an artistic expression, so that the character for dragon becomes a dragon (without losing its identity as a character), or a poem becomes a pictorial representation.

Chops or carved seals

A chop is a piece of stone with the owner's name or initials carved into the bottom for use as a personal signature. The type of stone varies but many types are used and the price corresponds to its rarity and to the beauty of its markings. Most have carved tops, for example the animals of the Chinese zodiac. The average chop is made of soapstone from Fuzhou Province. Cheap ones can still be very attractive, and your name in Chinese or Roman script can very quickly be carved into the base. The ink is a red paste, often found in delightful ceramic pots. Many shops, specialist and otherwise, provide this service, or you will often find a carver selling his services in hotel lobbies.

Other arts and handicrafts readily available are paper-cuts, dough figurine modelling, kites, porcelain, carpets (see 'Carpets'), jade (see 'Jade'). Some shops dealing in arts and crafts are:

— Shanghai Friendship Store, 40 Beijing Dong Lu.
— Shanghai Arts and Crafts Trade Fair at the Shanghai Exhibition Centre, 1000 Yanan Zhong Lu.
— Shanghai Arts and Crafts Store, 190-208 Nanjing Xi Lu.
— Yuhua Arts and Crafts Store, 929-935 Huaihai Zhong Lu.
— Arts and Crafts Research Institute Shop, 79 Fenyang Lu.
— Guohua Porcelain Shop, 550 Nanjing Dong Lu.
— Shanghai Changjiang Seal Carving Factory, 722 Huaihai Zhong Lu. Tel:211854
— Shanghai Jingdezhen Porcelain Artware Service, 1175 Nanjing Xi Lu, Tel:530885
— Shanghai Old City Temple Arts and Crafts Store, 1 Yicheng Lu. Tel:289850
— Duoyunxuan Painting and Calligraphy Shop, 422 Nanjing Dong Lu. This old shop, apart from its wares, was beautiful in its own right, but it seems to have been demolished. Whether it will be rebuilt is not known.

Many of the major hotels have shops selling a substantial number of wares, e.g. Peace, Jinjiang, Shanghai, Sheraton and Hilton. Prices are likely to be higher, however.

Silk

Silk is one of the bargains of China, and the best selection is to be found in Shanghai (silk is produced in the neighbouring provinces — see 'Shanghai Economy' under Sericulture). The Friendship Store and the Arts and Crafts Trade Fair in the Industrial

Exhibition Centre have good selections. Try, too, the Shanghai Silk and Satin Shop at 592 Nanking Dong Lu; or the Shanghai Number 1 Clothing Store at 650 Nanking Dong Lu; or Jin Men Silk and Cloth Store at 80 Nanjing Xi Lu; or Jin Long Woolen Silk and Cloth Store, 858 Huai Hai Lu. It is also sometimes possible to visit the Shanghai Silk Printing and Dyeing Factory, 1133 Chang Ning Lu. Tel:520709, which has a shop attached.

Tailoring

Hong Kong is well known for quick, cheap tailoring, yet many of the tailors there are originally from Shanghai. Today, after some years of decline, tailoring is set to make a return, although very much in its infancy. The choice of material may be limited, and you may have to produce your own design, but the price is probably right. It isn't always clear who does what, but try the Friendship Store, and some of the shops at the Bund end of the Nanking Road. Another shop that may oblige is the Baromon Suit Company at 284 Nanjing Lu. Tel:586798

Carpets

Shanghai is one of the centres of Chinese carpet manufacture, there being two factories in the city, one specialising in wool carpets, the other in silk. Manufacture follows three stages:

● The first stage is weaving. Most of the workers are girls, who take up their trade after several years training. They sit in front of vertical looms, following a rough pattern, with a crowd of balls of wool or silk dangling about their heads. Crouched over their work, they tie knot after knot with invisible clipped, darting movements. At the end of each row, the knots are pounded together with a heavy metal fork.

● Then the carpets are opened up around a large room. Workers crawl all over them, hunting and scouring for imperfections that are weeded out by hand.

● Finally the carpets are transported to yet another room and slung over tables slanted like scriveners desks. It is time for the electric scissors. Carpets from eastern China tend to have their design cut in relief, and machines like sheep shears with an electric cable chatter around peonies, bats, and double happiness characters.

The finished article is then displayed in the salesroom, or despatched to destinations around the world. Addresses of two carpet manufacturers are:
— Shanghai General Carpet Factory, 25 Cao Bao Lu. Tel:389713
— Shanghai Silk Carpet Factory, 342 Ling Ling Lu. Tel:375564
Both factories ship to your nearest port. Major credit cards are acceptable. Carpets are available in several other outlets, notably the Friendship Store and the Industrial Exhibition Centre.

Ming gate to the Temple to the City God. This is the way in from the south and leads to the bazaar and the Yu Garden.

Jade

To say that jade is a contentious subject is something of an understatement. Just what it is, and how good jade is distinguishable from bad, are questions that elicit a multitude of answers. The average Chinese, for whom jade has traditionally been an object of veneration, will say that appreciation of it is an entirely personal matter. This does not explain the extraordinary variation in price, which — as with any other precious stone — is where rarity, colour, and flawlessness play their part. It is often said that white jade is the purest, yet teardrops of emerald green fetch enormous prices. There is no answer to this conundrum except to look very carefully at the prices of what is on offer, and to develop a feel for quality. You are unlikely to be swindled in mainstream shops, but beware of people on the streets. Addresses of places where jade may be purchased are:
— Shanghai Jade Carving Factory, 33 Cao Bao Lu. Tel:388660.
— Shanghai Friendship Store (address above)
— Industrial Exhibition Centre (address above)
— Jia Hua Gold and Silver Shop, 1149 Nanjing Xi Lu. Tel:530609
— Tian Bao Gold and Silver Jewellery Shop, 645-647 Huai Hai Lu. Tel:264850
— Long Feng Gold and Silver Shop, 406 Huaihai Lu. Tel:203458.
— Shanghai Jade Carving Factory Sales Department Branch, 1828 Huaihai Zhong Lu. Tel:371375

Other shops

There is a multitude of shops in Shanghai, many of which are changing, being modernised, or moving, which makes them difficult to list accurately. Fortunately there is a new publication, something like 'Yellow Pages', that lists, in English, most of the shops, factories and other organisations of Shanghai. It is called 'Shanghai Chinese-English Edition Telephone Directory', published by the Shanghai Telephone Directory Corporation at 333 Jiang Xi Road North. Tel:255544. It costs about 25 yuan, and is quite comprehensive, although some of the list headings are a little eccentric, i.e. most restaurants are listed under 'Service Agents'. Still, it is to be recommended. Here are a few samples from Shanghai's wide range of shops:

Bicycles
— Yong Hua Bicycle and Motorcycle Traffic Store, 860 Yanan Lu.
Tel:536100

Leather
— Ai Jian Leather Ware Shop, 21 Da Du He Lu. Tel:577300
— Dong Hai General Leather Shop, 387 Xi Zang Lu. Tel:224387
— Jin Guang Leather Goods Shop, 727 Nanjing Xi Lu. Tel:531638
— Bo Bu Leather Shoes Shop, 753 Nanjing Xi Lu. Tel:535355

Fur
Frist Siberian Fur Co., 1137 Nanjing Xi Lu. Tel:532211

Chinese medicine
— Bao Da Ginseng Shop, 455 Henan Zhong Lu. Tel:229156
— Cai Tong De Chinese Medicine Store, 320 Nanjing Dong Lu.
Tel:221160
— Fu Chang Ginseng Store, 76 Xi Zang Nan Lu. Tel:283217
— Shanghai Number 1 Medicine Store, 616 Nanjing Dong Lu.
Tel:224567

Chinese food and drink
You can do worse than go to the Shanghai No. 1 Foodstuff Shop
at 720 Nanjing Dong Lu. Tel:222777, which offers a very wide
range of foods from all over China.

Foreign and imported foods
There are some available in the Friendship Store; there is a
supermarket in the Jinjiang Hotel (sells condoms amongst other
items) which is rather expensive; and other of the major hotels stock
bits and pieces, or run expensive 'delicatessens', e.g. the Hilton and
the Sheraton. Local shops are now selling things like instant coffee
and powdered milk but at high prices.

Photographic supplies
It is now possible to buy most types of film (except black and
white), but the supply network is limited. You are advised to bring
your own supplies. Video and cine film are extremely difficult to
find.
    Developing of standard colour print film is now very easy —
there are shops with the most modern equipment all over the city.
— Feng Guang Photographic Supplies Store, 258 Nanjing Xi Lu.
    Tel:538374

— Guan Long Photo Supply Co., 180 Nanjing Dong Lu. Tel:214015

— Shanghai Tri-Union Watch Optical and Photographic Apparatus Co., 46 Nanjing Xi Lu. They also undertake repairs.

Musical instruments
— Wan Li Musical Instruments Store, 420 Jin Ling Dong Lu Tel:283739

Music tapes
There are a number of shops selling tapes. As good as any is the Shanghai Music Bookstore, 365 Xizang Zhong Lu.

Bookshops
— 380 Fuzhou Lu for foreign language and second hand books.
— Shanghai Trading Association, 390 Fuzhou Lu — wide selection of foreign language books about China.
— Xinhua Bookstore, 345 Nanjing Dong Lu. Tel:212599
— Shanghai Science and Technology Bookstore, 221 Henan Zhong Lu. Tel:212156
— Shanghai Music Bookstore, 365 Xizang Zhong Lu. Tel:223829
The Peace Hotel has a good bookshop, as does the Jinjiang.

Opticians
Another fast-developing service is the making of spectacles. Many places have up to date equipment and the prices are low. Try Mao Chang Glasses Store at 762 Nanjing Dong Lu. Tel:223427

Theatrical costumiers (Chinese opera)
— 279 Nanjing Dong Lu.

The bazaar in the old town, in the vicinity of the Yu Garden, has a lot of shops specialising in things like tea, pottery, walking sticks and embroidery.

Sending things home

By mail
It is not easy to mail things from China unless it is something bought in one of the major retail outlets for foreigners. Places like the Friendship Store and the Carpet Factory will take care of the formalities involved; if you simply want to send something home,

you must take the item to a post office and wrap it in the presence of whoever deals with parcels to be sent abroad. It is not impossible, but not easy.

If you can, get it to Hong Kong, if it is on your route, where the task is much easier.

By air

This will be expensive, but possibly easier. Contact the airlines direct (see 'Useful addresses'). For cargo try Eas Express Aircargo System Co. Ltd., Room 106, Union Building, 100 Yanan Dong Lu. Tel:265275.

By sea

The slowest but cheapest way, provided you have enough goods to fill a crate. The only problem is to find out from where to send it — try going directly to 1 Jinling Lu and, if they should try to send you elsewhere, ask them to telephone for you in order to avoid unnecessary journeys.

TWELVE

A brief history

Shanghai, with a population of 12 million, is the largest city in China. It lies on the Eastern seaboard and, surrounded by the provinces of Jiangsu to the north and west and Zhejiang to the south, is one of three centrally administered municipalities, the others being Peking and Tianjin. It has a total area of 6185 square kilometres, of which 6045 constitute the suburban area, and 140 the city proper.

The city is situated on the banks of the Huangpu River, a tributary of the Yangtse (ChangJiang) which empties into the South China Sea a further 14 miles downstream. Shanghai, lying in the middle of the north-south shipping route along the mainland coast, is China's major seaport. Inland from the port, navigation is possible on the Yangtse, Huangpu and Wusong (Suchow Creek) Rivers, the last two of which have their source in Taihu Lake to the west.

Shanghai is connected by rail to all the major cities of China, e.g. Peking, Canton, and Urumchi, and by air to all the principal domestic destinations. There are international flights to the USA, Japan, Canada, Italy, Singapore and Hong Kong.

The major industrial centre of China, producing 15 per cent of industrial output, it lies about four metres above sea-level on low, open terrain , some of the most fertile in China. In the surrounding areas rice, wheat, cotton, rapeseed, vegetables and fruit are produced.

The city is divided into twelve municipal areas and ten suburban counties.

Humble beginnings

Before the middle of the nineteenth century, Shanghai was a city of only marginal importance. Its early name was Hu, and it is known that in the seventh century the area was a sparsely populated marsh, the home of small communities of fishermen. As time passed, small trading vessels began to ply the creeks and waterways of the delta, and further afield along the seaboard. Shanghai, which means 'above the sea', only gained its new name, and any importance, with the silting of the Wusong River (Suzhou Creek) and thus the need for a new harbour for the trading and agricultural communities around Tai Hu (Tai Lake) that during the Song Dynasty were expanding as hordes of northerners fled before the invading Mongols.

By the beginning of the eleventh century a customs office had been established, and by the end of the thirteenth century Shanghai had become a county seat, under the jurisdiction of Jiangsu Province.

During the Ming Dynasty, favourable natural conditions encouraged the creation of a cotton industry, and soon 70 percent of agriculture in the area was devoted to the production of cotton to feed the city's cotton and silk spinning industry, which by the end of eighteenth century was providing employment for twenty thousand people.

Commercial success had its drawbacks, however, and during the sixteenth century a series of attacks by pirates forced the construction of a city wall, which was to stand until 1911; thus protected, Shanghai remained a small port of middling prosperity, until the coming of the British in the mid-nineteenth century.

The Foreign Devils arrive

Opium for the masses

British merchants, such as Jardine Matheson and Co., were the independent successors to the East India Company that had dominated trade in the Far East for the past two hundred years. Espousing the values of Free Trade, sanctioned by religious conviction, as a civilising influence, limited business was carried out with the Chinese in the southern port of Canton. The bulk of the traffic was in opium, imported from India, and then sold, illegally, for silver. Understandably, the Manchu government, seeing the damage being wreaked both on their own people and on their reserves of silver, refused to allow foreign trade to expand any further, much to the displeasure of the eager merchants. The British

Prime Minister, Lord Palmerston, was persuaded that a display of power might have the desired effect.

Unequal treaty

When a British fleet made its way up-river towards Shanghai in June 1842, it met little resistance. Having taken Shanghai, the British moved inexorably on to Nanking, where the Chinese capitulated. On August 29 1842, the Treaty of Nanking was signed aboard a British warship. The main provisions are worth quoting:

- An indemnity of 21 million dollars was to be paid by the Chinese in instalments.
- The five ports of Amoy, Canton, Fuzhou, Ningpo, and Shanghai were to be opened up to unlimited trade.
- British and Chinese officials of corresponding rank were to be accorded the same status.
- British consulates were to be established in each of the five ports.
- The Cohong monopoly was to be abolished (the Cohong was a guild of Chinese merchants granted a monopoly by the government).
- Uniformly moderate tariffs were to be imposed on both imports and exports.
- Hong Kong was to be ceded to Great Britain.

As if this wasn't enough, the British were granted the right of 'extraterritoriality', which implied that foreign nationals were not subject to Chinese law.

The British, it seems, obtained as much as they could possibly have wished; the Chinese, too weak to resist, felt that appeasement was the surest way of containment. When, not long after, similar privileges were granted to the French and to the Americans, the Chinese had in mind that perhaps, at a later date, they could be turned against the British.

There remained the sticky problem of the opium trade, which, since it was illegal, could hardly be inserted into the treaty. In the end it was simply tolerated, and the drug was merely delivered to 'floating drug warehouses' anchored outside the port.

Down to business

By the mid 1850s, Shanghai had a foreign population of over three hundred working for twenty firms; there were eight consulates and thirty six missionaries. Three-quarters of the population was British and half the trade carried out by Americans.

The Chinese population was over half a million but it was the British who built up the economic structure of the Treaty Port — after all the whole purpose of being in Shanghai was to make money and to encourage free trade. There were two principal parties involved in this: the merchants, for whom anything that brought in money was fair game, and the Consuls, who had to administer the law and mediate with the Chinese.

Gradually, companies like Jardine, Matheson and Co. concentrated less on the opium trade and turned to banking, shipping and insurance. The heads of these companies (Taipans), relied heavily on their so called 'Compradores', Chinese who acted as go-betweens. These men, who at first were usually Cantonese as they had the experience, would secure market information, conduct exchange transactions, be responsible for all Chinese personnel and deal with the Chinese customs house. Many were able to generate substantial incomes from this, and went on to make their fortunes.

The British consul was not only responsible for the behaviour of Her Majesty's subjects but also for dealing with the Chinese authorities on certain matters. The job of interpreter, therefore, became highly important and the likes of Robert Hart and Horatio Nelson Lay, who were to play substantial roles in the future of Shanghai, began their careers this way.

Growing up

There was no looking back — within fifty years a city that was a mixture of Paris, London, and Liverpool was affixed to the east coast of China. Apart from the historical facts that brought about this transformation, there was the question of geography — for here was a port lying almost exactly mid-way along the north-south trading route, at the mouth of a river that was navigable for several hundred miles to the west and with a hinterland able to produce food for a large population. More extraordinary still, it was a success story achieved without the violent overthrow of a government, and without true colonisation, thanks to the legal framework of a treaty, and the ensuing need for order.

Concessions and settlements

The areas that were occupied by the foreigners were known as 'concessions', as they had been 'ceded' to them by the Chinese government. The first was the British. It established itself along the area known as the Bund, where the Huangpu meets Suzhou Creek, and worked westward, in the direction of today's Nanking Road. Originally it occupied an area of one square mile, but with the merging of the American Settlement (the area north of Suzhou Creek) in 1863, forming the International Settlement, by 1899 it was 8.35 square miles in size. The French Concession lay to the south of the British and grew to an area of 3.9 square miles. Permission was refused when applications were made to extend them in 1915, although the Treaty Powers' sphere of influence was nevertheless increased by the building of roads in the outlying districts.

Unlike in the other Treaty Ports, where areas of land were ceded to the foreign consulate in question, which then organised their distribution, in Shanghai foreigners negotiated perpetual leases directly with Chinese landlords. Thus, although Chinese were supposed, theoretically, to live in the old walled Chinese city, unless in the employ of a foreigner, in fact large portions of land were never transferred to foreign ownership.

A model settlement

Following the capture of Nanking by the Taiping rebels in 1853, thousands of refugees drifted into Shanghai and many ended by staying in the concessions. A curious situation thus prevailed, where foreigners became legally responsible for Chinese, who were only too glad to cooperate in every way possible, since their usual sources of income had been plugged by the activities of the rebels.

Life and death
With the unexpected influx of so many refugees, facilities were stretched to the limit — disease and crime were suddenly big problems that required a municipal authority, involving all the foreign communities, to cope with them. The Shanghai Volunteer Corps was thus formed to act as a police force, and regular meetings between residents were convened to ensure the maintenance of the roads, bridges, and drains.

There were other areas of administration that needed attention too. The Customs Service was hopelessly corrupt — simple connivance between the Chinese who were supposed to administer it and the foreign merchants who were supposed to pay it, ensured that if payments were made at all, they were rather smaller than they should have been. This suited neither the Chinese government, who were supposed to benefit from customs levies, nor the foreign consuls who were supposed to see that they were paid. In the end the Customs Service was more or less handed over to the Treaty Powers for reorganisation.

In 1854, an elective Municipal Council was constituted, for the governance of the concession areas. Ultimately, the 'Shanghai Municipal Council' superintended the affairs of the International Settlement only, since the French Concession had its own governing body. The Council was composed of nine members and excluded Chinese until 1928; such was their power, that on occasion Chinese troops were denied access to the concession areas. In spite of the occasional minor contretemps, by the 1890s the International Concession came to be known as the 'Model Settlement' — the suburban areas were patrolled by mounted police (usually Sikhs), the streets were cleared of rubbish three times daily, and the city was supplied with pure water from the waterworks three miles away. The streets were lit either with electricity or with gas.

Money for all
Although social discrimination between different ranks of the foreign community, as well as the Chinese, was an unpleasant fact of daily life in Shanghai, many Chinese tolerated it since it enabled them to remain independent of the Imperial Government and to make themselves rich. By 1913, 19.85 percent of all Chinese owned factories were in Shanghai, but well before the end of the nineteenth century, Chinese run shops were to be found in the fine streets behind the Bund, and wealthy Chinese were competing for British houses.

Until 1911, when the Manchu government fell, and the 1920s, when incidents occurred that betokened the beginnings of extraordinary events to come, Shanghai was rarely touched by the issues that bedevilled China — it merely prospered, and its denizens knew how to enjoy it.

The Devils at their ease

In the Shanghai of the early twentieth century, only misogynists and misanthropes would have been unhappy. If ever a city glittered, that city was Shanghai; it was exotic, it had style and, for the foreigner, it was cheap. The gourmet, the collector, the sportsman, the hedonist — all would have found something to their taste.

A genteel outpost

Before the end of the nineteenth century, the city skyline was not the distinctive one that even now gives Shanghai its peculiar character. In the late 1880s, for example, the Bund was a tree lined avenue, a thoroughfare that separated the lawns and wharves, on one side, from the villas and their gardens on the other. The lifestyle that went with it, in the International Settlement anyway, must have been the same that the British took with them all over the world — the daily ritual of afternoon tea would have been punctiliously observed and everything bought on credit, making use of the ubiquitous 'chit' system. A very few among the expatriate community would interest themselves in things Chinese, but on the whole the question of genteel avarice was paramount. Yet many among the British community lamented the fact that there was no longer any money to be made in Chinese business. Had they taken a deeper interest in the way things were done in China, and learnt to speak Chinese, they could have relied less on their 'compradores', and achieved more themselves.

Melting pot

Shanghai, however, was an international city. The Americans and the French were already in residence when a succession of different episodes somewhat broadened the mixture, turning the city into a cosmopolis, lightening the tone and introducing some dash and a note of exhilaration (and desperation) to proceedings.

In 1853 the Taiping rebellion obliged thousands of Chinese to flee their homes and many of them found themselves camping on the Bund, or in boats tied up at the jetties that were built along it. Many continued to live in the concessions long after the rebellion had petered out, building up businesses and trading with the foreigners. Despite the fact that in the foreign concessions there were now many more Chinese than expatriates, far from slipping back to Chinese jurisdiction, they became legal havens for the refugees, and all the more so when the Chinese walled city was captured by the Small Swords Society, another rebellious group from the south, in the same year.

This was followed by the First Sino-Japanese war, at the conclusion of which in 1894 many Japanese moved into Shanghai. The Russian Revolution in 1917 saw the arrival of large numbers of White Russians and in the 1930s, many Jews, escaping persecution under the Nazis, made their way to safety.

Simultaneously, Shanghai itself was not much affected by the same events (until the Japanese invasion in the 1930s) that produced waves of immigrants, who were able to settle down as best they might, earning their keep by contributing a motley variety of skills. Of course there was a tendency, for reasons of language or psychology, for people of the same nationality to stick together, providing for their own needs and traditions, but inevitably their ways of life spilt into the community at large. The Jews quickly adapted and did well for themselves, arousing the spite and envy of the Russian community who had found it harder to make a success of their exiles. Yet, as a newspaper pointed out at the time, there was room for everybody. This fantastic variety of race and background, combined with the dawning of the age of the motor car, the moving picture, revolution and emancipation, fashioned a way of life that may never be possible again.

The outdoor life

Apart from the villas, with swimming pools set into trim lawns, there were the clubs, of the gentlemanly sort, like the Shanghai Club on the Bund, or the Cercle Sportif Françcais in the French Concession; there were the horse races and the greyhound derbies; and there were parks, where gentlefolk could enjoy a country walk, without being bothered by riff-raff.

The main horseracing track was opposite the Park Hotel, and is now known as the People's Park. It is discussed in more detail in Chapter 16. Greyhound racing may seem a rather eccentric passion for Shanghailanders (as Shanghai's foreign residents called themselves), but it had the two ingredients most dear to the heart of the foreign resident of Shanghai, namely excitement, and money. It first was introduced in the late twenties, at the very time that student agitation was at its most active, which just goes to show how little politics interfered in a determination to enjoy life. At first the dogs were imported from Britain and Ireland, until a kennels was established in the French Concession. Interest and stakes were as high as for the horses: the wealthy had their own 'stables' of dogs, and in the case of Sir Victor Sassoon each animal carried his initials as in 'veiled secret', 'very soon', 'very slippy'. After a while, however, the Chinese tried to have it banned, as being immoral, and

Opposite: *An illustrious corner of Shanghai. The Waibaidu Bridge across Suzhou Creek, Shanghai Mansions (formerly Broadway Mansions), the Soviet Consulate, and the Pujiang Hotel (formerly the Astor).*

although those in the International Settlement gave way, the French refused. Thus the racing continued in the 'Canidrome', Avenue du Roi Albert and Rue Lafayette. In the late 1930s flagging interest was only revived by perching monkey jockeys on the backs of the dogs.

Outside the city, the homesick fox hunting man could indulge in paper-hunting, a sort of paper-chase on horse back; and there was even a pack of foxhounds who would set off in pursuit of a chemical trail that had the odoriferous qualities of a fox. It was up to the last man through to settle with the farmer in the event of any damage to crops.

For the refined mind

If it was music you craved, then orchestras abounded; the theatre, then you went to the Lyceum, if the cinema, the Carlton.

Shanghai attracted a number of international stars to its theatres, the singer John McCormack, and the comedian Sir Harry Lauder to name but two. Normally, even the greatest names in entertainment were prepared to accept just enough in the way of fees to cover their expenses, simply for the pleasure of playing in Shanghai. This meant that theatre tickets were exceptionally cheap. The story goes that when Sir Harry Lauder, the Scottish comedian, was performing there, he insisted that the prices be increased; as a result his audiences were so small that his run was reduced from two weeks to two days.

A visit to a Chinese theatre was an altogether different experience. Seats could not be booked in advance. Touts would set up stalls in the lobby and await customers a short time before the beginning of the performance. Many touts had their own regular customers, and it was accepted that there was to be no poaching. When, however, a new patron arrived, then he was fair game for all, and there was an almighty clamour as he was set upon, in the race to secure him as a regular. Whenever a partnership was struck, then the tout and his customer were left to discuss terms — the more generous the patron with his tips, the better service he would receive the next occasion.

The performance itself usually lasted for between five and six hours. The plot, as one might imagine, was rather complicated, and

Opposite: *Longhua pagoda. In front, the market that takes place every April; a massive and colourful affair.*

was carefully contrived so that the star performer, the principal attraction for many of the audience, need appear only during the middle two hours. The first part merely served as an appetiser, and many among the patrons sent their servants along for the first two hours, to keep their seats warm. Then, just as the star was about to make his entrance, there was a commotion in the auditorium as the servants made way for their masters, and on the stage, as the tawdry drapes of the introductory part made way for the gorgeous scenery of the climax. After the star had made his final exit, the same spectators who had arrived late would depart, leaving their seats to others. Compared with Western theatrical performances, an evening at a Shanghai theatre was an informal affair, and even now a Chinese audience is comparatively vocal and mobile.

After dark

Shanghai was 'whoopee town', really only waking up at night, a night that started with the tea-cocktail hour, "tea for propriety, and cocktails for pep", and finished at dawn, with a last swift one down at Blood Alley. The red light district was in Fuzhou Road, and the cabarets, with 'dance hostesses' of all nationalities, dotted all over town. And if all this should fail to please, there was always 'Great World', where the latest in the bizarre would be on display. In the late 1930s, an evening could could have been spent in the Tower night club, at the top of the Cathay (now the Peace Hotel) Hotel, drinking and watching the firework display of exploding shells, as the Japanese neared the city. The Park Hotel was where the young, modern Chinese liked to dance or throw parties, and the best meal in town was to be had at the Metropole, on Fuzhou Road.

Taxi dancing

The 'taxi-dance' was a typical Shanghai institution. The dance halls were immense, with an area for dancing surrounded by a great clutter of tables at many of which would sit the dance hostesses. A gentleman without partner could 'hire' a hostess for a dance upon the presentation of a ticket, a supply of which he would have bought as he came in. He could also buy her a drink, which would certainly be cold tea but billed at the price of whatever drink the girl had requested, from which she would earn a commission. There were dance halls that specialised in Russian girls, others in Korean girls, or some other nationality, or no nationality in particular; and there was rivalry between the American sailors, who were reasonably well paid, and the British, who were not.

Vodka and chopsticks

The twenties were the years when Shanghai became known as the 'Paris of the East'. Of course, being a port, Shanghai had never been a model of respectability, but until after the First World War, a certain modesty and decorum, hypocrisy perhaps, had held sway. After the war, the word 'emancipation' became fashionable in Shanghai as everywhere else. In Shanghai, however, a volatile element was added to an already steamy brew — the Russians.

As the Bolsheviks celebrated their victory over Czarist Russia, the defeated poured out of the country in their thousands, and a large number of them arrived in Shanghai, city of refugees. Some arrived clutching bags of coins, others with only the clothes they were wearing. These were the desperate ones, and they made money any way they could.

It was really the Russians who invented the 'cabarets' that supplanted the ballrooms. The first cabarets opened in the slum tenements of Chapei, one of the Chinese areas outside the Settlements. A Chinese owner would team up with a Russian entrepreneur and a Filipino dance band, and Russian girls would dance for drinks and commissions. Soon there were so many cabarets that it didn't matter if you were thrown out of one, since you couldn't help but sprawl into another. The girls very quickly sensed their power, and began to extend their services: jealous fights broke out, and armed guards were posted all over the area, which as a result came to be known as 'the Trenches'.

The cabaret was there to stay, however, and before long they were dominating the the the nightlife of the Settlement areas too, in the uninhibited atmosphere of Del Monte's, Maxim's, and Mumm's. There were floorshows — the 'Cossack Whirlybird', or 'Salome in Spangles'; and there was an explosion of domestic crises, as Russian women were cited in a large number of scandalous divorces. Even the Chinese were bewitched, so that Government employees on business were warned away from the corrupting influences of the cabaret. As a guidebook of the time pointed out 'There are three classes of cabaret — high class, low class, and no class'.

After 1927, when the Guomindang was finally established in Nanking, yet more demands were made on the night resources of Shanghai. Chinese from Canton, free of the constraints of traditional Chinese society, wanted jazz and Chinese dancing partners. Dancing academies sprang up all over the city, and 'singsong' girls became taxi-dancers, and opium smokers were roused from their reveries to play jazz. There was still a wide gulf separating the Chinese from the foreigner, but under cover of darkness a yearning for excitement brought everyone a little closer, although there was pompous talk in some quarters about damage to the image of the 'white man', as Russian girls flirted with 'the natives'.

Rickshaw boys and sing-song girls

When the Communists came to power, one of their first tasks was to abolish the rickshaw as a slight on human dignity. Before 1949 it was the cheapest and most convenient form of transport in Shanghai; and if anything is to be said in its defence, it is that it gave employment to men who would have otherwise become criminals, or who would have died of starvation.

Strictly speaking, a rickshaw driver was supposed to accept any fare, but obviously an overweight passenger was a challenge that the already overworked driver might prefer to ignore. In this case, the route and the charge would be worked out in advance to the last yard, but it was common to behold the driver and his fare arguing when it appeared to the weary pilot that he was being cheated.

Another hazard for the driver, as if he didn't have enough from his passengers, was from the grasping policeman, who would swipe the cushion from a rickshaw, and then fine the hapless driver for working without one, which was against the law. The driver should have paid the 50 cent fine at the police station, but a day might pass before the formalities could be completed, during which time the driver would lose not only his own income, but that of his co-lessee, since the drivers did not own the rickshaws, but rented them for twelve hours. It was ultimately cheaper to allow oneself to be cheated by the policeman and pay up on the spot the 30 or 40 cents he charged, for the privilege of having the cushion returned quickly.

The rickshaw driver's main enemy was the weather more than the pulling — after all, most of Shanghai is pretty flat, with only some of the bridges across Suzhou Creek presenting a problem; and there would always be a group of urchins ready to help for a few coppers. In the wet, however, the driver would often have to carry his fare from door to vehicle pic-a-back style.

The ordinary rickshaw was a simple, unprepossessing conveyance, but at night a notable exception was the private rickshaw belonging to the sing-song girl. The sing-song girl provided entertainment at restaurant dinner parties — her main accomplishment, as the name suggests, was singing, usually to the accompaniment of her one-man orchestra, who played the two string Chinese violin, the 'er hu'. He would follow her from party to party. Many of the girls were as celebrated, and as rich, as Hollywood actresses, and there was intense competition to have the most famous sing at one's banquet.

Every girl had her headquarters at a particular hotel, where she would always begin her evening to check for customer calls, since patrons at a given restaurant were not obliged to use the resident singers. If it was a large party, and many girls were required, then special invitation cards would be filled in, and restaurant staff despatched to track them down. Back would come the responses, some accepting for a later hour, others declining gracefully and sending their regrets.

The sing-song girl's rickshaw was an arresting sight. It would be of highly polished laquer, embellished with chromium plated, battery fed headlamps. The star sat demurely inside, snug in the shadow, but with true oriental flair for the cross between the modest and the dramatic, a bell might tinkle to announce her passage, and the onlooker would turn to see a silhouette whose face was brightly illuminated by a third lamp concealed beneath her feet, that would show to great effect the lotus in her hair, and the coils of glittering jewellery around her neck. The jewellery was real enough — not far behind the rickshaw ran a trusted guardian ready to provide protection whenever necessary.

Oddments

A walk around the streets of Shanghai would have displayed a rare mixture of the bizarre, mysterious and horrifying. On a corner of a street in the Chinese city a crowd of locals craning their necks in the same direction would have betrayed a public execcution — the victim kneeling, with his braid of hair, in the days when men were still expected to follow the Manchu fashion, held by the execcutioner's assistant to keep him still. Beggars were everywhere: women crying over dead babies that probably weren't their own but had been plucked from a rubbish tip; boys hunting cigarette butts to make up new cigarettes that could be sold singly to the stevedores at the docks; and urchins waiting for passing ships to jettison their leftovers. In the financial districts pedestrians were scattered by the low slung, four-wheel carriages of the exchange brokers, as they dashed from office to office as the rates rose and fell. The carriages

N

French
· · · · · · Concession
Boundary

International
-· -· - Settlement
Boundary

SEYMOUR ROAD

BUBBLING WELL ROAD

YATES ROAD

AVENUE FOCH

AVENUE DU ROI ALBERT

AVENUE HAIG

AVENUE JOFFRE

French
Park

RUE LAFAYETTE

AVENUE DU ROI ALBERT

ROUTE DE ZICAWEI

Cathedral

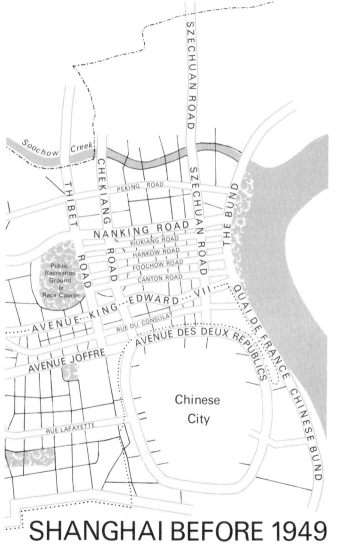

Soochow Creek

THIBET

CHEKIANG

SZECHUAN ROAD

PEKING ROAD

NANKING ROAD

ROAD

ROAD

KIUKIANG ROAD

HANKOW ROAD

FOOCHOW ROAD

CANTON ROAD

SZECHUAN ROAD

THE BUND

Public
Recreation
Ground
&
Race Course

AVENUE KING EDWARD VII

RUE DU CONSULAT

QUAI DE FRANCE

AVENUE JOFFRE

AVENUE DES DEUX REPUBLICS

CHINESE BUND

RUE LAFAYETTE

Chinese
City

SHANGHAI BEFORE 1949

Scale 1:34 500

0   1   2   km

were pulled by little Mongolian ponies, and each would sport a coachman dressed in all his finery. At night the city was radiant, but in the darker corners, mothers with daughters they didn't want, or couldn't afford to keep, deposited their children in an alcove of an orphanage wall rather than leave them to die on a pile of rubbish.

High life

For the expatriate, living in Shanghai implied a frantic, hectic social round of parties, lunches, gossip and speculation — is Soong Ai-Ling as tough as all that? Did the staff at the British Consulate *really* just leave their papers fluttering on their desks, as the Japanese broke through, and flee with their families? And, you know that beautiful Russian who is always with the American tycoon? Well, she used to work in one of the houses . . . yes, one of those houses! It would be unrealistic to suppose that everyone led a life of gloriously unbridled gaiety and dissipation, but it is obvious that a large proportion of the population did their best. Shanghai had that sort of reputation, for money, intrigue, and fun — that was why you went. Try as Shanghai people might to prolong this happy state of affairs, by assuming that they couldn't be touched by events in the world outside (a mentality fostered by the notion of extraterritoriality), in the end they lived in China, and in China changes were taking place.

All good things . . . . .

Until the 1911 revolution, Shanghai was rarely touched by the upheavals that were beginning to reveal the weaknesses of the government in Peking. On the contrary, Shanghai very often acted as a bolt-hole, both for unwilling participants looking for a new home, and for revolutionaries keeping a safe distance from their own fomentations. It acquired something of a neutral status, and in 1911 negotiations between the Republicans and the Imperial house took place there. After 1911, Shanghai was in many respects the boardroom where decisions were made that the city itself could mostly afford to ignore, if only temporarily, but which did determine the future of the country as a whole.

Waiting for the helmsman

The transition from dynastic rule to its revolutionary successor took rather longer than had been hoped — about thirty eight years in fact. During those years there were several so-called governments (sometimes simultaneously), heads of state, and capital cities. The Republic of China only had any coherent form after 1928, by which time it was too late to rule effectively, because of the constant threat of invasion by the Japanese, and the growing strength of the Communists. Between 1911 and 1928 Sun Yat-Tsen became President twice, but only for short periods, and at least two Warlords held the balance of power at various times. Although Nanking was to be the Republican capital, there was still a feeling that Peking was the real capital of China, and whoever happened to be there was generally recognised as ruler, at least by foreign governments.

The basic problem was that the country was impossibly divided. A social system that had barely changed in thousands of years was dissolving, and those who stood to lose by the changes that should have been taking place were jockeying for power. The Republican Party (the Guomindang) was split into factions representative of both Left and Right, and limped forward by means of a series of compromises.

Of the several elements in Chinese society that wished to have a say in the future, two were to be found in Shanghai — an industrial working class, and an intellectual middle class, mostly students, some of whom were for espousing Western ideas, Marxist and otherwise, and others who clung to the more traditional Chinese values. The 'May 4th' movement, an intellectual protest at the ceding of Shandong Province to the Japanese after the First World War, started in Peking, but quickly spread to the rest of the country; and in 1921 the Chinese Communist Party was founded in Shanghai, in the French Concession, at 76 Xingye Road.

The position of the foreigner was ambiguous, resented by the poor Chinese, but encouraged by the powerful. After the First World War, European and American firms returned with renewed vigour, but despite the growth of anti-foreign movements, were too valuable to cast out. Yet the poverty on the streets of Shanghai was indescribable — thousands of corpses were scraped up annually. Sooner or later there would be a reaction.

May 30th incident

On 30 May 1925, anti-Japanese demonstrations took place all over Shanghai following the shooting of a worker at a Japanese owned mill. Outside the Laozha police station on Jiujiang Road a large crowd gathered, and a number of students were arrested by the

British police. The Police Commissioner was on holiday in Japan, and his deputy was playing cricket at the race course; as the crowd swelled, the police panicked, shots rang out, and at least four demonstrators lay dead, with several others wounded. A general strike was the outcome, and a boycott of British goods. Over the next few days there were many more shootings, and a state of emergency was declared. As a direct result of this, Chinese were permitted to sit on the Municipal Council for the first time (in 1928).

The Guomindang arrive at last

In 1927 the Guomindang, by this time with Chiang Kai-Shek at its head, was finally moving northward and was within striking distance of Shanghai. This was a crucial time in China's development, for the Guomindang would soon be compelled to establish its political direction once and for all, decisions that were anxiously awaited by the foreign community, especially as the British had been forced to give up their Concession in Wuhan. Shanghai became an armed camp, and no one was allowed on the streets between 10 pm and 4 am. Strikes and demonstrations were commonplace. The police hacked at anyone who might be sympathetic to the Left, but large areas of the city outside the Concessions came under Leftist control anyway, led by Zhou En-Lai. They still hoped for support from Chiang, but not long after his arrival in Shanghai, Chiang unleashed a brutal attack on his former allies on the Left. It was a massacre. Zhou took refuge in the Commercial Press building, and thence to Wuhan.

When the Guomindang finally took the city, they stopped short of the Settlement areas. Chiang, now married into one of the wealthiest and most influential families in China, the Soongs of Shanghai, was conclusively not a revolutionary of the Left. When later he was proclaimed President of the Republic, the capital was once again Nanking, but the source of his power and his money was Shanghai.

The Left wing of the Party moved to Wuhan, and many of the Russian advisers with whom the Guomindang had cooperated in the years of indecision were expelled or executed.

Life resumed its familiar pattern for the expatriate community. Some thought thus: 'So wars come and go, but through the ninety years of its modern existence, Shanghai, although faltering at times, has never really been out of stride in its advance to its inevitable destiny.' Others must have had a suspicion that its destiny lay elsewhere, but another ten years were to pass before then.

The Japanese on the move

The Japanese had been a threat to China for many years, since the Sino-Japanese War of 1894. At the conclusion of the First World War, it was agreed amongst the signatories of the Versailles Treaty that Shandong Province would be ceded to Japan. Anti-Japanese feeling amongst the Chinese ran high, and the Japanese knew it. Japan was working towards the creation of a 'Greater East Asia', a Japanese dominated confederation of Asian states, free of Western influence, that would be an endless source of raw material for Japan. In 1928 Japan landed troops in Shanghai as a show of strength. Nothing came of that, but in 1931, Japan took over the whole of Manchuria.

In Shanghai, Japanese goods were boycotted. A Japanese priest was killed, an act which kindled a whole series of riots and scuffles between Chinese and Japanese, and finally a flotilla of Japanese navy ships entered Shanghai, ostensibly to defend Japanese residents in the district of Hongkou. In the ensuing battle, the Chinese 19th Army fought heroically but were unable to repel the enemy. Once again a State of Emergency was declared in the Foreign Settlements, although after a month of fighting, they remained unaffected. The district of Chapei, on the other hand, was badly bombed, and in the end the hundred thousand Japanese troops were too much for the under manned Chinese. A truce was signed, but a Japanese garrison remained in place.

Full scale war between China and Japan broke out only in 1937. Chiang Kai-Shek, in a much debated military ploy, lured the Japanese to Shanghai, but the ruse failed — the Chinese were unable to offer much resistance, and very soon Shanghai was an occupied city.

The residents of Shanghai were used to threats to their lifestyle looming up and vanishing without causing too much trouble; this time, the threat would hold good. Again, the curfew, again the Volunteer Force was put on the alert, and again there were more uniforms on the streets. Apart from that, the war remained in the distance at first; so much so that a popular story told of a bomb falling on the Bund, and a dazed pedestrian staggering from the rubble as he muttered: "Good Heavens! This will set extraterritoriality back twenty five years!"

Nevertheless, some people must have taken it seriously as quite a number were evacuated to Hong Kong, or even further afield. There were those, too, who found life away from Shanghai unbearable, and came back, Japanese or no Japanese.

Eventually, the Japanese occupied the area north of the Garden (Waibaidu) Bridge. Sentries were posted there, so that permission had to be granted to cross from the International Settlement to the areas beyond. There were, for example, refugees who wanted to reclaim belongings they had left behind. The guards enjoyed a little sport to relieve the tedium of their post — foreign men were frequently made to remove their trousers before being granted leave to cross, and everyone was expected to bow. Miserable though the situation was, a sense of humour prevailed — medals were awarded to those unfortunate enough to be on nightsoil duty.

The fighting moved on to Nanking, where the Japanese troops went berserk, staging a massacre the Chinese have never forgotten. Shanghai, outside of the Settlements, was under Japanese jurisdiction, but in practice the Settlements were affected too, since the Japanese refused to leave Hongkou which was the part of the International Settlement (north of the Garden Bridge) where most of the Japanese civilians resided. They had proved only how barbaric they could be, but had failed to win the respect they so badly coveted. When in 1937 they were still unable to obtain the third seat they wanted on the Municipal Council, one of the Japanese delegates vented his frustration by shooting one of the councillors.

The bitter end

Life resumed something of its normal pattern, but the city had had its confidence shaken. People were edgy, not altogether surprising when they had been brought face to face with a war that had seemed just a distant roll of thunder. Bombs had even fallen on the Bund, admittedly through the carelessness of Chinese pilots aiming for a Japanese warship, but bombs nevertheless, that had killed 1500 people. The British police deserted the suburban areas and the Japanese promptly commandeered 76 Jessfield Road as a torture chamber for dissident Chinese. In April 1941 the Japanese finally obtained their much coveted third seat on the Municipal Council, and took control of all Chinese organisations. They tried, too, to muzzle the press, by killing journalists. Finally, on 8 December 1941, the day after the bombing of Pearl Harbour, they occupied the city centre. The French Concession was spared, for the time being, as the Japanese wished to exert diplomatic pressure on the Vichy government; but in January 1943 the Western Powers renounced their treaty rights and in August of the same year the first

Chinese mayor of all Shanghai took charge, under Japanese tutelage.

No man's land

Shanghai was a deflated balloon — many of its factories had been destroyed in the fighting of 1937 and many of its businessmen had either left the country or transferred their affairs to the Free China capital of Chongqing. Those that stayed had their factories and premises taken over by the Japanese. Yet the industrial machine managed to keep going — there was no shortage of manpower or money, the only problem being to circumvent the Japanese levies and the difficulties of maintaining supplies. The Chinese kept going by doing business from their own homes, and the foreign owned spinning mills managed to stay profitable by importing cloth. Legitimate business, however, on its pre-war scale, was out of the question — only gangsters really prospered.

After the war nothing improved. All the available money was committed to the battle against the Communists and a variety of draconian measures to stimulate the economy merely stirred unrest. A common saying was 'business is better than working, hoarding is better than business, and speculation is better than hoarding'. In 1947 there were violent hunger strikes; sometimes the corrupt and desperate government was reduced to using tanks to quell the anger of exhausted factory workers; and imaginary Communist plots were discovered to justify repressive measures. It was all to no avail. The end had come, and the Guomindang retreated to Taiwan.

Revolutionary Shanghai

By the time the Communists came to power in 1949, they had acquired some experience in governing rural areas, but none of governing cities. According to Mao, 'the centre of gravity of the Party's work had shifted from the village to the city'. His revolutionaries, many of whom were peasant farmers who had never even seen a city, regarded them as bastions of conservatism and inequality. It is certainly true that in the great metropolises like Shanghai, unemployment, corruption, gangsterism, drug addiction and prostitution were rampant before 1949, and in the months leading up to the defeat of the Guomindang, when inflation was rising at 25 per cent a week, there were food shortages, riots, and looting. Factories were forced to close. Rickshaw drivers, too weak to work, refused to haul passengers. In short, chaos and despair. That all this was the fault of the Guomindang, or 'foreign imperialism' is a moot point, but anyway the victors, Mao's Communist Party, were now to attempt the reconstruction of their country.

Different reactions

'We had been ruled since '37 by the Japanese, and since '45 by the Guomindang, and during that time we lost everything. How could Mao Zedong be worse ?'

When the Communists entered Shanghai, they entered very quietly. There was almost no fighting, no looting, and the soldiery was excessively polite, even refusing cigarettes from the populace. Everybody, including the large foreign community, was told that they had nothing to fear. In short, there appeared to be a smooth transition of power.

Of course reactions to the coming of the Communists varied. Many residents, both Chinese and foreign, had fled when it had become obvious that the Guomindang were on the verge of defeat. One wealthy Chinese was said to have moved his business, lock, stock, and barrel, and all his extensive staff at more than $1000 a head, by air to São Paulo in Brazil, where a little Shanghai began to flourish. Most Chinese had no option but to stay whether they wanted to or not, but there were others who felt confident of their ability to manipulate the Communists in the way they had manipulated all the other governments that had come and gone in the preceding years. Still others, from more humble backgrounds, saw an opportunity to better themselves. Of the foreigners, most Americans felt that the Communists would renege on their promises, and that a swift departure was the best policy, whilst a good many British and Europeans reasoned, incorrectly as it turned out, that although there was bound to be change, it would not affect them a great deal.

An impressive start

During the first few months many things did, indeed, improve — corruption was all but eliminated, inflation was brought under control, goods that had been scarce once again became available, and hygiene was considerably improved. Women were encouraged to think for themselves, and take jobs (whenever any were available), and the rickshaw became a thing of the past. At the same time, there seemed, at first, to prevail an admirably pragmatic approach to solving many outstanding problems. Although it ran counter to Communist policy, pedicabs continued to ply their trade, and servants remained in the employ of their masters, to avoid adding to the already chronic unemployment. The Courts functioned without lawyers, with only a single presiding judge making decisions based on commonsense, a system that satisfied everyone at first. But before too long the changes became campaigns and the campaigns became close to persecution.

A light is extinguished

Very soon Shanghai began to lose its distinctive character. Not surprisingly the brothels were shut down and the prostitutes and taxi-dancers were rounded up and 're-educated'. Afterwards they would work in factories, or would stay at home to make matches or embroidered flowers. Nor did it stop there — all the ballrooms, all the cabarets, every establishment that had provided entertainment, lewd and otherwise, closed its doors and didn't reopen them. The Shanghai Film Studio continued to produce films, (the acting profession only lost its glamorous appeal in the Cultural Revolution), and Western dance music, strangely, was not proscribed. The spirit, however, had gone. Everything was arranged, organised, and controlled. The streets crackled, not to the sound of fireworks or neon lighting, but to loud-speakers forever exhorting people to work harder; or insisting that passers-by take part in exercises to keep the body lean and the mind alert. Everyone wore a boilersuit.

Increasing industrial production became the sole aim of society. In the first years, then, even if the methods were of questionable efficacy, there were solid, practical reasons for motivating the populace, which had nothing to do with class struggle. Since there was no possibility, in the early days, of providing a system of social services, people needed to be taught the value of community help, not previously a strong feature of life in Shanghai. Much of the early propaganda was aimed, not at political transformation, but at an economic transformation, which was badly hindered by the continuing blockade of the port by the Guomindang in Taiwan.

Shanghai posed a special problem for the Communists, since its whole raison d'etre was based on an economic system, and on an entrepreneurial spirit that was contrary to the ethos of Communism. The new Chinese government was far more inward looking, seeing the future of China tied in with that of the Soviet Union. Many people from Shanghai were sent to work elsewhere, and the city saw its second Russian invasion in less than forty years, as large numbers of Soviet personnel arrived with their families, as advisers and experts. In some respects the following years were going to be reminiscent of Soviet power in other ways.

The swinging fifties

Life became a series of campaigns, usually against rather than for something. For example the first was the 'Land Reform Movement' of 1950-52, a campaign against the former landlords, and an attempt to redistribute the land more fairly. This seemed a worthy and reasonable excercise, but was followed not long after by a movement against 'Rich peasants'. From one campaign, or movement, the Maoist government would swing to another, often opposite in nature to the one preceding. When in 1956 Mao started the 'Let a Hundred Flowers Bloom and Let a Hundred Schools of Thought Contend' campaign, it seemed that he was encouraging people to criticise and debate — yet the 'Anti-Rightist Campaign' that followed it, denounced the same people who had dared to speak out.

Before 1949 the typical Shanghai figure had been the eager opportunist. After, it was the bureaucrat. In old Shanghai the streets were alive with colour, fascination, and poverty. Happily the poverty was disappearing, but the fascination and colour were in anti-USA demonstrations, and in exhibitions depicting the cruelty of Taoist priests. For the foreign businessman, as well as for the enterprising Chinese who had stayed behind rather than flee, life became steadily more difficult. Ultimately, the foreigner was forced to sell out to the government, who would tax companies until they were worth almost nothing, and then buy them out. In 1955 a resident card system was introduced — every six months they came up for review, and reasons were quickly found for not renewing them. Yet there were some people still owning private property until the late 1950s, and some of the larger companies, like Shell, maintained an office until 1966.

The 1950s were, for Shanghai, a period of enormous change. Some would call it sad, others would regard it as nothing but nemesis — an alcoholic drying out. The average Chinese was materially more secure, and he could enter the old Shanghai Club without the outraged and apoplectic look of a blimpish Englishman. And yet there must be not a few who would have found less drastic changes easier to stomach.

The Cultural Revolution

The Great Proletarian Cultural Revolution was the last and most drastic of the political campaigns to sweep across China since the founding of the People's Republic. The real nature of this 'revolution' is still debated but the Chinese freely acknowledge, now, that it constituted a disaster of almost cataclysmic proportions. It may be summed up as two things — an attempt by Mao to stifle criticism of his leadership after the disaster of 'The Great Leap Forward', when millions died of starvation in the wake of ill-advised agricultural policies; and a final, all-out effort to eradicate the 'bourgeois' thinking of the masses and the tyranny of bureaucracy, both of which were the antithesis of Maoism.

It lasted for ten years (1966-76), although the violence and chaos were at their peak during the first three. At various stages every aspect of life was affected — factories ceased production, schools and universities closed, farmworkers neglected the land to travel to the cities and 'exchange revolutionary experiences' with workers and students. Millions of people died at the hands of their persecutors, who were at first Mao's 'Red Guards', and then a series of cliques who came and went as their star brightened and dimmed.

Shanghai played a highly significant role in the Cultural Revolution. All four members of the 'Gang of Four' had strong Shanghai connections and it was in Shanghai that first the students, and then the workers rallied to Mao's call to smash the 'four olds' — old culture, old customs, old habits, and old ways.

The January Revolution

When, in 1966, the 'Great Cultural Revolution' began, Shanghai was not only the most populous and highly industrialised city in China, but it was the most politically radical, and had the greatest concentration of working class people. It was ripe and ready to be swept up in the Cultural Revolution when it came.

Following the lead given by Red Guards in Peking, in the summer of 1966 students at Shanghai University began to form groups of their own. Soon, however, these groups were split by disputes and arguments, which somehow had the effect of making them still more radical — verbal attacks became wall posters and mass rallies, and eventually physical attacks on government offices. Mao had said 'dare to rebel', and although the students had no qualms about rebelling against the established Party bureaucracy, the workers were more circumspect. Past experience had taught them that precipitate action, revolutionary or not, was not always sensible. They knew, too, that a political dossier was kept on each of them and were not unnaturally concerned about how such a document might be used, should things go wrong. This was solved when the students seized the dossiers, but even when the workers were persuaded to destroy the Party infrastructure by rebelling in the factories, squabbles amongst them prevented the formation of a united front.

Despite their differences, everybody had one thing in common — a loathing of the Party bureaucracy that ruled their lives. By November of the same year an organisation calling itself the 'Headquarters of the Revolutionary Revolt of Shanghai Workers' had been formed, entirely separate from the student Red Guard, or the Government in Peking, which had envisaged a part-time revolution, a revolution out of office hours, so to speak. Shanghai, needless to say, was one step ahead of Peking and demanded direct rule by the Proletariat, immediately. In no mood to accept refusals, a group of workers commandeered a Peking-bound train, which promptly came to a halt just outside Shanghai. The hijackers stayed where they were for three days, until officials from Peking arrived and recognised the 'Headquarters' organisation as legitimate.

Girls in a shop. Chinese women, after a long period of austerity, are rediscovering femininity.

Nevertheless, with the erosion of Party authority, discipline weakened and violent rebel groups roamed the streets. Yet, when the 'Headquarters' organisation placed an appeal for unity in the local newspaper 'Wen hui bao', a million workers gathered in the People's Square and denounced the local Party bureaucracy. The Mayor and his cronies were publicly criticised, and then removed from office. They were said to have attempted to 'bribe' the workers back to work, reducing the Cultural Revolution to the level of a workers strike for better pay and conditions; and indeed it is probable that at first many workers major concern was just that. Only later did they aspire to a more 'revolutionary' cause.

The 'Headquarters' organisation remained united, eager to build a Shanghai Commune, along the lines of the one in Paris the previous century. Chang Chun-Qiao, a colleague of Mao's wife, was appointed by Peking to head this 'January Revolution' but of course the very fact that his power derived from the Party, and not from the local revolutionaries, meant that the experiment was doomed to failure. It seemed that Mao, for all his talk of rebellion and democracy, felt threatened by independent movements. Chang was recalled to Peking and told that 'Revolutionary Committees', an alliance of the Army, mass Revolutionary organisations, and pro-Maoist party cadres, were to be introduced, and that Communes were, in fact, reactionary. After nineteen days the Shanghai Commune became the 'Revolutionary Committee of the Municipality of Shanghai'; and power lay not with the people, but with Chairman Mao.

Apocalypse now

Once some sort of political direction was established, the fighting and the persecution became worse. Different factions outdid each other in revolutionary fervour, until life in Shanghai, and all over China, became a travesty, or worse, a perversion of civilisation. Anyone, or even relatives of anyone, who had ever been in contact with foreigners, was put on trial in 'people's courts', or subjected to all night indoctrination sessions, or simply flung in gaol to rot, or to be subjected to interrogation and torture. Many people, confused and terrified, threw themselves to their death from top-floor windows. In milder cases, the victim was paraded in the streets wearing a dunce's cap with the Chinese characters for 'Cow's Demon and Snake Spirit' written on it. These characters vilified any member of the 'Nine Stinking Categories', basically anyone who had been a subject of the various campaigns during the 1950s. Women had their hair cropped in the street if the style was deemed incorrect, and their shoes removed if the heels were provocatively high.

The frightening thing was that the government, far from trying to curb the excesses of the mostly self-styled revolutionaries, actually encouraged them — the newspapers, all mouthpieces of the state, urged its citizens on to still greater acts of brutality. So keen were people to be seen to do the right thing, that the houses of Red Guards were being ransacked while they were themselves ransacking the house of some so-called counter-revolutionary. Shops discarded their old names in favour of 'The East is Red', and the most prominent items in their windows were portraits of Mao. Streets had their names changed — the Bund, for example became 'Revolution Boulevard', and it was even debated whether to change the traffic lights so that red would signify 'go'.

Chang Chun-Qiao directed everything from the Peace Hotel, in close cooperation with Jiang Qiao, Mao's wife, who, as Minister responsible for the Arts, used the Cultural Revolution as a way of exacting revenge upon former colleagues who, she felt, had scorned her during her spell as a mediocre actress then known as Lan Ping, in Shanghai before 1949. There was a nation wide hunt for beautiful girls to fill the Shanghai harem of Lin Li-Guo, the son of Lin Biao. If spite, malice, and abuse of power were even only partly responsible for such chaos then the tragedy, already great, was incalculable. As the spires of the Catholic Cathedral were being desecrated, and the Ching En Tze temple demolished by students, children were writing big-character posters denouncing their parents as counter-revolutionaries. They were encouraged in this by their parents, who were attempting to protect their offspring from the wrath of the Red Guards.

Aftermath

By 1969 the streets were quiet again, the quiet that follows a bombing raid. The Red Guards had been sent to the countryside 'to learn from the peasants'. The Cultural Revolution was still in full swing, but the long, slow tussle for power that would only be concluded with the death of Mao and the arrest of the Gang of Four was just beginning. In the meantime equerries from Peking toured the country interrogating prisoners on the correctness of their political thinking. They all tried to get to Shanghai because, even in those hard times, the shopping remained the best. Gradually things returned to normal — a sign of change was the visit to China of President Nixon in 1972, and the signing of the Shanghai Communiqué.

Prisoners began to be released to the waiting arms of the Residential Committees who were now responsible for the reindoctrination of former 'criminals'. Thousands of people had died unnatural deaths in Shanghai, and many who had survived against the odds had their lives destroyed. The madness continued, nevertheless. At one point there was a movement to make sure that the trains always arrived late — punctuality might be construed as ambition, and taking the capitalist road. Under such conditions it would take time for life to return to normal.

Reconstruction

The persecution and the uncertainty only came to an end in 1976, with the death of Chairman Mao, and the subsequent arrest of the Gang of Four. Even now, it is not clear how events unfolded and who made the decisions that led to their removal. At the time, rumour, as always, was hard at work. It was thought, for example, that the Gang of Four, who all had strong Shanghai connections (Jiang Qing, former Shanghai actress and wife of Mao; Chang Chun-Qiao, journalist and director of propaganda in Shanghai; Yao Wen-Yuan, editor of the newspaper 'Shanghai Liberation Army Daily'; and Wang Hong-Wen, originally a Shanghai worker who helped to found the Shanghai Workers Revolutionary Headquarters and who rose to become a Vice-premier), were organising a private army in Shanghai to march on Peking and seize power. If so, they never had the opportunity, because others in the Politburo were quick to realise that China was once again on the brink of civil war.

A new Chairman (Hua Guo Feng) was elected by the Politburo, and Shanghai, with the rest of the country, got down to the business of rebuilding its shattered way of life. Shanghai, renowned for 'its glorious revolutionary tradition' had once again played the major role in a piece of Chinese history, but this time it was something that most wanted to forget.

Foreigners were once again to be seen on the streets of Shanghai, but as visitors, not taipans. New hotels, new industries, and a new prosperity were coming, in an attempt to come to terms with the past and revitalise the city.

1976-1990

In common with the rest of China, Shanghai has continued to develop and prosper. Deng Xiao Ping succeeded Hua Guo Feng as leader of the country and until 1989 presided over a programme of reconstruction that was allowing China, apparently, to make considerable progress, at least as far as the economy was concerned. Politically and sociologically the rate of change was far slower, reaching a low point in the early 1980s with a campaign against bourgeois liberalism and moral pollution. This did not last long and life returned to normal. By 1988, however, it was clear that there was discontent in the land. Inflation had become a problem, corruption was widespread and frustration simmered at the lack of political freedom.

All of this came to a head with the student demonstration in Tian An Men square in Peking. Demonstrations spread to the rest of the country, including Shanghai, workers joining the students in giving vent to their frustrations. One June 4th the troops were sent into Tian An Men square - carnage ensued. Shanghai escaped this fate although the city was threatened with the imposition of marshal law. 'We warn all the cliques and plotters that you must stop with your attempts to disrupt the city of Shanghai — otherwise you will be crushed.' The demonstration continued throughout the next few days. Public transport came to a halt as the buses were commandeered for use as barricades by the protesters. At this stage thousands of people were taking part in demonstrations, but defiance was shown in a variety of ways. A pianist at one of the luxury hotels interrupted the flow of insipid muzak to play the Internationale. Rumour was busy as usual — Deng Xiao Ping was said to have died.

By the 7th June the student movement, based at Fudan University, was becoming nervous. An orator was speaking from the top of a hi-jacked bus, but on the whole the movement appeared to have no operational centre. This was tactically sound as far as escape from the authorities was concerned but ensured too that the movement could not really mature. Nevertheless the Shanghai students constructed their own statue of liberty just as their comrades in Peking had done.

By the 8th the streets resounded to the slapping of hands on the flanks of newly arrived tanks as demonstrators implored the army to withdraw. By now only a thousand demonstrators listened to the protest speeches outside Party headquarters. The students were bombarded by propaganda, the Wen Hui Bao newspaper playing a leading role in this. The student movement was infiltrated by secret police rendering it 'unspeakably brave'. The mayor of Shanghai, Zhu Rong Ji, widely considered a moderate, appeared 'tormented and unhappy' when asking for calm on television, It was felt that the local Party Secretary, Jiang Zeming, who was not much liked, was behind the suppression of the protest movement.

The 10th June saw the movement still fighting for its life. A peaceful rally of between 50 and 100 thousand in the People's Square brought traffic to a standstill. A vow was made by the students to avenge their classmates who were killed in Peking and a call went out for copies of videos taken during the massacre. The Mayor was playing a clever game, diverting people's interest away from the protests by harping on the disruption caused. The student's attitude: 'We'll never forget'.

On the 13th a student activist was seized at Shanghai airport and by the 19th it was all over including the shouting. Old men in blue suits and caps anointed with a red star were the guardians of the peace — the hardliners had won the day and scenes that followed were faintly reminiscent of the days of Mao. These ageing militia men were posted every few yards. They dealt with any transgressions of 'socialist legality'. Before, when the student movement was at its height, the air was fresh and exhilarating, even if anarchy seemed to be imminent. A foreigner felt like the little boy in *'Empire of the Sun',* carried away on the tide. Now a muttered remark within earshot of the militia pensioners earned a slap and a chase along the zig-zag bridge in the old town.

The 22nd brought recriminations. Three men who had been found guilty of burning and destroying a train that had run over six demonstrators were publicly shot. There remains only the vow of one of the Peking leaders who escaped to the west — 'Black sun, I'm going to shoot you down!'

By the middle of July life had assumed its old rhythms. Church worship remained strong, implying that the crackdown was aimed mostly at law and order rather than at ideology. Thirty per cent of foreign businesses had re-occupied their offices. Come August Britain had withdrawn its official warning to British nationals about travelling in China. Calm has returned to the country. It is forced but the powers that be are strong. Shanghai can get back to the business of prospering. To visit Shanghai now, one would never know what had happened, and so it will remain for a few years until the next time.

THIRTEEN

Shanghai hands

The Soongs

In the space of two generations the Soong family had a profound influence on the history of modern China. The three girls, Ai-Ling, Ching-Ling, and May-Ling, who were each married to rich or influential men, H.H.Kung, Sun Yat-Tsen, and Chiang Kai-Shek respectively, wielded, or were thought to wield, enormous power over their husbands and thus over the destiny of China. Their brother T.V.Soong, was probably the richest man of his generation. To describe them as 'legendary' would not, for once, be an abuse of a potent word, for in the minds of a people that for thousands of years had known their rulers as 'sons of Heaven', the Soongs were touched by the mystique of imperial power.

Founding father

The Soong progenitor was Charlie Soong, born in 1866, who grew up on the island of Hainan, in the south, but who at an early age found himself in the United States of America. Benefactors, with the zeal characteristic of their time, were eager to make an educated Christian of him and in time he arrived in Shanghai as a missionary. One of the problems he encountered immediately was the absence of cheap bibles written in the vernacular. He set to printing them himself, and began to make money. Finally, he gave up his missionary work to devote his time to business; but he remained a devout Christian and married into a Christian Chinese family.

His faith didn't stop him from maintaining the traditional ties with secret societies dedicated to the downfall of the Manchu dynasty. Through them, he met Sun Yat-Tsen, a revolutionary and fellow southerner. Charlie, now rich but anxious to see the demise of the corrupt government in Peking, pledged support to Sun's cause. The revolution that finally saw off the Manchus was not a summary affair — in fact Sun was fund-raising in the United States when the first shots were fired in 1911. He returned to be appointed President of the new republic, but China was a country of fragmented loyalties, and real power was still in Peking, in the hands of a wily warlord, Yuan Shih-Kai, who had the tacit backing of Great Britain and her allies.

A compromise was reached. Yuan was to become President, but the young emperor Pu Yi, who had been placed on the throne to prolong the illusion of imperial power, was to stand down and the capital was to be moved to Nanking (as a symbol of the restoration of the Ming dynasty, whose first capital had been there); Sun, despite all that he had done for the Republican movement, was given the post of Director of the Railways. As the years passed, and as promises were broken by the government in Peking, Sun was all the more resolved to form an alliance of sympathetic warlords, march north and take Peking.

Precocious children

The Soong children were all educated in the U.S.A., and like their father were able to add worldliness to their natural store of intelligence. Eventually, Soong Ai-Ling, the eldest child, was married to a scion of a wealthy Shanxi Province family, and descendent of Confucius, H.H.Kung, a match that met with the satisfaction of her father; Ching-Ling, the second sister and dreamy idealist of the family, eloped with Sun Yat-Tsen, much to her father's disgust, for he was a personal friend and thirty years older than the bride. In 1918 Charlie Soong died, too soon to see his children immortalise his invented name.

In 1919, at the end of the First World War, the Versailles Treaty was signed and through an agreement reached between the major powers, Shandong Province was ceded to Japan. An intellectual revolutionary movement burgeoned amongst the students as a result, and in 1921 the Chinese Communist Party was formed in Shanghai, an event that was eventually to make its mark on China as a whole, but which in its early years would act as a foil to the corruption of the Soongs as they tightened their grip on the Guomindang (as Sun's Republican party was known).

The same period saw the rise of Chiang Kai-Shek, a military graduate and hellraiser, who had become associated with the Republican movement that, before the fall of the Manchus, was in exile in Japan. When Sun decided to move his centre of operations to Canton, and eventually open a military academy for the training of revolutionary troops, Chiang was invited to take charge of it. Not long before, he had met Soong May Ling, and resolved to make her his wife (although he had only recently divorced his first wife and married his second); and T.V.Soong, the ablest of the brothers, had been invited to strengthen the finances of the Guomindang. Slowly but surely, the Soong family was working its way into all the principal areas of influence in China.

Dream of Red Mansions. In modern China the links with the past remain strong.

In power

There ensued another three years of chaotic fighting, amongst the various warlords who controlled different areas of the country, and between the revolutionary government in Canton, and the puppet government in Peking. Finally in 1924 the ruling clique in Peking was toppled by Warlord Feng Yu-Xiang, who invited Sun to become President. Soon after his arrival in Peking, Sun died, without anyone to take his place. A long struggle for power began.

There were a number of candidates for the post, but of such wildly diverging political ideas and allegiances that Chiang Kai-Shek, whose ties were mostly military, was chosen to succeed Sun. His rise to power was not without its sinister side, and it has been alleged that the Green Gang, who controlled the Shanghai underworld and who were tightly bound up with the fortunes of the Soong family, played a considerable role in his election. Seemingly his revolutionary zeal was not entirely free of mercenary considerations.

During the next four years the Guomindang was in disarray. Two factions developed, one on the Right, led by Chiang, and the other more Leftist, championed by Soong Ching-Ling, who regarded it as closer to the ideals of Sun Yat-Tsen. Ultimately, the Leftists were pushed out into the cold, and in 1928 it was Chiang Kai-Shek who, in the new capital, Nanking, was proclaimed as the President of China.

'One loved power, one loved money,one loved China' — so the Chinese say of the Soong sisters. Yet it was the one who loved China, Ching-Ling, who was forced into exile in Moscow, whilst the others remained to abuse the power they had achieved in order to secure the money they craved. By marrying Chiang (with a glittering reception at the Majestic Hotel on the Nanking Road), May-Ling found herself in a position of power; Ai-Ling had married into money, and through her probable dealings with the Green Gang and the manipulation of her husband built up a massive fortune. The eldest brother, T.V.Soong had both money and power. Over the next ten years he held a variety of governmental posts, from Finance Minister to Premier, and accumulated enormous wealth in the process. The two younger brothers, T.A. and T.L.Soong, less rapacious than their siblings, made do with millions rather than billions.

Diaspora

Until 1949, when the Communists came to power, China lurched from one crisis to another. If it wasn't a showdown with the

Communists, it was the weakness of the economy; and if it wasn't the economy, it was an invasion by the Japanese. Finally the Guomindang allied itself with the Communists to expel the Japanese, but after the Japanese had taken Shanghai, Nanking was next on the list and the government moved to Chongqing. In the meantime May-Ling went to the United States to lobby for financial aid, which she obtained, and in so doing became enormously popular with Americans. The billions of dollars that the U.S.A. provided did not prevent famine, or equip soldiers, yet the Soongs increased their wealth. The husband of Ai-Ling, H.H.Kung, was minister of Finance, and responsible for budgeting.

By 1948, the Communist forces of Mao Zedong were in the ascendant, and the Soongs dispersed, May-Ling with Chiang to Taiwan, Ai-Ling Kung and her husband to the U.S.A., and T.V.Soong first to Hong Kong and then he too to the U.S.A. where the two younger brothers also made their permanent homes. Ching-Ling, who had returned from exile to assist the War effort, was the only one to remain in China. She became one of three non-Communist Vice Chairmen of the new government, and continued to live in her father's old house on the Avenue Joffre, in Shanghai. T.V.Soong died in San Francisco in 1971, T.A.Soong in 1969, and nobody is certain what befell the middle brother.

May-Ling still lives in New York. When her sister, Ching-Ling, died in Peking in 1981, May-Ling refused the invitation to attend the funeral.

If the Soong children had anything in common it was their fondness for flouting convention, something they presumably acquired during their years in the U.S.A., where their powerful personalities were allowed to develop, unhindered by the normal stifling conventions of Chinese society. Once home, there was no better setting than Shanghai for realising their ambitions, but only Ching-Ling, it seems, was able to keep them under control.

Pockmarked Huang and Big-eared Du

Through the years Shanghai, with its peculiar status as a Treaty Port, had acted as a haven for refugees. At the same time, it was a city that fairly reeked of money. It is a combination ripe for 'gangsterism', and gangsters were the dark shadows behind the pastel colours in the portrait of Shanghai. Two of them were linked to events in the Shanghai of the twenties and thirties in a way that, even for gangsters, borders on the incredible.

Secret societies

Gangs, in the form of secret societies, have always been an important part of the Chinese social fabric. During the rule of the last of the Chinese dynasties, many societies flourished dedicated to the subversion of the Qing, who were Manchurian and therefore foreign, and to the restoration of the Ming Dynasty, which had been established on the back of peasant insurrection. Central and southern China were the principal areas of operation, since Qing power was more firmly established in the north — even monks were involved, witness the Kung Fu sect that was formed at Shaolin Temple. The northern societies tended to be more fanatical, like the Boxers who at the turn of the century had caused so many problems for the government in Peking.

As time passed, hundreds of societies sprang up, providing cover for all sorts of outcasts and adventurers. In English they claim to be known as Triads, an approximation of their Chinese title which refers to the three sides of an equilateral triangle, representing Man, Heaven, and Earth. Inevitably whilst their original aim was never forgotten, these societies found that their very secrecy, in the tradition of the Mafia, could have its uses.

The Villains

In the Shanghai of the late nineteenth and early twentieth century, a society calling itself the Red Gang ran its underworld. Its gangleader was Huang Jinrong, otherwise known as Pockmarked Huang, who based his activities in the French Concession, not least because Huang was also the Chief Detective for the French Sûreté. Gangland in foreign Shanghai was the French Concession, partly because it was more accessible to the Chinese, and partly because the French themselves were involved in some of the gangs' activities. They were not averse, for example, to a stake in the opium trade.

Du Yuesheng (Big-Eared Du) was not much more than a waterfront tough when he met Huang, through Huang's mistress. Du, somewhat precociously, persuaded Huang of the virtues of the cartel in matters of drug running, and formed the 'Green Gang' that was to have such an influence on the destiny of China. Huang remained Godfather, but Du assumed the responsibility of manager.

It was said of Du that "a hundred thousand men in Shanghai obeyed his orders". Not only men, because he controlled half the city's prostitutes, as well as retaining exclusive rights to the drug running operations. As his power grew he was able to turn to another source of income — offering 'protection'. Those who considered themselves above 'protection' were reminded of the dangers of city life with the delivery of a coffin to their front door.

To the likes of Du, Communism posed a threat. Du's involvment with politics, particularly with the Guomindang, is certain, but the details are murky. Unquestionably he knew Soong Ai-Ling and Chiang Kai-Shek well, possibly ensuring the rise of Chiang as a hedge against the Communists; certainly he and Huang were honorary advisors to the Guomindang and were given the rank of Major General; and it is more than likely that he engineered massacres and assassinations with the connivance of people terrified of the Red threat. Yet he became a Christian in the middle of his career, and sat on the boards of all sorts of worthy institutions. No doubt he stood to gain much from such displays of piety, but, whatever the motive, it was his money that provided the wherewithal for a resistance movement against the Japanese in Shanghai during the 1930s.

After the war, he could see that big changes were afoot, and he lost no time in making himself scarce. He went to Hong Kong, where, in 1951, he died.

Everything about his life seems to have been created on a film set — opium dens, mobsters, political intrigue, and power — and yet Hollywood could have learnt a thing or two from him. As a waif from the wrong side of the River, he used crime to gain notoriety, when he craved respectability. Unable, or unwilling, to relinquish his hold on the power that crime had bought, he only had swank and infamy to sustain him. No other city but Shanghai could have bred him, and no other city could have tolerated so ritzy, so bizarre a lifestyle.

Part of the Donghu Guest House used to belong to Du Yue-sheng. See Chapter 6 for the address.

Several Sassoons and a Hardoon

Early days

The Sassoons were a Jewish family, originally from Baghdad, where their chieftain wore a robe of gold tissue when he rode to the palace of the Pasha, and the people in the streets bowed as he passed by. As the city fell into decline at the end of the eighteenth century, and the Jews began to suffer at the hands of intolerant rulers, David Sassoon left Baghdad and headed east for places he knew through trade, and where he thought he could make a new life. He alighted first at Bushehr, in Persia, and thence to Bombay, where fortunes were being made in the cotton trade. He was not a flamboyant merchant, but he had a quiet knack of doing the right thing. Traders liked doing business with him because he gave credit freely — they liked the credit but they liked to be trusted too. He saw the developing China trade, and bought wharf space so that he could load and unload when he wanted.

The Chinese connection

As his company prospered, he turned to China and the new treaty ports. His second son, Elias, represented the company interests in Shanghai; rather than rent them, Elias preferred to buy or build warehouses, so that David Sassoon and Sons soon had large interests in the choicest wharves in the Far East.

In the early days, before Robert Hart took charge of it, Shanghai was attributed with the most corrupt Custom's Service on the Seven Seas. Elias needed to keep his wits about him, but, fortunately, he was a sober minded individual, and although he patronised the Shanghai Club and attended the races, he was more interested in buying sites on the Shanghai mud flats at agricultural prices than indulging in idle gossip over a gin and tonic. He paid as little as £90 an acre for land that was to be worth £3,000,000 an acre when his grandson Sir Victor came to develop it sixty years on. He invested in housing estates, too, to house the refugees pouring in as they fled the civil war between the Manchus and the Taiping rebels. After a while Elias was replaced by brother Solomon, as he returned to the family firm headquarters in Bombay, where business was excellent.

In 1867 Elias broke away to form his own business, E.D.Sassoon and Co., and despatched his son Jacob to Shanghai to take control of his affairs there. Jacob continued to buy land and erected the first 'Sassoon House' on the Bund.

Silas Hardoon

When a penniless Jewish immigrant, also of Baghdad, joined the original company of David Sassoon and Sons as a wharf nightwatchman, nobody could know that he was destined to become one of Shanghai's wealthiest citizens. In 1880 he became manager of the Shanghai office, and by 1882 had decided to go into business on his own account. It was too early and he failed. He returned to the Sassoon fold, but this time with the newer branch of E.D.Sassoon, and ran their office when Jacob returned to Bombay to attend his father's funeral, and take his place as head of the company. Whenever a Sassoon boy was sent out to Shanghai to learn business, it was up to Silas to show them the ropes.

Gentry

In England the achievements and wealth of both Sassoon houses gave them London offices, knighthoods, and far reaching influence. It also meant that some of the newly monied younger members of the family took a less serious approach to business, preferring instead, much to the disgust of patriarch and matriarch, to race around England in their beloved roadsters; or, in the case of E.V., later Sir Victor, Sassoon, beloved aeroplanes. After graduating from Cambridge, he had been sent by his austere father, Sir Edward, to the Bombay offices of E.D.Sassoon, still run by the firm's head, and Victor's grandfather, Sir Jacob, who had taken over following the death of Elias, and to the Shanghai office, where he had been tutored by Silas Hardoon. By now the company had expanded in all directions, with interests in the importation of wheat and oilseed to China, and the development of trams, launderies, insurance and breweries in Shanghai. Victor, however, wanted to return to England. His father was displeased, but his grandfather in Bombay still had high hopes that one day Victor would settle down.

Aero and dynamic

Victor was one of the founder members of the Royal Aero Club in 1909, and became an accomplished pilot. During the First World War he was in an aircraft, as an observer, that crashed, crushing his legs and thigh. He was invalided out of the war with injuries that were to cause him pain for the rest of his life. Deskbound, he decided to go to Bombay again.

In Shanghai, meanwhile, Silas had done very well for the company, and for himself. He left, in 1920, to engage in speculation in property and public utilities, becoming a rich and controversial figure in the process — several attempts were made on his life. He had become interested in Buddhism, and taken a Eurasian wife, Loo Chia-Ling, long before it was considered acceptable. They were childless, but adopted a crowd of children of various nationalities, whom he had educated at his home, Hardoon Gardens. Each one became proficient in three languages — Hebrew, Chinese, and English. He never attended social functions, and apparently he never looked at another woman after his marriage, since he felt that his wife had brought him luck. Every morning would see him rattling along the Nanking Road in his old French car, on the way to his office.

Silas was replaced by Victor's cousin Reggie, who found steeplechasing a good deal more absorbing than commerce. Victor,

Monkey and master. Gradually the streets are coming back to life.

on the other hand, hadn't lost his appetite for fun following his crash, but had discovered a profound desire to succeed. In Bombay he learnt quickly, and soon displaced Reggie to run the operation in Shanghai, which was booming. The Sassoon go-downs (wharf warehouses) were filled with tea, silk, cotton, spices, rice, and sugar; and Victor took a leaf out of Silas's book by buying sites that were to be developed into factories, tenements, and, on the Bund, hotels and offices. A quote from the magazine *Fortune* in 1935 sums up some of the reasons for his success: 'Sir Victor was not interested in Society, or in great mansions like that of his cousin Philip outside of London with its peacocks and scented swimming pool: Sir Victor saw himself as the inheritor of a great tradition of international trade and finance, and he set forth to build the Sassoon edifice up to new heights. He ran, head on, however, into the post-war British tax collector. There was bitterness and recrimination. Sir Victor sat himself down to contemplate international law. Was there no spot where one could put one's money to work without paying more than half one's earnings to a government? He discovered Hong Kong. And he discovered Shanghai.'

In his personal life he was as obsessive as in business. He was convinced, as a result of his lameness, that no woman would marry him unless it were for his money and position. Yet he had plenty of affairs, about which he was tight lipped and discreet, for fear that they would interfere with business. Eventually, when he was in his seventies, and long after leaving Shanghai, he married his American nurse.

New Cathay

By the late twenties, Victor had all but moved from Bombay to Shanghai. A high proportion of Sassoon business was done there, the raciness of the city suited him, and it allowed him to indulge his other great passion of horses (after leaving Shanghai he was to breed several Derby winners). In 1929 he decided to build a skyscraper on the Bund to be the headquarters of the Sassoon empire. Built on land purchased by his great-grandfather Elias more than sixty years before, it was the second Sassoon House, part of which became the Cathay Hotel. Now it is known as the Peace Hotel, and remains Shanghai's most distinctive landmark (see Chapter 16. Bund, for more details).

In 1931 Silas Hardoon died. Lots of relatives, none of whom had ever shown their faces before, suddenly appeared in Shanghai to claim their share of his fortune. It was all left, however, to his wife, and it seems some went to his financial advisor, a priest from the temple on Bubbling Well Road. Victor, who was now concentrating on real estate, bought a good deal of Hardoon property that was being sold to pay off death duties. At one point his opinion that neither the depression nor the invading Japanese would have lasting effects on business seemed unduly optimistic; fortunately his cousin, Lucien Ovadia, arrived to act as financial advisor and prevented him from taking too many of the risks he so dearly loved. By the middle thirties he was richer than ever, and consulted for advice by the likes of H.H. Kung.

On the Hongqiao Road Victor had a villa built (known as 'Eve's' and 'Sassoon Villa') close to the golf course, and part of today's Cypress Hotel, only five minutes from the airport. It was built in old English country style, but Victor preferred to spend most of his time at Sassoon House, where he would give extravagant theme parties — guests, for example, were invited to attend dressed as if they had taken to the lifeboats, after a shipwreck.

End of an era

As the end of the decade approached the world was in upheaval. The Japanese army was marching through China, and Shanghai was filling with Jews fleeing the persecution of the Nazis. They received considerable help from Victor — he gave them jobs, provided medical care, and pledged large sums to refugee associations. Outspokenly anti-Japanese, he was persuaded in 1941, just before the Japanese took over the whole city following the bombing of Pearl Harbour, to leave until the war was over. When he returned the Cathay Hotel was still doing good business (even if his suite was occupied by an American General who was reluctant to give it up), but things were irredeemably different. In 1948 the company was put into voluntary liquidation, and Victor left Shanghai for good. Lucien Ovadia stayed behind for several years winding up company affairs and trying to reach agreements with the new government, to whom Sassoon House was leased, in perpetuity as it turned out.

Sir Victor placed most of his assets in the Bahamas, but was in New York when he was told of the Communist victory. " Well, there it is," he sighed. " I gave up India, and China gave me up."

Sir Robert Hart and the Chinese Customs Service

An institution responsible for collecting taxes would not, normally, be associated with the furtherance of an ideal, and the Chinese, and most probably the Westerner, of today, would look askance at the very thought. In the 1850s, however, a great deal turned on the collection of duty payable on goods entering and leaving the port of Shanghai, and at the apogee of its power, the Customs Service was the mainstay of the treaty ports' economic success. This fact has its origins in the agreement reached between China and the Treaty Powers at the Treaty of Nanking in 1842. One of the stipulations of that treaty was that the foreign powers would undertake to ensure the prompt and correct payment of import and export taxes to the Chinese authorities; but in the early days the organisation for an efficient service was entirely lacking. Thus two very important issues were at stake — the vitality of Shanghai itself, which was based on trade, and the nature of the uneasy relationship between the Imperial Court in Peking and the foreign powers.

Won't collect, can't collect

In 1853, the Taiping rebels were strong enough to take Nanking. Trade was at a low ebb, yet such was the corruption of the Customs Service that the Foreign Consuls became acutely worried — if traders were consistently seen to be paying little or no tax, the consequences for the future of Sino-Treaty Power relations could be catastrophic. The British Consul, against the better judgement of the British Government, who felt that help given to the Chinese Government might eventually compromise Britain's bargaining position, initiated a bonding system, whereby merchants signed a sort of I.O.U. This system was quickly abandoned, since the British were the only ones enforcing it, much to the anger of their merchants.

Rutherford Alcock, the British Consul, was of the opinion that the solution lay in administration by the Treaty Powers alone. Not surprisingly, the Chinese Government failed to greet the idea with any degree of enthusiasm, until Alcock mentioned that perhaps the British Government might see its way to paying all the duty that had not been collected during these months of confusion.

An unsatisfactory compromise

There was a conference on the subject. For the Taotai (the department of the Chinese Government responsible for the collection of excise and duty), the chief problem had been to find employees with the necessary probity, vigilance and knowledge of foreign languages. A solution was found — foreigners would be nominated by their respective consuls to act as customs inspectors, and work under the auspices of the Taotai. A new office was subsequently opened north of Suzhou Creek, in 1854.

Because of the unusual circumstances, the inspectors found themselves in an ambivalent position, employed by the Chinese yet, in the case of misdemeanour, responsible to their own government; and many traders resented the new arrangement because they were now obliged to pay tax that before had been easily avoided. The Chinese, however were satisfied by all the revenue that was coming their way — revenue, they now realised, that had been denied them until then, because of the corruption of their own customs inspectors.

The new service was only a partial success, however, because of the strange relationship between the new inspectors and their consuls. At last the dilemma was resolved once and for all when it was agreed that the responsibility for the selection and employment of foreign inspectors would be wholly that of the Chinese Imperial Customs Service. Robert Hart became the first Inspector General under the new arrangements.

Sir Robert Hart

Robert Hart was born in Portadown, County Armagh, in Northern Ireland. He studied both in Dublin, and in Belfast, at Queens University. Belfast was beginning to thrive and many of the suggestions that he would later make to the Chinese Government were inspired by his memories of his sojourn in a progressive city. Certain students of Queens were given the chance of becoming interpreters in the service of the government in China, and Robert Hart was one of them. He was posted first to Ningpo, where he learnt Chinese, and in 1858 was attached to the British Consulate in Canton. Apparently highly respected by colleagues and Chinese alike, he was invited by the Chinese Government to set up a Customs House in Canton similar to the one in Shanghai. At first he refused, since at the time the position in Shanghai was still far from clear, but once everything was settled he accepted, resigning his post at the consulate and entering the employ of the Chinese Government.

Under his leadership the Customs Service prospered until it became the financial backbone of the government — it even acted as a debt-collection agency on behalf of the governments of France and Great Britain who were owed vast sums of money, in the forms of indemnities, by the Chinese.

In 1865 the office of Inspector-General was moved to Peking, where Hart retained total control over all personnel according to regulations that he made and enforced. He was keen to point out to arrogant members of his staff that they were paid by the Chinese

Young Priest in the Jade Buddha Temple. Priests have surplus energy too.

Government and were therefore its servants. Duties collected were paid over to Chinese customs banks under the control of Chinese superintendants, but the assessments and compilation of the accounts were all performed by Hart's staff. So efficient was his management that 20 per cent of Chinese tax revenue came via the Customs.

A special relationship

Hart was one of the few foreigners ever to win the respect and trust of the Chinese. Not only was he entrusted with the reform of the Customs Service, but he became a sort of advisor on foreign affairs, and was sometimes able to influence policy. He was successful, for example, in persuading the Chinese of the need for diplomatic representation abroad, and of the usefulness of teaching maths and science in schools. His vision, however, of a strong and advanced China could not compete with the nervousness and suspicious nature of the Qing court, who more often than not rejected his proposals (most of his ideas about education, for example) or severely watered them down (allowing foreign engineers to work on Chinese projects, but stopping short of full Sino-Western cooperation). Despite these setbacks he entertained a love and respect for the Chinese all his life, even on occasion entering into lawsuits against the British Government on their behalf when agreements relating to customs matters were infringed.

A great legacy

When he died in 1911, an imperial edict conferred upon him the posthumous title of 'Guardian of Heir Apparent' (T'ai-tsu T'ai Pao). A statue of him stood outside the Customs House on the Bund until it was destroyed by the Japanese in 1942. On one of the bronze plaques at its base was written 'Inspector General of the Chinese Maritime Customs. Founder of the Chinese Lighthouse Service. Organiser and administrator of the National Post Office. Trusted counsellor of the Chinese Government. True friend of the Chinese people. Modest, patient, sagacious, and resolute. He overcame formidable obstacles and accomplished a work of great beneficence for China and the world.'

FOURTEEN

Economy

Industry

Shanghai is China's leading industrial and manufacturing centre. When the Communists started governing the country in 1949, one of the main problems they had to face was the absence of an industrial base — China was essentially a peasant economy. In certain areas that had fallen into foreign 'spheres of influence', industry, albeit usually of the most exploitative kind, had taken root. Manchuria was the industrial powerhouse, but Shanghai, which owed a lot of its wealth to shipping and banking, had great potential, and much stress was laid on its development.

That Shanghai was so quickly able to take the leading role in China's industrial advancement is due to a number of factors. Foremost among these is its location, the very thing that made it attractive to the foreigners a century before — a deep water port equidistant from the north and south of the country, with comparitively easy access to the interior, and a fertile hinterland able to provide food for a large population. Moreover, Shanghai had a sizeable workforce that was both skilled and technologically innovative, out of which grew a good scientific research base supportive of industry; and finally there was a tradition of cooperation among producers (even during the Cultural Revolution).

The main developments are the following:

- The growth of an iron and steel industry in Shanghai has encouraged the development of machine manufacture, i.e. multiple use lathes, wire-drawing dies, equipment for the assembling of computers, precision instruments, and polymer synthetics.
- The chemical and petrochemical industries are well integrated — there is good cooperation among individual factories in all

aspects of production, ensuring that supply reflects demand as accurately as possible in enterprises that are run by the State. The main products are plastics, synthetic fibres, dyes, paint, pharmaceuticals, agricultural pesticides, chemical fertiliser, synthetic detergents, and refined petroleum products.

● The government has made efforts to reduce the pollution problem by the encouragement of light industry in recent years. Textiles, therefore, have become more important than ever, and consumer goods, as a result of the government's dalliance with a market economy, have assumed a new significance, in the form of watches, cameras, radios, pens, glassware, stationery, leather goods and hardware.

Commerce

In Shanghai, which has traditionally been China's trendsetter in matters of fashion and lifestyle, there are some 35,000 shops and 2,500 restaurants. Overall management of the retail trade is in the hands of the First Commercial Bureau, but each commodity is represented by a specific bureau. Yet another bureau controls the major retail outlets, and there are still others responsible for particular districts.

Finance and trade

With the adoption of the so-called open-door policy, China's trade has increased many times over, and Shanghai is of course an important conduit for imports and exports. The main imports entering China through Shanghai are unprocessed food grains, petrol and coal, construction materials, industrial raw materials like pig iron, salt, raw cotton, tobacco and oils.

As the volume of trade with the rest of the world increases, doing business should become easier for foreigners. One of the problems has been the level of interference from bureaucracy, and the consequent inability on the part of individuals to make decisions. The Chinese government is well aware of these problems, and is making efforts to simplify matters. There are, in any case, not a few foreign companies already involved in multi million dollar enterprises in Shanghai, and there promise to be many more. One solid indication of that is the large number of foreign banks that are now represented in Shanghai (examples are given in Chapter 10).

The Shanghai municipal government has established several offices specifically to facilitate investment in the city, i.e. the Shanghai Municipal Foreign Investment Administration and others. Special zones, with the necessary facilities, have been designated in the Shanghai area for the building of factories and the development of foreign trade, e.g. Minhang Economic and Technological Development Zone.

Enterprises interested in doing business in Shanghai are invited to contact the nearest Chinese Diplomatic Mission or directly to Shanghai Foreign Investment Development Agency, Bldg. no.1, 33, Zhongshan Dong Er Lu, Shanghai, P.R.C.

Silk production

Before the arrival of the foreigners in 1842, Shanghai's prosperity was partly based upon the spinning of cotton and silk. The production of silk is still an important part of China's economy, and the Yangtse Valley one of its main sources, although Shanghai these days is mostly involved in silk dying and the manufacture of silk carpets.

Nevertheless, all aspects of silk production take place within striking distance of Shanghai, and so an explanation of the main processes is given here.

History
Nobody knows the precise date of the discovery that the cocoon of a worm could become transformed into beautiful cloth, but in most historical records that mention silk there is usually mention of the Empress Hsi-Ling, who it seemed in the year 2640 B.C. at least encouraged the breeding of silk worms on a wide scale, and may therefore be accredited with the launching of an incipient industry. In any case, the Chinese were able to keep a monopoly on the industry for almost 3000 years, until some refugees took the secret with them to Korea, and thence to Japan. That India managed to get in on the act is explained by the perfidy of a Princess who married the Prince of Khotan and insisted on taking some silk worms with her to her new home — word soon got round and passed across the frontier into Kashmir. Finally the West obtained knowledge through two Christian missionaries from Persia, who brought back some worms concealed in a bamboo staff, for the pleasure of the Emperor Justinian.

Sericulture

Sericulture is the breeding of silkworms and the production of raw silk. The word derives from the Greek for silk, serikos, which in turn derives from the Chinese word for silk which may be best rendered by 'sse'. In the provinces neighbouring Shanghai, the farmers grow mulberry and breed silk worms, and deliver the silk cocoons to the spinning factories, where the raw silk is drawn onto bobbins, ready for commercial use.

A silkworm is the caterpillar of the moth Bombyx mori, a native of China. One moth may lay up to five hundred eggs. When the caterpillar emerges, it is black, or dark grey, later turning creamy white, with a brown head. Its immediate and only aim is to eat, and its preferred food is mulberry leaf (the only food given for commercially spun silk). The eggs are hatched in incubators, or open trays, at about 72 degrees Fahrenheit, and strips of mulberry are given to the worms as soon as they hatch. They are fed every three to four hours. Four times the worm anchors itself to the tray or leaf with silk, sleeps for anything up to 36 hours, and then sloughs its skin. After five weeks they are three inches long. Sensitive though they are to smells and noise, when they are fully grown they leave their food and become restless. At this point small straw frames are placed on the trays, into which the worms climb, and spin their silk cocoons. The silk is produced by a pair of long tubular spinning glands in the caterpillar, each of which secretes a single fibre, at first fluid, that is joined together with the other by muscular contraction. A gummy coating is still preserved around the fibre, which holds the cocoon together. Ten days later the cocoons are in the spinning factory. Ten percent are retained for breeding purposes.

Reel silk is best

In the spinning factory, the cocoons are sorted, and any with flaws discarded.

After sorting, the cocoons are steamed to kill the live chrysalis within and so preventing them from emerging and spoiling the thread.

A cocoon is a continuous thread from six to nine hundred metres long, a thread that alone is too fine for weaving, and therefore has to be combined with others. This is the 'reeling' process. Six or seven cocoons are placed in a basin of hot water, which has the effect of loosing the thread and reducing the gumminess. The various threads are plucked out of the water and are mechanically reeled upwards as one, bound together by the gum that hardens as it re-emerges from the water. At the top of the machine the new filament is wound on to a winding reel. The raw silk is ready to be thrown.

Throwing silk

The term 'throwing' refers to the process where the threads, newly reeled from the cocoon onto a winding reel, are transformed into yarn suitable for weaving and knitting. The word 'throw' comes from the Anglo-Saxon word 'thraw', meaning to whirl or to spin, and here covers the whole range of operations by which reeled raw silk thread is twisted and doubled into a more substantial yarn. Doubling and twisting gives greater durability and strength, but to what degree depends on the use to which the yarn will be put. For example, there is an optimum point for twisting, after which the silk loses its smoothness and is left with a pebbled surface — this becomes the cloth known as 'crepe'.

The twisting is done by machine. In a factory you will see row after row of machines, seemingly engaged in the pointless task of transferring the thread from one bobbin to another. Indeed this is what is happening, but since the bobbins are moving at different speeds, the thread achieves the twist that it needs as it is 'thrown' from bobbin to bobbin.

Thus silk thread comes into being, and will go on to be used for weaving into cloth and carpets. Hangzhou is the region's centre for cloth weaving, and the reeling and throwing processes (referred to as spinning in China), are carried out in Suzhou and Wuxi. In Suzhou the Silk Embroidery Institute produces finely embroidered screens and tapestries, and in Shanghai there is a silk dying factory and a silk carpet factory — see Chapter 10.

Agriculture

China is famous for its communes, but in fact the 'commune' as a concept no longer exists in China. A commune implied collective ownership, with decisions made by local officials who might well not know a great deal about farming. Thus, between 1977 and 1984, the land was redistributed among the farmers, who were then given greater freedom to make their own decisions and at the same time to earn more money for themselves. The term 'commune' was discarded in favour of 'township'. Production has increased and the farmers have become richer, but the reforms have confronted the government with a new set of problems.

In simple terms, these problems are the following: how to increase the size of the farms, so making the introduction of new technology worthwhile, without throwing farmers out of work; and how to ensure that farmers do not turn too much to the growing of cash crops (like vegetables), at the expense of staples like rice that are needed to feed the massive population. Thus, in some townships in the rural areas around Shanghai, some of the most fertile and productive in China, the local bosses, in order to honour contracts they have made with vegetable companies (part of the new policy of encouraging entrepreneurs), have deprived local farmers of their apparent independence by telling them what they should grow. In some respects therefore, things have turned full circle, as the discovery has been made that there is no easy solution to the problems facing China. If a true free market economy is still a long way distant, it is nevertheless a fact that many farmers now are able to improve their lot, if only because the idea of one farmer making more money than another is no longer frowned upon.

For the foreign visitor however, rural life in China seems to go on as it always has — straw hats bent over rice under a boiling sun, water buffalo tugging doggedly on a plough, and acres of glistening paddy fields. You don't have to venture very far out of Shanghai before you find yourself in the midst of it all, and some of the townships permit visits by foreigners. Such visits need to be arranged in advance, through either CITS or one of its rivals.

There is no end to the variety of crops grown in the Shanghai region but the principal ones are winter wheat, cotton, rapeseed, vegetables, fruit and, most important of all, rice. The paddy field is almost synonymous with China, so an explanation of the production of rice is given here.

The cultivation of rice

In the first century A.D. the main population centres were gathered not around the Yangtse, but further north around the Yellow River, which has always been considered the cradle of Chinese civilisation. The people living around the Yangtse and the south of China were not Han (the northerners of the time, and the vast majority of today's population). It was they who grew rice, but their methods were unsophisticated — they didn't, for example, use irrigation. The Han, on the other hand, had some knowledge of intensive farming and irrigation, but they didn't grow rice. The characteristics of 'wet-rice' cultivation therefore only emerged later when the Han moved south in the fourth century, prompted by disturbances in the north. Leaving their sheep behind, which were unsuited to southern conditions, they brought with them pigs and intensive farming, and combined them with the rice cultivation, poultry, and water buffalo of the native southerner. By the eighth century, half the population of China lived in the Yangtse Valley, and rice was well established as a staple food.

Preparation

Rice is not a particularly demanding cereal — it is tolerant of a wide range of soils, and gives a high yield in a comparatively small area. Certain criteria do have to be met, however. Rice needs an average temperature of at least twenty degrees centigrade over a period of three to four months, and at least 1778 mm of rain during the growing season. The period of the summer monsoon in the Shanghai region is suitable on both counts.

Wet rice, as opposed to upland rice, must be submerged beneath water to an average height of from 100 to 150 millimetres during three quarters of the growing period; and this water has to be of equal depth to ensure even growth. For this reason small levelled fields ('paddies', from the Malay word 'padi' for rice in the straw) surrounded by low earthen bunds that keep the water in, and are quickly breached to let it out, are favoured in wet rice cultivation. Although hillside terracing is often associated with the growing of rice, it is far from typical — most is cultivated in deltas or in the lower reaches of rivers, where it is inexpensive to level fields, and where water is near to hand. The further away from water, the greater the need for irrigation.

Having got the water in the paddies, it is essential to prevent it from draining away. The earthen ramparts surrounding the fields stop it from slopping over the sides, but the sub-soil has also to be impermeable to prevent downward loss. Since rivers tend to deposit heavy, fine-grained material in their lower reaches, heavy, water resistant soils predominate in the sort of farmland found in the Shanghai region.

Cultivation

Rice farming is labour intensive, and requires the participation of the whole family. At the beginning of the growing season dykes, bunds, and irrigation canals have to be repaired; and the soil must be reduced to a muddy consistency, usually with the help of a water buffalo and a plough.

One tenth of the paddy fields are set aside as nurseries, where the seedlings are carefully cultivated and manured. After four or five weeks the seedlings are transplanted to the paddies, where they are arranged in rows for easier weeding.

As the harvest season approaches, the fields are drained, and after reaping the landscape is alive with the scurrying of farmers gathering the sheaves, and feeding them into wooden threshing machines that are operated by a treadle. Finally the stalks are ploughed back into the soil, and the paddies fertilised with mud, compost, rice stalks, and night soil.

Secrets of paddy fields

Wet rice farming allows the same paddy field to be used year after year without rotating the crops, and without loss of production. There are a number of theories explaining this phenomenon. First, the water protects the soil from the heat, from high winds, and from the direct impact of tropical rains, which means that soil erosion is reduced to a minimum. Then, the high water table limits the vertical movement of the water, and so the loss of plant nutrients by percolation. Lastly, flooding and irrigation bring silt and other nutrients which stimulate the soil every year.

Most rice is hard with a starchy grain, but some 10 per cent of rice that is grown is glutinous, with a large soft grain, and much prized throughout Asia.

Opposite: *A smiling salesman. Traditional Chinese shops are making a comeback.*

FIFTEEN

An aspect of Chinese life: acupuncture

In recent years, following the re-emergence of China from its isolation, and in view of a certain disenchantment with Western medicine, Chinese traditional medicine has been treated with something more than idle curiosity. Although remaining a controversial subject, it is generally accepted that there is much more to it than mere quackery, and that if allied to a modern scientific approach, it may well have a great deal to offer. That in certain cases acupuncture works is beyond doubt — just why it works is rather less obvious.

The theory

The Chinese explain the efficacy of acupuncture by using a number of concepts that are hard to define, and for the Western mind, suspiciously lacking in scientific substance.

The best known of these is 'Yin' and 'Yang'. The original meaning of Yin was the the 'sunny side of a hill', or the 'north bank of a river', whilst Yang referred to the 'dark side of a hill' or the 'south bank of a river'. Gradually their meanings came to be extended so that Yin was regarded as a female element, symbolising cold, rest, passivity, decrease, and interior and downward movement; and Yang as the male element, and heat, movement, vigour, increase, and upward and outward movement. Although they are superficially opposite in nature, they are thought of as being interdependent. The well known symbol of two fish in an interlocking embrace demonstrates this. One's health is thought to rely on their equilibrium, and treatment is based on the idea of

Opposite: *Chinese crocodile on the Nanking Road. Children are roped together to avoid the crush.*

correcting imbalances.

The concept of Yin and Yang is the premise upon which Chinese traditional medicine bases its application. This broad idea has to be translated into criteria more precisely related to the human body.

Other theories

An important concept is that of 'chi', a word that has no exact equivalent in English, but which could be imperfectly rendered as 'energy', or 'force'. Chi is thought to be that which adjusts the body to change, provides immunity to disease, converts food into energy, and generally sustains life and health in the body.

'Chi' is theoretically pumped around the body by means of a system of vessels that are connected to the organs. These are not

Children on a balcony. Shanghai has the most chronic housing problem in China. Two flats lead off this balcony.

necessarily the same vessels that carry blood — chi is yang, blood is yin. These vessels are known as 'medians', and can be described as an underground irrigation system, which is accessible at certain points through a series of wells. Acupuncture treatment takes place at these points, mostly, but certain points are not along these median lines. There are 365 points in all.

The organs of the body are thought of rather differently in China from in the West. They are divided into those that are 'yin' (heart, lungs, spleen, liver, and kidneys), and those that are 'yang' (gall bladder, stomach, small and large intestine, and urinary bladder).

Diseases are thought, broadly, to be caused by three factors and influences — environment, emotions, and way of life. Emotions are considered to be governed to a certain extent by the other two. Environment refers to wind, cold, heat, and dampness. Way of life refers to diet, and physical and sexual activity.

Diagnosis and treatment

When a Chinese doctor examines the patient he will take into account his medical history, his general appearance, and his state of mind. The tongue comes in for special scrutiny, but it is the pulse to which the most attention is paid. The pulse may be felt in a dozen different ways, which relate to the internal organs.

Treatment will be decided mainly according to indications from the pulse readings. The aim is to re-establish the correct flow of 'chi'. Great care should be given to finding the exact point for the insertion of the needle, and to the manner in which it is handled. Some points are supposed to sedate, others to galvanise. The pulse is regularly checked during treatment, and the reactions of the patient carefully monitored. The doctor can himself feel certain sensations as he manipulates the needles, enabling him to modify the treatment as he proceeds. When it is not possible to give such personal treatment, needles may be inserted in a number of median points, or the stimulus may be enhanced by the use of electricity. A good doctor will also take into account the time of day or month, which is supposed to have an effect on the metabolism.

Moxibustion

The word refers to the burning of the leaves of the Artemesia species which are burned to provide a heating effect around the median points. Moxibustion is supposed to be better for chronic cases, that is to say in cases of diseases which are deep-rooted and long-lasting. Acupuncture is supposed to be more efficacious in acute cases, that is to say cases which come very quickly to a crisis. The 'moxa' (burning leaves) may be held close to the skin, for warming purposes, or placed on a layer of soya sauce, garlic, or ginger for insulation. For some conditions the moxa is permitted to become hot enough to burn.

China's old are hardy but cheerful thanks to good food and a belief in traditional medicine.

SIXTEEN

The former Concession areas

Unlike other cities of China, whose names are evocative of fabulous examples of China's imperial past (the Forbidden City in Peking, for example, or the Terracotta Warriors in Xian), Shanghai conjures up a way of life. The skeleton of that life still exists — a magnificent waterfront (the Bund), and behind it, a network of avenues that are little changed since the Concessions were given up in 1943. The aim of this chapter on the old Concessions is to give an idea of what is there and what to look for. Apart from the Bund and one or two other key items, the visitor will probably want to discover Shanghai alone. That, after all, is one of the joys of the city. It is a vast living museum of the recent past, full of curiosities and unanswered questions. Some of them can be resolved here but not all. It may be tempting not to read the history section (Chapter 12), yet Shanghai, despite its comparative youthfulness, will only properly come alive if its *raison d'être* is understood.

In the early part of the twentieth century, Shanghai could have been, broadly speaking, divided into three areas — the Chinese city (the original Shanghai), the French Concession, and the International Settlement. The Concessions and Settlements were those areas ceded to Great Britain, France, and the United States of America by the Imperial Chinese Government following the signing of the Treaty of Nanking in 1842 (see Chapter 12). Pieces of land bordering the Huang Pu river were apportioned to the Foreign Powers, after which perpetual leases were negotiated between individuals and the Chinese landlords.

The International Settlement was the result of the amalgamation of the British Concession (the first of the Concessions) with the area north of Suzhuo Creek, known as Hongkou, which was a loose mixture of foreign nationals dominated by Americans. The French Concession was always administered separately.

Most of what is now central or downtown Shanghai was the original British Concession — that is, the area that extends south and west from the confluence of Suzhuo Creek with the Huang Pu river. It was bounded in the east by Zhongshan Dong Lu (the Bund), in the west by Xizang Zhong Lu, and in the south by Yanan Dong Lu, this last being built over the Yang Ching Pang canal that separated the British from the French Concession. "The French boundary is an undesirable creek, running past the east gate of the native city, between which and the Huangpu are crowded and unsavoury suburbs," observed Isabella Bird in the late nineteenth century.

The best place to begin a tour of the Concessions is the Bund.

The Bund and environs

The fulcrum of old Shanghai was the Bund, and for the modern visitor so it remains. This waterfront strip, whose name is derived from the Anglo-Indian word meaning quay or embankment, is an eloquent testimony to the presence of the Western powers in Shanghai until 1943. Like a medieval citadel, it is a proud proclaimer of what lies behind, in this case a city built on a grid pattern, almost wholly European in style. By standing opposite the Peace Hotel, and looking west along the Nanking Road, or scanning the embankment from Shanghai Mansions in the north to the modern office block in the south, the onlooker witnesses two generations together — young Shanghai where foreigners are visitors, and where New China is in the ascendent; and old patrician Shanghai, where big business and tycoonery were manifested in the waterfront palaces, and which spawned, for the foreign resident, a lifestyle of legendary opulence. Flowing beside the Bund is the Huangpu River and its attendant hubbub, and fourteen miles downstream is the yawning mouth of the Yangtse.

The Bund (excluding the former French and Chinese waterfronts) is three quarters of a mile in length; you can walk it in fifteen or twenty minutes. But it's a better idea to combine it with other visits, devoting a half day, even a complete day, to the area of the Bund. On the Bund you find the Peace Hotel, where, apart from enjoying a grand relic from Shanghai's past, you can take a coffee in the old bar; one of the best Friendship Stores in China is only two minutes from the waterfront; and the boats which offer cruises on the Huangpu, through the docks and as far as the mouth of the Yangtse, cast off from just south of the Waibaidu bridge. (Details of this are given separately — see Chapter 18, 'Touring the Huangpu River').

Walking the waterfront

A convenient point of departure for a stroll along the Bund is Shanghai Mansions, the 22-storey brick pyramid hotel that overlooks Suzhou Creek just to the north of the Waibaidu Bridge. The hotel is in what used to be the American Concession (before it combined with the British Concession in 1863, forming the International Settlement) and used to be called 'Broadway Mansions'. It was built in 1934, to be an exclusive residential hotel, and accommodated the Military Advisory Group of the U.S.A. on its lower floors, foreign newspaper reporters who had flats on the higher floors, and the Foreign Correspondents' Club of China. The entrance and interior have been modernised, but the general effect of the exterior is powerfully reminiscent of pre-liberation Shanghai. There is a coffee bar on the mezzanine and an excellent view across the harbour from the upper floors where, according to a current brochure, 'the excellent sealing and sound insulation have now completely removed the long existed sheer trouble of the noises and bad odours from the rivers'.

Turning left out of Shanghai Mansions, and walking across the Bund Road (Zhongshan Dong Lu), still north of the bridge, you meet two other buildings of the pre-war period, one on the left, and one on the right which overlooks the river and the Bund. The first is what is now a budget hotel, the Pujiang, but in its prime this was one of the finest hotels of Shanghai, the Astor House, when a double room on American plan (meals included) would have cost 20 Mexican dollars (Mexican silver was the standard currency). It is badly run down at the moment and it requires some imagination to picture it as a sophisticated meeting place of glamorous and wealthy patrons, but on a weekend evening the entrance is once again thronged with wedding guests photographing the bride and groom before continuing inside for the feast. Occasionally there is a sort of cabaret in the dining room, acrobatics, perhaps, or song and dance.

Opposite the Pujiang Hotel stands a building in Russian style that, before 1960, housed the Soviet Consulate. Then it became the Seamen's Club (now in the Dong Feng Hotel at the other end of the Bund), and since 1987, as relations between China and the Soviet Union improve, it has once again become the home of the Soviet Consulate. Now a red flag flutters on the roof, and Russian-speaking tourists have returned to the streets of Shanghai. During the Cultural Revolution, this street, because of its association with the Soviet Union, was renamed 'Anti-Revisionist Street'.

On the other side of the Consulate is a modern building, the Seagull Hotel, built on the site of the old German Consulate. For the walker the main attraction is a bar/coffee shop overlooking the harbour in the annexe on the right as you enter the courtyard, and the view from the top of the main building.

Before the International Settlement

The American Concession was originally the area to the north of Suzhou Creek. It grew up haphazardly, a result of over crowding in the British Concession more than anything else, but 1848 is the accepted date of its foundation, when a Church Mission was established in what was then a swampy riverbank, and is now Hongkou. The American Consulate was originally in this area, but by the 1930s it had been moved to Jiangxi Lu, in the International Settlement. North of Suzhou Creek, the International Settlement was bounded by the railway line and in the west by what is now Xizang Bei Lu, but of course these boundary lines became academic and the foreign community spilt out well beyond them. As time went on this area became known as 'Little Tokyo', since it was the part of the International Settlement dominated by the Japanese. Here was the Japanese Temple, the Japanese School and streets of Japanese shops. Nevertheless, the Hongkou district maintained a number of institutions that served various sections of the community, e.g the Chinese Public School to the south of the railway station, the Mixed Court (redundant after 1927), the Temple of Heaven, dairies, a Russian post office, and some of the cabarets. The main artery of the area was, and is, Sichuan Bei Lu, the next major road east of the Bund.

A walk northwards along Sichuan Bei Lu would eventually bring you to Hongkuo Park (described elsewhere), and industrial Shanghai, which is rather a long way (about an hour on foot). Whether you care to do that depends on your appetite for exploring. The main advantage to walking around this area is that you are likely to be the only foreigner in the vicinity. The old buildings are less spectacular than in the downtown areas, but curiosities of style abound, and by wandering off into the back alleys, you can have a glimpse of contemporary Chinese life (the grandmothers of the households gathered under a street awning against the sun, gossiping and peeling prawns) amidst the solid residences of old Shanghai.

Just off Sichuan Bei Lu, on Kunshan Lu, is the Protestant church where Chiang Kai Shek wedded Soong May-Ling.

The industrial area north of Honkou is Zhabei, previously spelt Chapei. This area was very badly bombed by the Japanese during the Sino-Japanese war in the 1930s.

Back to the Bund: a bridge and a garden

Waibaidu Bridge spans Suzhou Creek and leads to the Bund proper. The creek is actually the Wusong River which joins the Huangpu River here. Originally, the Wusong River was the source of the area's water borne prosperity, until it began to silt up badly enough to force the local fishermen downstream. However, for small craft, it remains an important link with the canal network of the interior, although far fewer folk are these days so devoted to their work, or so needy, that they spend their lives aboard their sampans, as many did when travellers journeyed west almost one hundred years ago. Then, the Creek was a teeming, noisy spectacle, bright with streamers and flags, and vibrant with clanging gongs, as processions of family businesses chugged from below the British Consulate towards Hangzhou, Suzhou, and the Grand Canal.

The Waibaidu Bridge was known as the Garden Bridge, because of the park that nestles on its eastern side. Now known as Huangpu Park, it was once simply called the Public Garden, and was the first in Shanghai. For the British, who built it, it was a corner of a foreign field that was forever Regents Park. Outside, stood the infamous sign that allegedly forbade entrance to 'dogs and Chinese'. The sign did not, in fact, read quite like that: 'The small public gardens, laid out on a shoal that appeared in the river near the Soochow Creek, were reserved for the foreign residents who came there in the evenings to listen to the Filipino band . . . and the little children with their amahs had a safe and healthy playground there. It is quite untrue that a notice was put up at the garden entrance opposite the British Consulate saying that Chinamen and dogs were forbidden to enter. . . . There was a notice that the gardens were reserved for foreigners, and it gave some four or five by-laws about picking flowers etc., and saying that no dogs were allowed inside except on a leash. Some wit at the club bar once made a remark about Chinamen and dogs, not knowing that this would fly round and round the world . . .' (William J. Oudendyk: *Ways and By-ways in Diplomacy*). Eventually, the rules were altered to accommodate a certain 'class' of Chinese.

Anybody may enter now for a payment of 3 fen. Upon giving up the 3 fen you will be given a plastic disc, which is to be thrown into a container, as proof of payment, under the watchful gaze of an elderly attendant. This small waterside park is, in common with most parks in Shanghai, a wonderful place for observing the Chinese at their leisure and, in this case, the harbour at work. There is an enormous statue of an eagle, a pretty waterfall and,

The Bund: not the busy waterfront of its heyday but its fame is undiminished.

sometimes, shows and exhibitions for which you may have to pay a little more.

There appear to be two interpretations of the meaning of 'Waibaidu', the current name of the former 'Garden Bridge'. One is 'bridge of the outermost crossing', referring to the most northerly ferry dock that was close by; the other is 'outer toll-free bridge'. In its present form it dates from 1906, but it was preceded by others of timber construction, and in the earliest days a toll was charged. The first iron bridge was built in 1871 but it collapsed before completion.

It has always been symbolic of a border, even with the merging of the American and British Concessions. After the occupation of Shanghai, during the Sino-Japanese War, which started in 1937, a Japanese soldier was posted continuously at the northern end of the bridge, from whom permission had to be obtained before crossing, and all vehicles and packages were subject to meticulous searches. For the Japanese soldiers, it was an opportunity to show off their feelings of superiority to the Chinese, and make fun of the Westerners.

The British Consulate

Opposite the Huangpu Park, at number 33, are the grounds of the former British Consulate (the address of the new one is found in Chapter 10). It was built on the site of the fortifications that had so unsuccessfully defended Shanghai against the British in the first place. The original was destroyed by fire, and this was built to replace it in 1870. 'But the British! They had, as usual, the best quarters in town for their consular staff. The British are that way; they take care of their officials and they are farseeing about such things as buildings and other external appearances in foreign countries. In Shanghai they had held onto the the best site they could possibly have owned, a large tract of land fronting the Bund down at Soochow Creek, and running back a whole long block. There were houses there for the staff beside the large building that constituted the consulate.' (Emily Hahn: *China to me*). The buildings, that seem to have been recently repainted, are magnificent, and the lawn fit for a game of cricket (or perhaps croquet). There is even an old lawn-roller rusting away in one of the herbaceous borders.

Now the buildings house a number of offices, including the Shanghai Centre of International Studies. The officious individuals at the gate may be reluctant to let you in if you wave a camera at them, but if it can be made clear that your purpose is more serious, there should be no problem.

In recent years the grounds were used for the Friendship store. This is now in new premises nearby, on Beijing Lu. At the back of it is another gate into the old consulate grounds which is sometimes open.

The Bund proper: a taste of money

The buildings that front that part of the Bund which was the International Settlement all date back to before 1949. When it is remembered that the stewardship of Shanghai was entirely in Chinese hands by 1943, and that it was under the control of the Communists by 1949, the self-confidence and optimism of the builders of these money factories is staggering. None of them date back to before the beginning of the century, and some were built in the early thirties, only a few years before the collapse of the system that supported them.

The first generation of buildings on the Bund were comparatively humble, something along the lines of the old consulate. Nor were they cheek by jowl, but sat like villas in their own grounds; looking south, the walls of the Chinese city would have been clearly visible beyond the Bund, itself a leafy avenue, broken by creeks and streams gushing into the Huangpu (or Whangpoo as it was then written). Nor was there any river wall at the beginning — instead there was a sort of greensward sloping down to the river, interrupted by a series of jetties. The jetties remained until the 1940s. In 1908 the first tram service was inaugurated, and one of the routes was along the Bund. Unfortunately the trams have gone, although the service still popular in Hong Kong demonstrates what it was like. There were three classes and tickets, as on today's buses, were cheap — the cost was from three to ten copper cash. The number of coppers to a dollar varied from day to day 'but these coins are only used by the poorer class and in travelling by bus and tram . . . so the visitor need not worry about the vagaries of copper exchange' (*All about Shanghai* — a standard guidebook, 1935). Like today, too, getting on and off public transport was a problem. The trams made only the briefest of stops. The Chinese refer to the Bund as 'Waitan', although it was briefly rechristened 'Revolution Boulevard' during the Cultural Revolution.

The first generation of offices along the Bund were mostly occupied by British companies. As time went on some of them survived to build more magnificent palaces, others were eclipsed by rising stars. Thus, in the 1930s you would have found the Nippon Yusen Kaisha (Japanese Mail) Shipping Line in number 31. They offered a fortnightly service to London for £99 first class. The journey took five weeks.

Many of the buildings along the Bund were banks. Number 29 was the home of the Banque de l'Indochine, and in 26 you would have found the Mercantile Bank of India, as well as the Danish Consulate. Now it has become one of the many offices of the Shanghai Foodstuffs Corporation. But in number 27, now a restaurant, were the offices of the company that started it all, Jardine, Matheson and Co., who had kept an office on the site from the beginning. Of course for many years they, having practically founded modern Shanghai on the importation of opium, were the hated symbol of foreign imperial aggression; but times change, and Jardine, Matheson and Co. are once again in residence in Shanghai. In number 24, another sign of the developing strength of the Japanese, you would have found the Japanese Chamber of Commerce and the Yokohama Specie Bank. Now you find a company developing photographs, and selling Japanese film.

Taking it to the top
As you approach the Nanking Road, two buildings evidently competing with each other in their reach to the sky stand close by each other, separated by a narrow street. At number 22 is the Bank of China, and beyond, at the corner of the Nanking Road, is the old Cathay Hotel. It is as well to walk across the road for a view of these two: the bank is in the style of an early New York skyscraper, capped by a Chinese roof; and the hotel (now the Peace Hotel) is pure art-deco, with beautiful wrought iron windows and distinctive pyramidal roof. It is said that there was a tremendous battle between the proprietor of the Cathay, Sir Victor Sassoon, and the director of the Bank of China, H.H.Kung. Kung wanted the bank to be taller than the Cathay, but Sassoon was having none of it. Such was the power of the foreigner in old Shanghai that Sassoon won; but the top of the bank was brought to within a hairsbreadth of the hotel, and some might say that it is fractionally higher. The bank is still the Bank of China and anyone may enter, to change money for example, or simply to look at the awesome interior.

The Peace Hotel is the combination of two former hotels, the Cathay, which was actually only a part of Sassoon House, and the Palace Hotel which was much older (1906) and stands on the south corner of the Nanking Road. The Palace hotel was always one of the best and in the middle thirties you could have had a double room for twenty four Mexican dollars. Now it is definitely the inferior half of the Peace Hotel as far as the rooms are concerned, although the best coffee is to be had in its new 'Peace Café'.

When the Cathay opened in 1930, it was the place to stay. Sassoon had decided in 1929 to erect a building in the most modern style on the Bund, on land bought by his forerunner Elias (see 'Several Sassoons and a Hardoon' in Chapter 12) in the 1860s. The mud of Shanghai would not, in those days, tolerate a true skyscraper of American proportions, and Sassoon was forced to compromise with a ten-storey building constructed of ferro-concrete covering an acre of ground. It was not only to be a hotel, but the headquarters of the Sassoon empire, and some floors were to be let to those organisations that could afford them. Many could; they were happy to pay for the latest both in technological excellence and in fashionable architecture. The ground floor was rented by two banks (the Netherlands Trading Society was one) and a variety of exclusive shops. The next two floors were offices occupied by the Dutch Chamber of Commerce, the Chinese Government Radio Administration, and R.C.A. Communications Inc., amongst others. The third floor was taken by E.D.Sassoon and Arnhold & Co., and the fourth by the American Women's Club of China. The rest was to be the Cathay Hotel.

Sassoon wanted it to be the best hotel in the East. He enticed the manager of the Taj in Bombay to Shanghai to supervise the opening. Three floors were given over to panelled rooms and suites with services superior to the best in Europe — guests could summon a drinks waiter, room boy, maid, dry cleaner, valet or laundryman by lifting the telephone. There were baths of marble from whose silver taps gushed pure water from the Bubbling Spring Well. On the eighth and ninth floors there were a ballroom with sprung floor, a restaurant, grill room and kitchens. The bar, the 'Horse and Hounds', was the most fashionable meeting place of the city, and leading cabaret artists from around the world performed in the ballroom. In 1930 Noel Coward stayed here and wrote *Private Lives*.

During the Sino-Japanese war, the Cathay was not only one of the gay, extravagant haunts of the beau-monde, one of the pillars of the legend of Shanghai, but a rendezvous for spies and political informers, including the Japanese. Sassoon, however, was outspokenly anti-Japanese, and in 1941 it seemed like a good idea to absent himself for a while. At the end of the war he returned to find that the Cathay was doing good business, but that some American army officers who had been conducting the war effort were reluctant to evacuate his personal suite. It made no difference. Everything was about to change, anyway, and in 1948 Sassoon went into voluntary liquidation. Sassoon House was leased to the Chinese government, and eventually appropriated in lieu of unpaid taxes.

The Cathay became the Peace Hotel, and settled to a more banal existence, until the Cultural Revolution, when the Gang of Four used it as the base of their Shanghai operations.

Staying here is not quite the experience that it was before 1949, but pleasant nevertheless. The interior is still delightful, with its marble balconies, and corridors suffused with the dim light of an Egyptian tomb. Many of the original fittings are still on the walls. If you are not staying there, go anyway one evening for a drink and to listen to the Peace Hotel Jazz Band (North Building — cover charge added to the bill). Otherwise, the bar is open during the day for drinks, coffee and snacks, there is a billiards room, a good bookshop, accessible lavatories, barber, and one of the better taxi desks. CITS have an information desk in the main lobby.

Diversion
Before reaching the Peace Hotel and the Bank of China you will have passed Beijing Lu. One hundred yards down here on the right you will find the Friendship Store. The first turning on the right after this is Yuan Ming Yuan Lu. This is a fascinating little street for its array of curious examples of 'modern' (modern for the 1920s and 1930s) architecture. Originally you would have found the Rotary Club at 133 and the YWCA at 55. The Hong Kong and Shanghai Bank have their Shanghai office here now, at number 185, in marked contrast with their original premises on the Bund. At 149 are now the offices of Wen Hui Bao, one of the popular Shanghai dailies, an important organ during the Cultural Revolution. Continuing to the end of the street, turn right into Suzhou Lu. This street follows the curve of the old British Consulate wall, bringing you onto the Bund once again by the bridge. It was known, for obvious reasons, as Anti-Imperialist Street during the Cultural Revolution. Along here, at number 107, is what used to be the Union Protestant Church, which appears to have become a clinic of some sort. At number 71 is an example of the new competitive spirit of the Chinese economy, the Tianmu Travel Service, independent of CITS, and perhaps more helpful.

The Bund again
The Bund is notable for the lack of statues. On a waterfront so proud and self-congratulatory one might have expected to find some of the city's more illustrious denizens immortalised in stone. There are none now, but this was not always the case. Until the war there

were at least a couple, and one of them used to face the Nanking Road from the riverside. This was a monument to Sir Harry Parkes, Envoy Extraordinary and Minister Plenipotentiary to Japan and to China. He stood in full regalia on a pedestal, looking commandingly down the Nanking Road.

Continuing along the Bund, past the old Palace Hotel, you arrive at number 18, which now is the home of Shanghai Home Textiles Branch of the Import and Export Corporation, and used to be the premises of the Chartered Bank of India, Australia and China, and of Credit Foncier d'extreme Orient. Next door, at number 17 you would have found the British, Canadian, and General Chambers of Commerce, and the North-China Daily News, the principal English language newspaper of China. It was not the oldest but, founded in the 1960s, it was to last some seventy years, outliving most of the others. The American writer Emily Hahn worked on the staff of the paper during her stay in Shanghai in the 1930s. She enjoyed working on it because it made her feel that she was near the more colourful parts of the British Empire, but she found, too, that the tone of its contents were wholly British — the Chinese simply did not exist. You won't be able to pass the doorman, but have a look into the entrance at the mosaics and the marble rising sun.

Many of the other buildings were banks, of course, like the old Bank of Communications at number 14 (still going at 200 Jiang Xi Lu). One of the most influential, one that could be said to have had almost as much influence on the prosperity of Shanghai as the opium trade, was the Customs House at number 13. This was built in 1927, replacing the previous one that was in the style of a Tudor mansion, and which itself had been built on the site of a Chinese temple. The brass plaques proclaim, in English, that the building still serves the same purpose. On the opposite side of the road, also marked 13, is the old warehouse for holding bonded goods, now a coffee bar and small shop. The roof of the Customs House is surmounted by a clock tower that used to be known as 'Big Ching'. It was built to play the Westminster chimes, but had not worked for many years, when, in honour of the visit by the Queen of England in 1986, the old mechanism was brought back to life.

A statue of Sir Robert Hart, the man who organised the customs service on behalf of the Chinese Government (see Chapter 12), used to stand outside, but it was destroyed during the war. If you step inside the building (nobody seems to mind), look up at the ceiling at the splendid mosaic pictures of marine scenes featuring Chinese junks.

At number 12 next to the Customs House, is the old premises of the Hong Kong and Shanghai Banking Corporation. This was built in 1921, and was considered to be one of the finest buildings in Asia — its opening was one of the social events of the year. The Corporation was established in Hong Kong in 1864 and opened in Shanghai soon after. It was the principal British bank of the Orient, and since in the early years commerce in Shanghai was mostly in the hands of British traders and officials (who also managed the Imperial Customs Service), it prospered. When the Chinese Government needed to borrow money, guarantees in the form of tax revenue had to be deposited in this bank. It was the Hong Kong and Shanghai Bank who organised the 450 million silver tael indemnity payable as reparation for the Boxer uprising in 1901. When the Japanese occupied the foreign settlements in 1941, the bank's activities were severely curtailed, to two hours a day; and of course by 1949 all operations had been moved to Hong Kong.

The entrance to the bank used to be guarded by the famous pair of bronze lions. Their paws were burnished by the strokes of endless Chinese pedestrians, who believed that to touch them was to draw on their power, and who believed, too, that gold had been used erroneously in their casting. There is no sign of the lions now, although it is said that they survived the war and were stored in the vaults of another bank. There is no prospect of entering the building now — it houses the Shanghai Municipal Government.

After passing what used to be the China Merchant Steam Navigation at number 9, the Commercial Bank of China at number 7, the P.& O. Banking Corporation at number 6 and the Canadian Pacific Steamship Line at number 4, you arrive at another venerable institution, the Shanghai Club at number 3, now the Dong Feng Hotel and the Seamen's Club. The Shanghai Club was actually the British Club, although it was open to other nationals (except the Chinese). Visitors, having been proposed and seconded by members, had the privileges of the club for 14 days. Members of the Bengal, Singapore, and Hong Kong clubs had visitors' privileges. Built in 1911, it was said to have cost 450,000 taels and, at one hundred feet, to have the longest bar in the world. One end of this bar was reserved for the 'Taipans', the bosses of the great trading companies. It was the most exclusive, not to say snobbish, of all the clubs in Shanghai. In her book *Shanghai, Crucible of modern China,* Betty Peh-T'i Wei tells a story illustrating this. A businessman who was not a member was passing the club when he was caught in a cross-fire of bullets during the fighting of 1949. He recognised an acquaintance inside who was a member, and expected to be allowed in. He was told that this was impossible as he did not belong to the club and the door was closed on him. Some minutes later the door reopened and he was permitted to enter — he had been voted a guest-member. It remained a bastion of British male snobbishness to the end, although other clubs, led by the Americans, eventually opened membership to the Chinese.

The exact location of the famed Long Bar is not clear; and no one on the premises today seems to know. However, it is there, if somewhat shorter than before, but it could be in either of two rooms, one downstairs, the other upstairs. The upstairs room is still a bar and with its English colonial flavour seems a likely candidate. One room on the ground floor is used for 'dance parties' sometimes, with live music. Others are now restaurants.

Number 1 the Bund was the McBain building. The McBains were originally from Scotland and had made their money from the importation of petroleum products. George, the first of them, married a Eurasian woman — their descendants continued to run the company, and some still live in Hong Kong.

Nanking Road

This is one of the few streets that has retained its original name (although the modern transliteration is 'Nanjing'), and it is traditionally the shopping street not only of Shanghai but of China. Like most of the streets of Shanghai, it was originally cobbled. The name was a celebration of the signing of the Treaty of Nanking in 1842, which ceded areas around Shanghai to foreign control. For the Chinese, however, it was always the Great Maloo, meaning road built for horses, since the road was built for use by horsemen. In its heyday it was included by the American writer John Steinbeck in his list of the seven most interesting streets in the world. It no longer fascinates in quite the same glittering way, but nearly all the buildings that flank it were built in the first half of this century, and many of them are fine examples of the sort of architecture that now collects preservation orders in the West. They are almost exactly as they were in Shanghai's heyday, and highly evocative of its past. The government seems to have awakened to their historical value, too. Many of the buildings have been or are being repaired, with not too much adulteration. One or two have been pulled down, however, but it is hoped that the intention is to rebuild them in their old image.

What is now Nanjing Dong Lu (Nanking Road East) corresponds

to the original Nanking Road — this is the busiest section, so much so that bicycles are forbidden here during certain hours. What is now Nanjing Xi Lu (Nanking Road West) corresponds to the former Bubbling Well Road, which began just before the People's Park at what was then called Thibet Road (Tibet), and is now called Xizangzhong Lu (Chinese for Tibet Middle Road). Bubbling Well Road derived its name from the well that was found in the middle of the road by the Jing An Temple. The total length of the Nanking Road is some six miles. Really it is the main east-west artery of the city, but at various points it is intersected by, or runs parallel with, other streets and avenues that were well known for particular trades or landmarks.

Walking the Nanking Road

An uninterrupted walk from the Peace Hotel to the Park Hotel, which stands opposite the old racecourse, would take something like forty-five minutes.

The Peace Hotel, that combination of the old Palace and Cathay Hotels, has already been mentioned in some detail. The most interesting part is the northern wing, the former Cathay, but the southern wing is worth looking at for two reasons. The first is that the building is one of the older remaining ones on the Nanking and Bund Roads, and that its design is typical of early Shanghai. At the beginning of the century, the Bund and the Nanking Road would have been lined with offices and mansions built in like manner, only being replaced by grander and more pompous versions as the century wore on. The second reason is the Peace Café and Bakery, a recent addition to the hotel, which dispenses drinks, snacks, and good coffee during the day, and meals and live music (for a cover charge) during the evening. This is not to be confused with the famous Jazz Band that plays in the bar of the other building.

In the immediate area of the Peace Hotel, the Nanking Road is flanked by shops specialising in clothes, shoes, computers, cakes, and various foodstuffs. On the north side of the road, in what is part of the Peace Hotel, there is one item of practical interest, a post office from where telephone calls abroad (including collect or reverse charge) may be made quickly and easily, and which is apparently open 24 hours a day.

A little further down on the south side, at the junction with Sichuan Lu, is the Deda Restaurant. This is of German origin, and although the clientele is wholly local these days, the food has international pretensions. Beyond the Deda, at 143, is another restaurant whose history is manifested in the items on the menu.

This is the Dong Hai Fandian specialising in coffee, borsch, cakes and lemon meringue pie.

Many of the other establishments on this part of the Nanking Road have both practical and curiosity value. If you run short of film the Guan Long Photo Supply Co. at number 180 may meet your requirements. If, on the other hand, you are thinking of purchasing a cloisonné (enamel) fountain pen, then you had better repair to the Hong Feng Fountain Pen Shop at 204, or perhaps to the Shanghai Pen Co. a little way beyond it. The Chinese are avid stamp collectors — many gather at the China Stamp Co. at 244, and if you are unable to find what you want in the shop, they may be able to give you pertinent information. At 262 is the Heng Da Li Watch and Clock Co. which apart from being able to effect repairs has an interesting old sign at the back which testifies that there has been a watchmaker's on the site since 1865, and that the original firm was called Hope Bros. At 238 is the Lao Ri Sheng Knitting Repair Shop should you need their services.

Go into number 279. This is Shanghai Theatrical Costumiers. The ground floor is not particularly interesting, except for a good line in embroidered evening bags, but the upstairs section (the stairs are at the back) sells all the paraphernalia associated with the

Theatrical Costumier on the Nanking Road. If you are thinking of going to any fancy dress balls during your stay ...

extravagance of Chinese opera — beards, masks, shoes, costumes, swords, etc.

The Xinhua Bookshop is at 327. The top floor sells foreign language publications, both from abroad (examples: *The Complete Works of Aristophanes* and *The Cosmic Code — Quantum Physics as the language of nature*) and from China. There is Moslem literature, translations of Chinese classics, maps, and posters.

The Sichuan Ginseng Shop is at 392. This used to be the premises of the Women's Commercial and Savings Bank in the 1930s, and was a testament to the changing role of women in Chinese society, since it was entirely owned, managed and run by Chinese women.

Nanking Road East becomes Nanking Road West (the old Bubbling Well Road) where it meets Tibet Road (Xizang Zhong Lu). Up to that point there are a good many shops worth visiting. At 536 Nanking Dong Lu is the Laodafang Provision Store, already famous before 1949. At 533, on the corner of Fujian Lu, is a shop built in Chinese style, that used to be a tobacconist, with a tea shop on the top floor. Perhaps it was the haunt of opium smokers and sing-song girls, but now it is a seller of bits and pieces including, for example, abacuses. At 550 is the Gua Hua Chinaware Store, eighty years at the same trade; at 592, the Shanghai Silk Shop, that was originally a jeweller's.

At the junction of Zhejiang Road there are two large buildings that are unmistakably relics from old Shanghai. The needle shaped one is in part, as it always was, a hotel, called the Seventh Heaven. The pile next door, at 635, is now called, following extensive refurbishment, the Hua Lian Commercial Building. Before 1949 it carried one of the most famous names in Chinese commerce, 'Wing On', a name which lives on in Hong Kong. Following the establishment of a new government in 1949 it became the Number Ten Department Store, retaining this name until 1987. Now it is one of the most modern and comprehensive department stores in the country, complete with restaurant and café. There are three other large department stores in the vicinity, each of which used to carry famous names which no longer survive in Shanghai. At 690 is the Shanghai Number One Clothing Store (Shanghai Fu Zhuang Shangdian), which used to be the 'Sincere' Company; at 720 the Number One Provisions Store (Shanghai Shi Di Yi Shi Pin Shangdian), which was formerly the 'Sun Sun' Company, and which now carries a vast selection of foodstuffs from all over China; at 830 the Number One Department Store (Shanghai Di Yi Baihuo Shangdian), which used to be the 'Sun' Company, and which has traditionally been considered the best department store in Shanghai and therefore in China. Before 1949 all four of these institutions would have been bestrewn with banners and pennants, music would have been playing in loud competition to attract customers, and inside there would have been variety shows and opera performances too. On occasion there were even turnstiles installed to regulate the flow of people. Now they fall some way short of their former glory, but at least some note is being taken of their architectural worth, and the quality of the goods for sale is improving.

A few other famous specialist shops are to be found at 740 (Ying Ye Shi Jian, for sheets and blankets), and at 768 (Wang Sin Kee, a celebrated seller of fans, now dealing in toys as well).

New World

At the junction of the Nanking Road with Xizang Lu there are two identical buildings at the northwest and southwest corners of Nanking Road. These used to be known as the 'New World' (Xin Shi Jie) and were the precursor to the 'Great World', the distinctive structure similar to a wedding cake that is visible from this junction about half a mile to the south. 'New World' was essentially an amusement centre, and was opened in 1915 by Huang Chujiu, an enterprising merchant. It was a place of sideshows and novelties, but the arrival of the larger and more extravagant 'Great World' ensured its gradual demise. Now it is made up of flats, shops, and a children's palace.

Looking westwards along what was the Bubbling Well Road, there are a few imposing buildings on the northern side, where the road begins to describe a curve following the contours of the old racecourse. At 104 Nanking Road West is the Overseas Chinese Hotel. Originally this was the China United Assurance Building which also contained the China United Appartment Hotel. Number 150 was the Shanghai branch of the YMCA, and 170 was the Joint Savings Building, containing the Park Hotel. It is still the Park Hotel (although for a period it was known as the International), and was reputed to be the tallest building outside the Americas when it was completed in 1934, and in fact remained the tallest building in China until the 1980s.

The race course

If anything attested to the lifestyle of the wealthy in Shanghai it was the square mile of real estate in the heart of the city that until 1949 was the Shanghai Race Course, also known as the Recreation

Ground. It is still clear where the race track was, although it has been given over to other uses. One half is the People's Park (Renmin Park), and the other People's Square. The entrance to the park is opposite the Overseas Chinese Hotel at the eastern end of Nanjing Xi Lu.

The first race course was in the area of today's Henan Road, but as Shanghai expanded, so the race track was pushed progressively westwards. The final site was apparently the area where the American adventurer Frederick Ward and his 'ever victorious army' fought off the Taiping rebels in 1861. It is said, too, that the area for the track was laid out in 1862 by a foreigner on horseback who traced out a large oval with a sword, and proceeded to buy all the land encompassed by it.

There was racing during much of the year in Shanghai (except at the height of the summer). The season began with the New Year Meet on 1 January, and finished in December with the 'China Gold Vase' meet. The most important events took place during the first weeks of May and November. Every Wednesday was Champions' Day, when sporting members among the spectators might win anything up to $125,000.

The majority of the riders were 'Gentlemen Jockeys', that is to say private owners-trainers-riders. Others were 'griffins', young company employees, clerks perhaps, who wore the company colours and who hoped, by winning, to increase their standing with their employers. In any case, clerks might well have been racing on equal terms with Taipans, owing to the way that the ponies were allocated when a shipment of them arrived. Members of the Racing Club were not able to select the ones they fancied — the ponies were distributed through a lottery system. It was, therefore, one of the few areas of social life in Shanghai where all those taking part were equal before the starting gun. Nevertheless, one of the best known riders was a Taipan, a certain Eric Moller, of Moller Steamships, who at the age of 60 remained a tough competitor.

This vast area had other uses too, apart from being a race course. In its centre were a swimming pool, a cricket ground, a golf club, a baseball field, tennis courts, and rugby and football fields.

Evidence of a racing past is few and far between in today's People's Park. Beyond the Park Hotel to the west, on the south side of the street, is a curving building with a clock tower, that used to be the grandstand, and now houses a municipal library of some six million volumes. The park itself is pleasant enough, however, and for a few fen you join in with the locals as they relax, walking their children, practising their English, or doing their exercises.

People's Square, to the south of the park, is a vast concrete plain that was used for parades and political demonstrations. These are fortunately out of fashion at the moment, but not so long ago, in 1966, this square was the scene of a massive rally, at least a million strong, when workers and militant students gathered to denounce the municipal government, in the early days of the Great Proletarian Cultural Revolution.

Along and around the Bubbling Well Road

The western portion of the Nanking road (today's Nanjing Xi Lu) has changed more than the eastern portion since the departure of the foreigners. It was always different anyway — the further west one went, the more residential the road became. Yet, in the late thirties the shops were beginning to encroach further west, and were much in evidence as far as today's Shimen Lu (formerly Yates Road). Beyond this point those who had made their fortunes in Shanghai were able to indulge their fantasies by building the palaces and villas they desired.

Going west from the Park Hotel there are still a great many shops. Just across the way, on the corner, is a shop whose ground floor is aimed at the local market, and whose first and second floors are very obviously aimed at the foreign market. This is the Shanghai Arts and Handicrafts Store. It is worth having a look, if only to stock up on film or to have an ice cream.

There is a cinema just along the short street that runs between this shop and the Park Hotel. This is the old 'Carlton'. As Shanghai rediscovers its heritage, some of the original names are being reintroduced, albeit a little eccentrically. This is currently advertised as the 'Cariton'. Continuing along this street and bearing left at the first junction you will come across the 'Guling Subdistrict Cultural Centre'. This is only a small room really, but the sign outside proclaimed that evenings of 'bluis waltz' were forthcoming attractions. This could refer to the 'Blue Danube' or, who knows, to a new tolerance towards Blues music. At any event, it is not unusual to see musicians and performers here at practice.

Back on the Nanjing Xi Lu, at number 216, is a cinema, originally christened in the 1930s 'The Grand'. It was, and is, considered one of the best cinemas of Shanghai under its new name 'Daguangming'. Then you have the 'Renmin' fast food outlet, and next to that a counter which sells, amongst other things, bottles of mineral water and drinking yoghurt. Further along is a shop selling

Market scene. This huge market in the old town sells an extraordinary array of comestibles.

Western musical instruments, another dealing in photography, and another by the name of 'Quanxin' dealing in clothes. Just by this is an alley that leads to an example of the secluded residential areas (otherwise known as 'Shanghai lanes') that were built before 1949 and which still have to cope with Shanghai's chronic housing problem.

The fish and flower market.

Opposite these shops is one of the last relics of the racecourse, the old clubhouse and grandstand which, surmounted by a clock tower, curves around the corner from Nanjing Xi Lu into Huangpi Lu. This is now the Municipal Library, said to be home to more than six million volumes. The Shanghai Art Gallery used to be in part of this building, at 226 Huangpi Lu, but this has been moved to new premises near the Acrobat Theatre. However, it may be worthwhile having a look at the various rooms at 226 as they are sometimes used as rehearsal rooms (performers may be rehearsing Chinese opera in full costume, for example) or to house temporary exhibitions.

The fish and flower market is very close to here; entering Huangpi Lu from Nanking Xi Lu, it occupies the first lane on the right, opposite the old clubhouse. A walk along here is interesting, anyway, for the atmosphere of an old Shanghai residential street but it is the market that animates it. Here are streetsellers and stallholders selling the glistening, irridescent pebbles that are a speciality of Nanking, terrapins, ornamental fish, crabs, stone seals, flowers and roots, bonzai, marble balls (worked on the spot), and miniature clay figurines that are works of art in their own right, but which are generally used to enliven rock and bonzai scenes. This market operates every day and is privately run — bargaining is therefore acceptable.

Back on the Bubbling Well Road

Beyond the junction with Huangpi Lu, the Nanking Road continues to be, with a few exceptions to the rule, a shopping street. On the north side of the road, just after the junction, is the 'Shanghai Hua Niao Shangdian'. This is a conventional relative to the fish and flower market, for here they sell fresh flowers, silk flowers, bird cages, stuffed and live birds, peacock feathers, plants, fishing tackle, and fish.

Not long after, still on the north side of the street, is a large open area containing three modern buildings. The round one is the home of the renowned Shanghai Acrobatic Troupe. The middle one is the

Xian Le Theatre, and the other is the new Shanghai Art Gallery.

Walking onwards will take you past a varied collection of shops, cafés and organisations. You will, for example, soon come across a café with a strangely European name 'Kiessling'. This is one of two in the street bearing this pre-liberation name. Mr Kiessling has long gone, but his style of cake is still sold here. At 620 there is a shop specialising in buttons and at 742 the old Embassy Cinema, still boasting a fine period lobby. Should you need business cards, the Xin Cheng Computer Printing Co. at 624 has the latest equipment.

One of the grander relics of Shanghai's past is to be found at 722 — now it is the Friendship Club and the Shanghai Chinese Overseas Friendship Association, but it was built as the American Marine Club.

Shimen Lu

At the junction with Shimen Lu there is a tall building in art-deco style. This was originally 'Medhurst Mansions', a twelve storey appartment hotel. In the 1930s a double room could have been had for $16 a day. Shimen Lu, when it was Yates Road, was given the soubriquet of 'Petticoat Lane' because of the number of shops specialising in ladies' silk underwear and things of the sort. Number 332, for example, was one of them, run by a certain Ken Kee. There is even today a proliferation of clothes shops, though the wares on display are rather less racy than their predecessors are likely to have been. However, one of the more picturesque shops on Shimen Lu is not a clothes shop at all, but a grocery shop specialising in dried foods, not strikingly beautiful, but rich in the charm associated with traditional Chinese shops. Once, most of the shops of Shanghai would have been similar, and happily it seems that there is a gradual reawakening to the fact that presentation is an important ingredient in the art of selling. This shop is called 'SanYangChengNanHuoDi' and is at number 113.

Nanjing Xi Lu again

The road is still mainly flanked by shops, interrupted by the occasional landmark. The other Kiessling Coffee House is at 1000, opposite the beginning of Nanhui Lu. At 1041 is the Guo Guang leather shoe shop; at 1141 a post office, should you need one. Close to this is a 'Newsstand' which sells magazines with optimistic titles like *Better Life* or, for the reader with specialist interests, *Journal of vibration and shock*.

At 1157 is a rather curious underground café and at 1175 a

porcelain shop selling, amongst other things, some rather good imitation antiques.

Shaanxi Lu runs to the south here, from the Nanking Road. The house at 186 Shaanxi Lu is a surprise. It was the rather elegant home of a Chinese textiles magnate, adorned with stained glass windows and a pretty garden with a traditional Chinese pavilion in the corner. The surprise is that apparently the family, now living abroad, still own it, and that it is now the Shanghai headquarters of the non-Communist democratic political parties like the Guomindang.

Returning to the Nanking Road, 1266 is an example of the changes that are taking place in Shanghai, and indeed in China. With the encouragement of private enterprise, small bars and cafés have sprung up all over the city. There is very little to distinguish one from another, but in a few cases there are signs of imagination and flair. This looks to be one of them. Care has been taken to preserve the building's original character, at least on the exterior — it has been painted in a green that is ritzy without being garish, and striped awnings add a dash of raciness. The staff are enthusiastic and courteous, and seem to have some knowledge of foreign languages.

Shanghai Industrial Exhibition

Another five minutes walk westwards will bring you to this massive institution. In many cities it would sit very uneasily with its surroundings, but in Shanghai it could almost be mistaken for yet another indulgence by a wealthy parvenu. In fact this was built in the 1950s, some years after the last capitalist had left, by the Soviet Union, and until 1960, when China decided to dispense with the services of the USSR, it was known as the Palace of Sino-Soviet Friendship.

The site has an interesting history, however. It used to be called Hardoon Park, and the mansion that used to stand here was the private residence of Silas Hardoon, the Jew from Baghdad who arrived poor, but died the richest man in Shanghai (see Chapter 13). It was 26 acres of fantasy in Chinese style, with pavilions and all the trappings of a traditional Chinese garden. This was explained by the fact that his wife was Eurasian, and he became a devout Buddhist. When he died the legal squabbles between his heirs (his many adopted children), and between them and the new government after 1949, continued for many years; and the mansion itself was destroyed by fire during the Sino-Japanese War.

The Exhibition Centre now houses a permanent display dedicated to the progress China is making in the fields of industrial and agricultural technology, and it is used for temporary exhibitions as well (although a new exhibition centre is being built, with Japanese help, just to the north of the old one). The west wing is called the Shanghai Arts and Crafts Trade Fair, but everything on display is for sale. It competes with the Friendship Store for the best selection of goods in the city. The middle building also has a large display of goods for sale. There is a lift that can take you up to the fifth floor, where the Friendship Restaurant is situated as well as a rooftop coffee bar with commanding views across the city. On the sixth floor there is another bar/café (covered). The restaurant is open from 11.00 to 14.30 and from 17.00 to 21.00. The bar is open from 09.00 until 21.00.

Two of the most magnificent villas from old Shanghai are located opposite the Exhibition Centre. Highly distinctive, and very similar one to the other, they sit back from the Nanking Road at the point where it meets Tongren Lu. Since they seem to be used as government offices you probably will only be able to admire them from afar.

The Jing An Temple

Bubbling Well Road was originally Jing An Road, named after the temple (Jing An Si) which is a few blocks to the west of the Shanghai Industrial Exhibition, at number 1686. In English it would be called the Temple of Tranquillity. For many years it was put to other uses, but in 1984 it was restored to its original purpose. There has been a temple on the site for about 1700 years, but the current structures, some of which are still under restoration, are mainly from the Qing and Ming dynasties. The temple is somewhat larger than it first appears, so don't be put off if at first you cannot get beyond the restaurant with the pagoda bedecked with Christmas lights and the picture of tourists on the Great Wall. One chapel is prettily decorated with artificial lotus flowers, and others have some splendid religious statues. There is accommodation for fifty monks, and services are performed at 0830 and 1630. The vegetarian restaurant is open between the hours of 1100 and 1300; and the temple itself is open to the public from 0800 until 1600. One of the guardians, Mr G.K.Cheng, speaks good English. A 'Bamboo Fair' used to take place nearby, selling only items fashioned from bamboo. The old Bubbling Well itself was very close to this temple, just at the point where Nanjing Xi Lu meets Huashan Lu (the former Avenue Haig which was the boundary of the French Concession). The old Bubbling Well Cemetery used to be opposite the temple and is now covered by Jing An park. In the park, full of life in common with all the parks of the city, there is a tea house, and a little pavilion in Greek style like a miniature temple, which was perhaps one of the mausoleums of the former cemetery.

New owners. This old mansion, formerly owned by the wealthy Kadoorie family, is now the Municipal Children's Palace.

The Children's Palace

There are a number of Children's Palaces in Shanghai, one for each area of the city. An idea inherited from the Russians during the 1950s when relations between China and the USSR were more cordial, they are basically after-school entertainment for gifted children, and tend to be housed in the old pre-1949 mansions. The finest, however, must be the one used for the Municipal Children's Palace, which is very close to the junction of Nanjing Xi Lu and Yanan Zhong Lu. This used to belong to people called Kadoorie, another Jewish family whose origins were in Baghdad and who made their fortune in old Shanghai. The family is still well known in Hong Kong — one member is currently head of the China Light Co. Of course the 'Marble House', as it was called, is rather run down through years of neglect — it wasn't built to withstand young hordes gallivanting about its premises — but retains a certain grandeur. The lines are still intact, along with some of the more solid decoration. There is a fine terrace, reached from the house by an array of French windows that are surmounted by a pretty balustrade. All would have been illuminated on hot tropical evenings by the ornate art deco lamps that still line the terrace, and which stand in bizarre contrast to the statues of revolutionary youth that are a more recent adornment. You could probably slip up the drive for a look without anyone minding, but Children's Palaces are open to the public at certain times, usually at about 9 am. If in doubt, consult CITS. The address of this palace is 64, Yanan Xi Lu. Tel:525537.

Beyond this point the Bubbling Well Road petered out into the Concession boundaries, and the beginning of the Chinese countryside. Officially, foreign jurisdiction ceased beyond Avenue Haig (Huashan Lu), but in practice many foreigners lived beyond it, or enjoyed themselves at the golf courses and riding stables that were to be found to the west and southwest of the Settlements. Legally, these outlying areas fell under the province of Chinese law, when in fact it was the British police that patrolled the streets until the Japanese occupation.

For interest's sake, here are a few of the establishments that used to flourish on the Bubbling Well Road: the Majestic Ballroom (254); Italian Consulate (515); Bubbling Well Home Appartments (196) ('15 minutes by rickshaw to the Bund'); Embassy Cinema (742); 'Little Café' (741); American Women's Club (150); Shanghai Railway Office (407); Continental Butchery (1202); Spanish Consulate (1205).

The vicinity of the Nanking Road

Whilst the Nanking Road is very much the main thoroughfare, there are, particularly in the area between the Bund and the old racecourse, several streets running east-west and north-south which are worth exploring. As always in Shanghai, it is the search for traces of its faded past that is so interesting, and thus it is important to look for the details that hint at it. The great monuments are few and far between, but wandering the streets in search of modern Chinese daily life in the shadow of a past that is recent, yet mysterious because it has entirely vanished, is a rewarding experience.

Most of the streets of Shanghai have been given new names since 1949 — now, the streets running north-south are named after provinces, and those running east-west after cities and towns. Before, they were named after places, sovereigns, statesmen, and people from all the foreign communities who had made a contribution to Shanghai life.

It is worth bearing in mind that much of the arrangement of life in Shanghai is the same as it always was; only today, in less flamboyant times, differences are not always obvious. For example, a casual walker may not notice that he has arrived in a Moslem area, until he looks a little more closely at the food, the presence of Arabic script, or the shape of local faces. In the same way, it is possible, by careful scrutiny, to see into the past — taking the example of Moslems yet again, one might be able to detect what used to be former Moslem areas by the shape of windows. Some streets used to be associated with particular trades and even now, despite the cataclysmic events that have so violently shaken China in recent years, the connections are still there.

Shanghai lanes

History and the peculiar arrangement of life in Shanghai gave rise to a particular phenomenen — the lanes. From the end of the last century until the middle of this, about 75 per cent of the population lived in them. They came about primarily as a result of thousands of Chinese entering the Foreign Concessions as they took refuge from wars involving the likes of the Small Sword Society and the Taiping Heavenly Kingdom. To cope with this, the lanes came into being, which were basically a smaller version of the Peking courtyard dwelling. At first these houses were constructed with a small but high wall, and a large black two-leaf front door fixed on a granite or Ningpo red stone frame with a small courtyard behind. Most of them had two floors, each with three rooms. Those that faced the street were used to conduct businesses on their lower floors — behind were dozens of these houses forming the 'lanes' and 'sub-lanes'.

In the 1920s the lanes continued to be an important part of Shanghai life, but were built according to a more western design — the walls were lower, with an iron gate replacing the door, and a garden replaced the courtyard.

Almost every aspect of Shanghai life took place among the lanes. There were hotels, bathhouses, brothels, opium dens, small industries, printers and publishers, bookstands (a few shelves of books and some stools — story pictorials were rented out to the public), and small theatres and story-telling halls, especially in the areas around the Great World on Xizang Lu, and the New World on the Nanking Road.

The 'lanes' are still very much in evidence, and in fact a great deal of local life is still concentrated among them, in a city that has a chronic housing problem. In the streets to the south of Nanking Road, and between the Bund and the People's Park, inconspicuous alleys very often lead to warrens of these lanes. Most date from the 1920s, but some of the older ones remain in the area of the southern end of Sichuan Nan Lu.

Landmarks: symbols of power

At the Bund end of Nanjing Dong Lu there are a number of landmarks. Just to the south, at number 6 Jiujiang Road, is the Peiguang Middle School, which used to be the infamous Laozha (Louza, as it was then) Police Station, scene of the so called May 30th incident of 1925, when police opened fire on a group of protesting students, several of whom were killed. The students, it will be remembered, were protesting at the death of a Chinese worker in a Japanese mill during a confrontation between management and the workers. All the senior officers were either on holiday or at the races, and the officer in charge was panicked into shooting wildly into the crowd, wounding many, and killing several. Although it wasn't realised at the time, this incident marked the beginning of the end for the foreigner in Shanghai.

Two streets further south you meet Fuzhou Lu (formerly Foochow Road), and at the point where it meets Henan Lu (old Honan Road), sits an enormous pile of magisterial aspect, that sprawls some way down both streets and has a porticoed entrance at the corner. This was the former headquarters of the International

Settlement Municipal Council, until 1928 made up exclusively of British and Americans, who took all the decisions pertaining to the organisation of the Settlement. Of the many departments in this building, one of the most famous was that of the Volunteers Corps, originally formed not long after the arrival of the foreigner the previous century, when it was realised that the occasional case of anti-foreign fever was likely to break out. It was in this building, too, that a Japanese delegate, frustrated at not being able to gain a third seat on the council for his country in 1937, shot one of the other members. The foreign dominated Municipal Council relinquished its powers in 1943, and the building has since been used to house departments of the People's Municipal Government; but drama was to come its way once again during the Cultural Revolution, when fanatical Red Guards thronged the surrounding streets, chanting quotations from Mao's 'Little Red Book' as they waved copies of it above their heads before finally taking over the building and control of local government.

Jiujiang Lu (formerly Kiukiang Road)

This street, running westwards from the Bund, immediately south of the Nanking Road, was known as the 'Wall Street' of Shanghai before 1949. American Express had their offices at number 158, Chase Bank at 80, The Italian Bank in China at 186, and Mitsubishi at 36. At 113 there were several firms of stockbrokers — Levy & Co., Rosenfeld & Son, and Shahmoon & Co.

Number 41 (now the offices of Xinming Wan Bao, the New People's Evening News) still has the imprint of a company crest visible, but not clearly enough to decipher. Number 89, now the Chemical Industry Supply Company, used to be the German and China Bank. At the junction with Sichuan Zhong Lu is what used to be the Continental Bank (now the Bank of East Asia), and directly opposite this is the entrance to the old Central Market. It seems a rather gloomy place, but walking its length will deliver you to a clothes market, a shop selling cassettes and an alley of little restaurants, mostly offering dumplings and noodles.

Back on Jiujiang Lu you will arrive at a small but shady park, and just beyond it, at 219, the old Holy Trinity Cathedral, a former Church of England which used to play the Westminster Chimes. It now houses the People's Government of Whangpu. It was known as the 'red temple' (Hong miao) after the strong colour of the bricks used in its construction. A church built on this site in 1845 had been damaged by a storm in 1850; the 5000 silver taels used in repairing it were to no avail, since the roof fell in once again in 1862. The eminent architect Sir Gilbert Scott designed another church and the current building, in thirteenth century Gothic style, was consecrated in 1894. It was to become the principal Anglican church of the city.

There is a useful item at 556 if the accommodation situation is critical and you need a bath. The bathhouse here is open from noon until 20.30. Finally, at that part of Jiujiang Lu that runs behind the Seventh Heaven hotel on the Nanking Road, there are a number of small independently run shops in good examples of the older balconied buildings in Chinese style.

Hankou Lu, Zhejiang Lu and the Moslems

Hankou Lu was well known as a haunt of publishers and booksellers, who found the concept of 'the freedom of the press', as understood by the British, to provide convenient protection from the censorship laws of the Chinese government as they advocated, in a variety of publications at the turn of the century, the overthrow of the Qing empire.

Towards its eastern end there are examples of the 'lanes', mostly in the area contained by Zhejiang, Fuzhou, and Hankou roads. One, for example, is called Hui Le Li, famous, apparently, for its low life, for which Hankou Lu had something of a reputation.

Towards the junction with Zhejiang Lu the windows of some of the buildings take on something of an arabesque. This is because most of the Moslem population of Shanghai resides along Zhejiang Lu and certain of the buildings in neighbouring streets used to be or are still occupied by followers of Islam. That you are, along Zhejiang Lu, in the Moslem 'quarter' is not immediately obvious, until you notice the Arabic script, the complexion of the people on the streets, and the kebabs and pancakes for sale from streetside vendors. The domed roof just south of the junction with Guandong Lu used to cover a mosque — it is now a hotel. The main mosque is at 372 Fuyou Lu, not far from the Yu Garden.

Fuzhou Lu

This was the notorious Fourth Maloo. Part of Shanghai's reputation as the 'Whore of the east' was founded on the establishments that lined the street, particularly after the junction with Henan Lu. There were brothels in abundance, some of which were attached to restaurants, and opium dens with sing-song girls in attendance. It was also another street known for its bookshops, of which even today there are several. At 380 there is a foreign language bookstore, dealing in second hand books particularly. At

390 you will find the Shanghai Trading Association on whose upper floor is probably the best selection of foreign language books, mostly concerning matters Chinese, in the city. A few second hand books are for sale too — eighteenth century leather bound copies of the *Spectator* magazine have been spied there. Paper cuts, paintings, and cuddly pandas are sold too.

At number 44, near the Bund, there is a very curious pseudo-Tudor building. This was built by a Mr Zheng Guang He, who built up an empire founded on soft drinks in old Shanghai. It is difficult to say what it is now — the guards on the gates are very secretive, but since it backs on to the Municipal Offices, it must be assumed that its business concerns local government.

At number 180 is the Xingcheng Hotel, with its old-fashioned lifts — this was the Metropole Hotel, supposed to offer the best meal in town in the 1930s. Beyond, at 209, is the former American Club, the first to admit Chinese guests. It is now a courtroom.

There is a good restaurant at 343 — this is Xing Hua Lou, easily distinguishable by the rather miserable looking snakes in the window. If you require only a snack, excellent dumplings and cakes are for sale downstairs.

Beyond the junction with Fujian Lu there are many older buildings built in the Chinese style.

Guangdong Lu

Guandong Lu (formerly Canton Road) runs east-west four blocks to the south of Nanking Road. In this street could be found the Masonic Club at 93 (before the 1930s it had been located at the junction of the Bund and Beijing Lu, adjacent to the British Embassy), the American Chamber of Commerce and the Dollar Shipping Line at 51, and the Hamburg-Amerika Shipping Line at 20. The Peninsula and Oriental Steam Navigation Co. (P & O) was at number 17.

Where it meets Sichuan Lu at number 93, there is a building that was evidently a bank and which has much of the rather extravagant decoration in the lobby well preserved. There are marble friezes, mosaics, and some fine art deco stained glass. You should be able to step into the entrance for a look.

The Shanghai Antique and Curio Store is at 218-226. This is one of the best antique shops in Shanghai, and has a long history. Originally a bazaar, carved up into stalls, it became one operation after 1949. One of the English speaking assistants, Mr Wang Yong Fu, used to be a stall-holder there — he and his colleagues are most helpful. At 440 there is a 'Jingshoushi', a dealer in jade, gold, and silver rings. The selection is not wide, but the prices may be lower here than in some of the foreigner-orientated shops.

Henan Zhong Lu
At 29-31 there is a shop selling maps, at 90 an old shop selling painting and calligraphy equipment, and at 186 a repair shop for bicycles.

Henan Nan Lu
On the corner with Renmin Lu, almost into the old town, stands a pottery shop with a few more unusual items. For anyone interested in the ceramic rubbish bins in the shape of animals (dragon, panda etc.) that dot the city, and China, this could be the place.

Sichuan Lu
Running north-south one block west of the Bund, this was formerly named Montauban in the French part becoming Szechuan Road in the International Settlement. The Norwegian Consulate used to be at 110, the Norwegian and Danish Chambers of Commerce at 220, and the Austrian Consulate at 330. The Dutch Java-China Lijn had its offices at 133. At 623, opposite the Navy YMCA a Doctor Duncan specialised in venereal problems and piles. In 1935 one of the top Cabaret Ballrooms, the Venus, was to be found on North Szechuan Road, 'scene of the Sino-Japanese hostilities', as the glamourous advertising went. There, curfew or no curfew, you could have danced until dawn to the music of the Venus Rhythm Boys.

This is the main north-south thoroughfare in the city, and a stroll along its length will introduce you to many facets of Shanghai. The southernmost end, which was originally Montauban and ran as far as today's Yanan Lu, begins close to the old 'Chinese' town, and continuing north will take you past some of the older style Chinese housing, the 'lanes', with their balconies and stone arch fronts on the lower floors. A little further north is the former Catholic St Joseph's Church, now a primary school. You pass the colonnades of Jinling Lu before leaving the old French Concession to enter the former British one at Yanan Lu. At the junction with Yanan Lu is the new Union Building, with some shops that may be of interest, and the YouYou restaurant and coffee bar. Opposite this is a building that has a distinctively 1920/30s facade. This was the Qi Ye Bank, now the Shanghai Department of Light Industry. At the junction with Guandong Lu is the building with the interesting lobby (see Guandong Lu). Continuing northwards will take you through the heart of the old financial district and bring you to Suzhou Creek. On the other side is a massive structure with clock tower — this was the Chinese Head Post Office, and a post office it remains. Beyond lies Hongkou, and eventually Hongkou Park, with the tomb of Lu Xun (see 'Parks'). Not far north of Suzhou Creek, Kunshan Lu runs east off Sichuan Bei Lu. At 135 is the Jinling Church where Chiang Kai Shek married Soong May-Ling.

Jiangxi Lu

This street, formerly Kiangse Road, runs north-south across the Nanking Road, two blocks to the west of the Bund. The American Consulate stood at 248-250, The Italian Chamber of Commerce at 278, and the Lloyd Triestino Line at number 170 (Hamilton House), opposite the old Metropole.

The French Concession

Shanghai was, in the popular imagination, at least two things — a swanky city of urbane swells and a refuge or paradise for adventurers. It was, by all accounts both of these, but the swells tended to keep to one side of the tracks, the International Settlement, and the adventurers to the other side, in the French Concession. There was, of course, a good deal of overlapping, but on the whole national stereotypes ran true to form. The international Settlement was British in character, a curious mixture of class consciousness and eagerness to do the right thing, and the French Concession, quintessentially Gallic, cosmopolitan, stylish perhaps, and rather disreputable.

It was clear, almost from the start, that the French Concession would be something of a maverick. When the settlements were first established, all three (American, British, and French) were, in theory, under a loosely applied joint administration, but it was an agreement that was never ratified by the French, and a proposal to unite the French Concession with the International Settlement was not accepted by them. "It is apparent that France regards her concession as a colony rather than a settlement and she has lately urged her claims for an extension of it in a most selfish and indefensible manner," wrote Isabella Bird in 1899. Evidently the French were determined to maintain their own identity. In the end, the chauvinistic attitude of the Treaty Powers did not interfere with the smooth running of Shanghai, but rather served to heighten the fascination of the place.

The International Concession was not, by any stretch of the imagination, a model of sobriety and modesty. But, on the whole, it was efficiently policed in the English manner, and somewhat conservative. Revolution, smuggling, the Bohemian lifestyle — they were to be found in the French Concession. On the right bank, the City of London; on the left bank the Latin quarter of Paris.

Former British Consulate. In the foreground office workers are following a Tai Qi class.

Chinoiserie

The French Concession stretched from the southern half of the Avenue Edward VII (today's Yanan Lu) in the north to Route de Zikawei (today's Zhaojiabang Lu) in the south. It was bounded in the east by the Huangpu River and, skirting the northern part of the Chinese City, reached its most westerly point at Avenue Haig (today's Huashan Lu). It had an area of 2525 acres, a little less than half that of the International Settlement.

The French had their own Municipal Council, comprising sixteen councillors, of which nine were French, five were Chinese, and two were British. The resident French Consul General was the supreme local authority, exercising the power of veto over the decisions made by the council, and answerable only to the French Minister to China, and to the French Government. They had their own police force and laws, their own fire brigade, and their own judicial system (with courts of appeal in Hanoi and Saigon). Of course the electrical system changed from one concession to another, and since the French Concession and the International Settlement met in the middle of Avenue Edward VII, westbound traffic was subject to French regulations and eastbound to British/American regulations. Fortunately, driving on the left was common to both concessions.

Quai de France

The waterfront area of the French Concession, known as the French Bund among anglophones, was officially named 'Quai de France'. Now it is the Zhongshan Dong Er Lu, which begins where it meets Yanan Lu. As far as shipping was concerned, it was always far busier than the Bund, and one of its landmarks was the signal tower that displayed the weather forecasts for the China Coast as they were relayed from the Siccawei (Xujiawei) Observatory, which was run by the scientists of the French Jesuits. The signal tower stands opposite the beginning of Yanan Dong Lu, and the observatory still stands in Xujiahui, towards the southwest of the city, today housing the Shanghai Municipal Meteorological Department. The Quai was also the site of some of the important French institutions — at numbers 9-10 were the offices of the Messageries Maritimes (French Mail), and at number 1 the flagship of the French banking community, the Banque Franco-Chinoise. Big-Eared Du, who was to become one of Shanghai's most flamboyant gangsters in later years, started his career as a young apprentice on the wharfs of the French Bund. Today there is not very much left of its past, although it has, as before, the atmosphere of a busy wharf. Traces of the original cobbled road are visible here and there, a few old warehouses remain, and there is an eel market on one of the alleys that lead west from the main road.

Avenue Edward VII (Yanan Dong Lu)

Avenue Edward VII, the boundary of the two concessions, was one of the main streets where the three principal communities (French, Chinese, and Anglo-American) converged. Shops and businesses from all three were to be found here. For the French it was a convenient location for some of their important offices in the financial world. At number 9 you would have found both the French Chamber of Commerce, and the offices of an estate agent, Foncière et Immobilière de Chine. Estate agents were, of course, an important part of Shanghai life. This was never more true than in the French Concession of the 1930s, which was becoming increasingly attractive to residents who found the International Settlement rather too crowded. At 183-189 stood the offices of a financial organisation of a different sort, the National State Lottery Administration. The lottery was run by the Chinese Government, and the profits were poured into a fund for the improvement of the road system. Tickets cost $10, and the best prize was $500,000.

As always in Shanghai, the serious and the lighthearted were never far from each other. The Nanking Cinema stood at 523, and two of the major cabarets of Shanghai were the Palais Café ('High Class Drinks, Good Service, Foreign Management') at number 57, and Ladow's Casanova ('Dance to the strains of a good orchestra') at 545.

Blood Alley and the Great World

Two of Shanghai's most infamous dives were on or close to Avenue Edward VII. Today's Xikou Lu, reached off Jinling Dong Lu, used to be called Rue Zhu Baosan, but it was known under the soubriquet of 'Blood Alley'. A small cul-de-sac, it was a succession of murky bars, the haunts of piratical sailors and loose women. Unlike the cabarets and bars elsewhere, with their glamorous veneer, the bars of Blood Alley were unambiguously and unashamedly salacious, and tense with the expectation of the eruption of violence. Apart from crumbling coats of arms and the traces of dates on the walls, there is nothing left of its infamous past. The bars are now mostly garages and storehouses.

Where Yanan Lu meets Xizang Lu, on the south corner, stands a building whose centre point is a tower that, for once, could well be described as 'wedding cake' style. This was the 'Great World', a burlesque curiosity, and a funfair in vertical layers, catering to the love of the Chinese for the bizarre. It was started by a certain Huang Chujiu, who had been involved in the management of the New World (see Nanking Road), and who decided to go into competition. His operation was to be much larger, and the French authorites readily gave permission for its construction in the expectation of attracting yet more money to their concession. The Great World was inaugurated in 1917, and its services were available from noon until late at night. Each floor specialised in different aspects of the lascivious and the weird, from sing-song girls and peep shows, to a stuffed whale and imported lavatories with a resident expert in their use. A Great World newspaper kept customers informed of coming attractions. Huang Chujiu began to lose money through extravagant gambling, and when even speculation in properties he had built in the neighbouring area of the Zhejiang Road failed, he was forced to sell Great World to no lesser figure than Pockmarked Huang, the gangster. It subsequently became known as 'Rong's Great World', but in 1954 it was taken over by the local government. Now it is the Shanghai Youth Palace, providing more wholesome entertainment for the young of Shanghai. Sometimes acrobatic performances are given there; and there is a coffee house on the ground floor.

Rue du Consulat

Just to the south of Avenue Edward VII was Rue du Consulat (now Jinling Lu). As the name suggests, this street was where the administrative offices of the French Concession were to be found. It was also well known for its variety of Chinese run shops. At number 2, at the junction with the Quai de France, stood the French Consulate, and at 25 the Dutch Consulate. Between the two were the offices of the francophone newspaper, *Le journal de Shanghai.* At the corner of Montauban (now Sichuan Lu) was the Hotel des Colonies. The French Municipal Offices stand at the corner of the former Rue de l'Administration, today's Shandong Lu (behind the Museum). One of the pillars of that institution was a certain Big-Eared Du, the gangster, who somehow managed to acquire a reputation as a philanthropist. At the junction with Quai de l'Ouest stood the French police station. It will be remembered that the highest ranking gendarme in the French Concession Police was Pockmarked Huang (Huang Jinrong), who was also at the head of the Green Gang, a secret society not unlike the Mafia, which controlled the opium trade. All this was an open secret. Only in Shanghai could such a situation obtain; but it was thought to be the lesser evil, since any police officer would have been bought off by Huang and his gang. This street is one of the very few that was built in the old fashioned but practical way, with porticoes.

Avenue Joffre and the heart of the French Concession.

Avenue Joffre is now called Huaihai Lu, and is one of the main thoroughfares of modern Shanghai. Before 1949 it was the main business street of the French Concession. It lies to the south of the western portion of the old Rue du Consulat, beginning at the northwest corner of the Chinese city. The first part of the road, as far as Xizang Lu, used to be called Rue de Ningpo. Just to the south of this stood the Ningpo Guild, of which only the gateway remains, the rest submerged beneath a housing estate. The old guilds, something like a cross between a trade union and a masonic lodge, were an important part of business life in the Chinese community. They consisted of men who grouped together according to their trade or their home town. This clannishness was, and is, a feature of the Chinese outlook on life. The guilds had their origins in the secret societies that sprang up following the rise of the Manchu Dynasty (see Historical section, 'Pockmarked Huang, and Big Eared Du') — some developed into criminal gangs, others into fraternal and philanthropic guilds. The Ningpo Guild was the comradely organisation of one of the most influential groups of businessmen in Shanghai. Ningpo (now more commonly spelt Ningbo) lies on the coast about 70 miles to the south of Shanghai, and before the rise of Shanghai was one of the busiest ports on the coast of East China. As Ningpo began to decline, so many of its traders brought their acumen to Shanghai, playing an important role in its growth as compradores and bankers. The Ningpo Guild provided burial grounds for its members and their families, or schooling, or loans, or indeed help of any sort whenever it was needed.

Many of the merchants and shopkeepers of Avenue Joffre were of Russian origin, and the signs over their shops were all written in Cyrillic. So great were their numbers, about 25,000 in 1935, that the area was known as 'Little Russia'. They arrived as refugees from the October Revolution of 1917, often with nothing more than the clothes they were wearing. It was a few years before they were able to establish themselves, but one way or another establish themselves they did, whether as dancing hostesses or as postage stamp dealers, as jewellers (G.Stepanoff at number 800) or as drapers (Grigorieff & Co. at 860). There were two Russian language newspapers, one revolutionary (*Slovo*) and one Czarist (*Zaria*). *Slovo* had its offices at 238 Avenue du Roi Albert (Shaanxi Lu) and *Zaria* at 774 Avenue Joffre. The unpleasant snobbishness that prevailed in Shanghai revealed itself most strongly with the arrival of the Russians. Poor and desperate as they were, many dying in the struggle to make a living in Shanghai, they were heavily criticised for the menial tasks they took on and for being willing to fraternize with the Chinese.

Jiujiang Lu. Many Chinese lived in the Foreign Concessions too; and happily the tendency is to restore the old buildings.

The Russian and French was a happy convergence of styles. The French Concession was characterised by its wide avenues fringed by plane trees, which are still a feature of Shanghai and other towns of the region. There was a profusion of cafés where pleasurable hours could be idled away drinking coffee or aperitifs and keeping an eye on the immigrés of aristocratic bearing dreaming of the salons of Imperial St Petersburg. One was Altmans Café at 752 Avenue Joffre. Plenty of shops catered for those with a hankering after the latest in Parisian fashion. Dressmakers were always on hand to offer suggestions at Maison Honorine at 662, and Maison Lucile at 813. The Lightfoot Shoe Company was at 722, the Georgette Gown and Hat Shoppe at 821; and, for that special occasion, the Maison Ando Beauty Salon at 868 would have added the final touches. If you were eager to impress, then a few lessons at Waldemar's Dancing Academy at 1272 might not have gone amiss, and the Cathay Cinema was at 868.

Looking around
Huaihai Lu and vicinity is one of the most interesting areas to explore. Where you start is of little consequence, but a good place seems to be Fuxing Park, from where you can wander north or south taking in a good slice of Huaihai Lu and visiting the likes of the Site of the First National Congress of the Communist Party of China.

Fuxing Park
This was originally a private garden belonging to a certain Mr Gu until in 1908 the French bought it and turned it into a park, calling it the French park. As always there were the regulations concerning dogs and Chinese that in the years following Liberation were used to such effect in the propaganda war. In 1928 the regulations were changed however. During the Second World War it was used as a military parade ground by the Japanese. When Shanghai was handed over to Chinese control, the park was renamed 'Daxing', and then 'Fuxing' ('revival') after 1949. The layout is very much in the Parisian style with wide paths flanked by trees.

It is now one of the favourite gathering places of the old and retired. Some of them have stories to tell and are quite willing to tell them. Interpreters are not too hard to find in Shanghai — it is often sufficient to look foreign (not difficult in China!) and to wait patiently in one place for the approach of a student who is eager to practise English. The old gather in a corner, argue about the comparitive merits of the past and the present and lament the passing of the old tea-house, which has now become a restaurant that is far too expensive for them. Further round there is a small pavilion on a mound — here people often gather to sing airs from traditional operas.

The revolutionaries

Because Shanghai was not in a sense part of China, it was always very attractive to revolutionaries of one persuasion or another. The French Concession was particularly expedient because of its more cosmopolitan racial mix, its flexibility in legal matters, and its cavalier attitude towards the Chinese Government.

The houses of some of these revolutionaries still stand and for the likeminded generations that have followed they have become shrines. They stand, it is frequently said, as a testimony to 'Shanghai's glorious revolutionary tradition', a boast that has become less proud since the Cultural Revolution.

Near Fuxing Park are the former residences of two of the great figures of modern Chinese politics, Sun Yat Sen and Zhou En Lai. Sun, the founder of the Republic of China, although a Cantonese, spent much of his political life in Shanghai, not least because he was married to one of the daughters of a great Shanghai family, the Soongs (see Chapter 13). He lived at what is now 7 Xiangshan Lu, a small street a little to the west of Fuxing Park, with his wife Soong Ching-Ling throughout most of their married life. It was here that Chiang Kai Shek met Soong May-Ling.

There is a selection of memorabilia and photographs, and the house is open from 1300 until 1630.

Zhou En Lai was head of the Shanghai branch of the Communist Party during the 1940s, and lived at what was 73 Rue Massenet and is now 107 Sinan Lu, again just to the west of Fuxing Park. Although Mao was 'the Great Helmsman', it may be that Zhou was really the more astute politician. In Mao's declining years it was probably he that encouraged the visit by Nixon that was to change China's stance in world affairs. The house is open from 1330 until 1600.

The site of the First National Congress of the Communist Party of China

This is at 76 Xingye Lu, which is a little way to the northeast of Fuxing Park. That the Communist Party of China should have formed in Shanghai was hardly surprising. The social conditions were right for it (an industrial working class, plus the existence of radical intellectual groups); and the French Concession, which was outside the immediate jurisdiction of the Chinese Government, provided a convenient cover for subversion. There were actually two wings of the party, one in Peking, the other in Shanghai. The first Marxist Society had been launched in Peking in 1919, with a young library assistant, Mao Zedong, as one of its early members. Peking however, was too dangerous and so, with Soviet advisors in attendance, the Chinese Communist Party was formally inaugurated at the first Congress in July 1921 at what was then 106 Rue Wantz. This house belonged to one of the delegates, Li Hanjun. After some days the meeting was infiltrated by a spy, and the delegates were forced to adjourn to a houseboat on a lake in Zhejiang province. Just who, and what, all the delegates were has been the subject of not a little debate, and even the address has been called into question. Of the names generally associated with the meeting, only that of Mao Zedong is immediately familiar.

The room where they met has been arranged with twelve seats around a table set in a businesslike way with teabowls and ashtrays. In other rooms there is an illustrated history of the Chinese Communist Party, which is fascinating for the aficionado of revolutionary memorabilia. It is open from 0830 to 1130 and from 1330 to 1630.

Going to Huaihai Lu

Not far from the former residence of Sun Yat Sen is Gaolan Lu. Along here is to be found one of those curiosities with which Shanghai abounds — a small disused Russian Orthodox Church. In fact it is used — not for worship but for the storing of washing machines. However, it is still very clear what it was, and the staff may let you in to have a look around. The upstairs part is in good condition. Despite its new role, such relics are apparently not to be destroyed until it is settled that they are truly defunct. It is perhaps unlikely that this particular church will spring to life again, but it does hold out hope for plenty of others of other denominations and religions.

Continuing towards Huaihai Lu by way of Ruijin Er Lu, you will pass, at number 71, Shanghai Huaihai Old Ware Store, where you may find second-hand furniture to your taste.

At the junction with Ruijin Lu, you are joining Huaihai Lu about a third of the way along from the east. Continuing north you would eventually pass along Shimen Lu and arrive at the Nanking Xi Lu a little to the east of the Industrial Exhibition Centre. Huaihai Lu is still at this point essentially a street of shops and restaurants becoming more residential further to the west, replete with old villas and apartment flats. It may be wishful thinking, but there seems to be a more lighthearted air in this part of the city, a hint of the old Gallic influence still present after forty years. One of the more substantial reminders of the foreign presence in the area is the number of restaurants selling what purports to be Western food. This comes mostly in the form of pastries and cream cakes (for example, at 'Laodachang', number 377), but there are some establishments that keep a more varied menu, as at the Shanghai Western Food Restaurant at 845. Not far from this is the old Cathay Theatre, now a cinema, shop, and coffee house.

Continuing west you will come to Maoming Nan Lu (the former Rue Cardinal Mercier). A short walk along here will bring you to the Jinjiang Hotel, and just beyond it, on the corner of Changle Lu, a theatre. Rue Cardinal Mercier was the site of two of the most important landmarks of the French Concession. The Lyceum Theatre, which is now the Shanghai Arts Theatre, at number 57, was the finest in the city. This building, the last in a long line, was constructed in 1931, and was the home of the Shanghai Amateur Dramatic Society. Before films became overwhelmingly popular the Lyceum played host to a whole range of international stars, from Sir Harry Lauder to John McCormack, but in its later years was more a cinema than anything else. Today you are more likely to see a local opera or a visiting dance troupe.

Next door, at 59, stands the Jinjiang Hotel, originally a private hotel for French residents dating back to 1931. It was here that the Shanghai Communiqué was signed by President Nixon and Premier Zhou Enlai in 1972. It is still a first class hotel, with an excellent shopping area which includes a foreign languages book shop, a branch of the Friendship Store, hairdressers, and a silk shop. The main building boasts an English pub, and a coffee shop.

Opposite the hotel, at 58, are the remains of the Jinjiang Club, the old Cercle Sportif Français, which was the French club in Shanghai. It was considered the most cosmopolitan of all the clubs. Women were admitted, but membership was limited to forty. There

Opposite: *The park. Shanghai parks are a retreat for the old, and for the visitor, an opportunity to see the many aspects of Chinese life.*

was a roof garden for dancing in the summer, and during the winter Sunday afternoon tea dances were held in the ballroom on the first floor. In recent years it was known as the Jinjiang Club, offering entertainment (bowling etc.) to foreign visitors, but it is currently being converted into a hotel, and although the splendid façade is being preserved, the massive construction rearing up behind it is inappropriate.

International sports

Returning to Huaihai Lu, the next junction is at Shaanxi Nan Lu, the former Avenue du Roi Albert. West of the point where Avenue du Roi Albert met Avenue Joffre (Huaihai Lu) was mostly residential — many wealthy Russians, Chinese, Germans, Americans, and British built mansions in this area, if only to escape the overcrowded conditions of the International Settlement. In fact in 1930 there were more British (2,228), Russian (3,879), and American (1,541) residents, than there were French (1,208) in the French Concession. Yet there were almost twice as many rickshaws in the French Concession as in the International Settlement for half the number of people. That part of Shaanxi Lu to the south of Huaihai Lu was notable as the site for a pair of unlikely sports that became immensely popular in the 1930s. Greyhound racing and Hai-alai had been both banned in the International Settlement under pressure from the Chinese, who were concerned at their potentially corrupting effects. The powers that be in the French Concession were not impressed by this argument and, fortunately for the punters, both sports flourished happily there. The home of greyhound racing was at the Canidrome or the Champs de Courses Français, which was at the junction of Avenue du Roi Albert (Shaanxi Lu) and Rue Lafayette (Fuxing Lu). This is now Culture Square and functions as a theatre with 18000 seats. One of the most popular cabarets was close by, calling itself the Canidrome, so if the dogs cleaned you out, consolation was not far away.

Hai-alai was a fast indoor game imported from Spain. There were tournaments every night, and of course bets could be placed on the players. Games took place in the Auditorium, which stood on the Avenue du Roi Albert, just off Huaihai Lu. The building is now the district indoor stadium. Turn south into Shaanxi Lu, and it is a little

Opposite: *A stall in the Flower and Fish market. This busy market, in an old street behind the Nanking Road, deals in pottery too.*

way down on the left. Opposite, at 328 Shaanxi Nan Lu, is a shop with a small selection of leather and fur items at reasonable prices. The quality of the styling is variable, but there may be something to suit. On the corner of Shaanxi and Huaihai is a good fruitshop.

Crossing Huaihai Lu and walking along the northern portion of Shaanxi Nan Lu will lead to three items of interest, a restaurant, a villa, and a shop. The restaurant is The Red House at number 37, the former Chez Louis, still cooking steak au poivre and soufflé Grand Marnier after all these years. The villa is at number 30, now seemingly something to do with the Communist Party Youth Movement, but a glorious example of the extravagant eccentricity of pre-war architecture in Shanghai. Its origins are obscure, but the design seems to owe something to Transylvania, with its gables and spires. The shop, the Shensi Old Wares Store, is at the junction with Yanan Lu, and has a goodly selection of fob watches and old embroidery.

The Huaihai road again

Once back on Huaihai Lu you will pass the Harbin Grocery at 919 and bakeries selling traditional Chinese sweetmeats such as green rice dumplings stuffed with red beans, which are made especially for the Qing Ming Festival on 5 April, when dead relatives are remembered. At 999 is a little shop that sells different types of Chinese tea. The staff are very friendly and will let you sample one or more of their teas, especially if they expect your visit. They normally stock the most famous of Chinese teas, from neighbouring Zhejiang Province, 'Long Jing'. The telephone number is 376382.

A little way to the east of the tea shop, on the other side of the road, is Shanyang Park. This is one of the most delightful of Shanghai Parks. It is small, with the distinctive outline of a large Russian Orthodox Church as a backdrop (this church, now a warehouse, is on Xinle Lu, to the north of the park) and adorned with carefully cultivated flower beds. Late April sees the garden dense with blossom. A little shop at the back sells cakes, chocolate and beer, and the tea house and its terrace are usually packed with retired men playing chess. One of the reasons, apparently, for the care taken in the cultivation of the garden is that the head gardener has been working there for many years, since it was a private garden owned by a certain Mr Xie.

At 1074 Huaihai Lu there is the Swan Pavilion Restaurant which claims to specialise in Italian cooking, but which includes on the menu 'fresh sausage roll à la Germany'.

Gradually the road becomes more residential. At the junction with Donghu Lu is one of the entrances to one of the villas that go to make up the Dong Hu Guest House. This is villa number 7 and is the former home of the Al Capone of Shanghai, Du Yuesheng (see 'Big Eared Du and Pockmarked Huang' in Chapter 13). When renovations are complete, it should be possible to catch a glimpse of the interior. To the north, where Donghu Lu meets Xinle Lu is a rather unassuming local restaurant with no name that deals mostly in dumplings — they are exellent. If luxury is required, the newly completed Hilton is within walking distance to the north. However, if you are going in that direction and in search of liquid refreshment, head for 'Jam's Bar' at 506 Wulumuqi Lu. This is yet another example of the changes taking place in Shanghai as people are encouraged to work for themselves. The owner, Mr Zhou Jing Gang, used to be a factory worker but seized the opportunity to start his own business. His first effort, the 'Smiling Bar' is at 449 Wulumuqi Lu. Success enabled him to open another, hence 'Jam's Bar'. Both are rather small, but well laid out, and comfortable. People like Mr Zhou have nothing with which to make comparisons, so this is a fine effort. There is imported beer at prices lower than in the hotels, music that does not impose, and attentive service. Mr Zhou's wife speaks some English. The bars are open from noon until late (depends upon business), and noodles and coffee and tea are available at Jam's until late. (See p.85).

Returning to Huaihai Lu

If you need cash, there is a branch of the Bank of China at 1162. Credit cards may be used to obtain FECs as well as travellers cheques and foreign currency. Closed on Sundays, it is open at other times from 0900 to 1130 and from 1300 to 1630.

Although the road becomes more residential, there are a few other shops of possible interest before reaching Soong Ching-Ling's former residence. At 1274 there is the Xinkang Second Hand Furniture Store; at 1297-1305 the Chong Shin Old Arts and Crafts Store; at 1324 the Yong Long Grocery, which sells 'Moon cakes'; and at 1834 the sales outlet of the Jade Carving Factory.

The former residence of Soong Ching-Ling

This is at 1843 Huahai Lu. After the death of Sun Yat Sen, his wife Soong Ching-Ling continued to play an important role in the shaping of China's destiny. She became disillusioned with Chiang Kai Shek and the Guomindang and, when it split into left wing and right wing factions, she sided with the more revolutionary of the two and went to Moscow. She returned later to help with the war effort and, when the Communists took power she was made an honorary President of the People's Republic of China. She was allowed two homes by the state. One was in Peking, where she died in 1981, the other at this address, where she lived mostly between 1948 and 1963. She is buried in the Wanguo Cemetery on Hongqiao Lu in the family vault.

The house was built by a Greek boat captain in the 1920s. It is furnished as it was on the day she died, with discreet elegance, mostly with gifts that she had received over the years from eminent visitors to her home. There is, for example, a carpet that was given her by Chairman Mao, bamboo work from Kim Il Sung, the North Korean leader, and a portrait by the Russian painter Jaspar. Her bedroom is furnished with what was part of her dowry. There is a well tended garden and apart from anything else the house is a fine example of the pre-1949 villa.

The entrance is on the main road, but security is rather tight, and you may need to press the bell on the large metal doors. It is open from 0900 to 1100 and from 1330 to 1600. The entrance fee is 2 yuan. There are sometimes English-speaking guides available.

Huangpu Park. The oldest park in Shanghai, once the preserve of the foreigner, is now open to all.

SEVENTEEN

The old town and the Yu Garden

Shanghai acquired its predominately European character only after the Opium Wars and the signing of the Treaty of Nanking which granted the use of certain areas to the foreign powers. Before that, Shanghai was a typical Chinese walled town of moderate importance, occupying the section of the city now known as 'Nanshi' (formerly 'Nantao', meaning 'southern market'). The walls were razed in 1911, but their old course is clearly marked by what is now Renmin Lu and Zhonghua Lu, and the old town remains somehow distinct from the rest of the city, like an off-shore island connected by a causeway. Within, it matches the popular conception of a Chinese town — a maze of alleys and narrow thoroughfares squeezed between odd little shops and steamy restaurants serving dainties, morsels and titbits, all savorous and delicious. Together with this, the Yu Garden, erroneously known as the model for Willow Pattern china but still one of the most complete examples remaining of the traditional Chinese garden, is historically and topographically inseparable from the town itself.

Chinese Bund, a market, and a way to the old town

The Chinese Bund is what is now the southern extension of Zhongshan Er Lu, beginning at Fang Bang Zhong Lu. If it used to be one of the busiest streets of Shanghai, it no longer is. Before, it was home to dockyards, hospitals, and shipping, timber and rice offices. The wool merchants had their guild-house here, with its temple and theatre; a market with peep-shows and story-tellers used to thrive in a square just behind; and the Cathedral of Tungkadoo, with its fine organ, was close by. All that has gone, and in fact this part of the waterfront is the least interesting nowadays. It is interesting only to note that the Yangtse steamers and ships serving

Chinese coastal cities berth at the large terminal that stretches along a goodly part of the harbour front. Nevertheless, one may enter the old town from here and there are good reasons for doing so, for as you go westwards along Dongmen Lu, you meet Wai Xiang Gua Jie ('Salty Melon Street') on your left. This is the food market street, huge and fascinating. It is divided into sections — fish, turtles, dried foods, seeds, eggs, sea creatures of a mysterious nature, poultry, bamboo, and fruit. Small restaurants serve stallholder and customer alike. It is open every day from the early morning onwards.

Continuing westwards will bring you to Fanbang Zhong Lu. Try to find a stall selling Luo Buo Ci Bin, which is a kind of delicious pasty. There are a few peculiarities along here — for instance, a factory making screws, and the Yi Cheng Traditional Medicine Shop, in classical Chinese style. A little beyond this is the old entrance to the heart of the old town — the Temple of the City God and the streets around the Yu Garden.

The Temple of the City God (Cheng Huang Miao)

The history of this area is rather confused. What follows is a distillation of conflicting accounts.

When Shanghai achieved the status of a county, it was considered essential that the spirit of a great man of the past be invoked to guard the city against evil and misfortune. That spirit was to be Qin Yu Bo, born in 1295, who had lived at the end of the Yuan dynasty and beginning of the Ming. He entered government service at the age of 49, and was considered a wise and able administrator. He was invited by the new Ming emperor to join his court, but refused on the grounds that it was an act of disloyalty to serve two dynasties, especially when mourning his mother — how could a man who was both disloyal and unfilial serve the emperor? Following his death the emperor pronounced him as guardian of Shanghai city. Over the ensuing centuries the worthiness of Qin has been questioned but the temple was built and rebuilt many times anyway, each time bigger than the last, and by the end of the eighteenth century it even had its own garden (the inner or East garden of today's Yu Garden). As for the original Yu Garden, it was built by one Pan Yunduan, a native of Shanghai, who had been in public service in Sichuan, to please his father. Occupying about 12 acres (five hectares), it was started in 1559 and completed in 1577 (Ming dynasty), by which time his father was already dead. The garden, built in the classical Chinese manner, with rockeries, bridges, lakes, and pavilions, fell into disrepair, however, as the fortunes of the Pan family declined. In the eighteenth century the East Garden (today's inner garden) was added, and quickly became part of the temple, whilst the West garden (which includes the famous tea-house, or mid-lake pavilion, an eighteenth century addition), was sold to merchants, who used the pavilions as offices and shops. It is uncertain who financed the construction of the East garden in 1709 (presumably members of the Pan family), but it seems clear that by the end of the eighteenth century it was the merchants who were financing its upkeep. Shanghai was, after all, prospering and the Temple of the City God (Cheng Huang Miao) was already part temple, part bazaar. It seems probable that the construction of the tea-house was sponsored by merchants too, who used it as the main meeting place for the discussion of business. It became a tea-house only at the end of the last century. As for the original Yu Garden, it was to serve as headquarters for two rather disparate groups: one, in 1842, was that of the British land force led by Liutenant-General Gough, as part of the campaign to open the treaty ports; the other, in the 1850s, was the 'Small Swords Society', a group of rebels wishing to restore the Ming Dynasty.

The temple today

Thus the ornate gate off Fangbang Zhong Lu is the original Ming entrance to the City Temple. In front of you is what is left of the temple itself. This is the latest in a long line of reconstructions, and dates back only to 1927. Now it is a large shop, retaining a bazaar atmosphere. It will be remembered that the whole area had become something of a market place by the middle of last century, as well as a gathering place for the townsfolk. In the 1930s it was an area of refreshment stalls, incense shops, toy salesmen, and jugglers. At the far end of the temple/shop is a good jade/jewellery shop, and others dealing in fans, silver chop sticks, calligraphy brushes with porcelain handles, and leather.

At the northern end of the Temple, turn left, or west, bringing you on to Yu Yuan Road. You will pass, on your right, a bird and plant shop, next to the Lubolong dumpling restaurant at 131. Adjacent to that is the Nanxiang Dumpling House. On your left you will pass a clothes shop, a magazine seller, a snuff shop and another clothes shop. Behind this is the Hong Guang Button shop, and next to that, around the corner, Ningbo Tang Tuan, famous for its exquisite sweet Ningpo 'pigeon egg' dumplings, and for 'Zhong zhi', glutinous rice and meat wrapped in lotus leaves. Nearby is 'Gui

Hua Ting', at 108 Yu Yuan Lu, well known for noodles. The tea-house (Huxinting) is clearly visible from here, sitting astride the 'nine zig-zag bridge'(zigzag to foil devils), and surrounded by water alive with dense shoals of glittering goldfish. The tea-house is famous in its own right, but has received additional attention following the visit of the Queen of England in 1986. Apart from its historical value, it is worthwhile taking a pot of tea here to cool down and to enjoy the surroundings. Old Chinese buildings were constructed with the climate in mind, and thus are shady and attractive to whatever breeze is around. Tickets for tea are purchased at the entrance: three yuan for first grade green tea upstairs or one yuan downstairs; two yuan for second grade upstairs or 80 fen downstairs; and one yuan and fifty fen for red (black) tea upstairs and fifty fen downstairs.

The Yu Garden

As we have seen, the original garden was a Ming dynasty construction, and has had something of a mixed history. It is hard to identify the precise boundaries of the Pan family garden since different accounts give different dates and some of the facts do not tally. If the above account is correct we can say that the tea-house and the 'inner garden' (i.e. the part adjoining the old Temple of the City God) are eighteenth century additions to a sixteenth century garden which covers the area from the entrance (north of the tea-house and the zigzag bridge) to Fuyou Lu on the north side, Anren Lu on its eastern side, and the beginning of the inner garden on its south side. The exit is in the inner garden and brings you back on to Yu Yuan Lu, hard by the Temple of the City God and the dumpling shops. It seems, too, that the garden originally extended further westward, taking in some of the present day bazaar.

Despite these complications, the present day garden is an excellent example of miniature landscaping. The real Chinese gardens, with pavilions, landscaping, and variety of flowers and trees 'are integrated works of art, lyrical and picturesque. The overall appearance, though man-made, should appear to be formed by nature'. It is not necessary to reproduce entire scenes — it is enough to hint at a scene, provided that the angle is right, and that skilful use of water and rock create the restful illusion of hill and lake. Flowers and trees play a similar role. Although they may, of course, be appreciated in their own right, in the landscaped garden they are to create a particular effect. They give life to a scene, yet their colour and texture soften the hard outline of water and rock — thus their position and shape are also important. In fact, straight lines are to be avoided as much as possible, especially in the case of paths and corridors, to enhance the illusions of length and depth. Pavilions should be positioned in accordance with their relationship with the rocks and water. They should never, therefore, be placed at the summit of a hill, but against it, so that the harmonies of scale are maintained. Furniture should be in the traditional style, whether of wood or stone, again for the purpose of harmony. Nevertheless, in some ways the pavilions must act as a draw for the visitor, since the Chinese garden is essentially a place of human contemplation,

The Dragon Wall in the Yu Garden. A symbol of ancient imperial power winds its way around the walls.

where man can coexist with nature without being overpowered by it. Whether the theory works in practice is for the visitor to decide.

The first pavilion immediately in front of the entrance is Three Ears of Corn Hall. Apart from being the vestibule and greeting place for visitors, it was here that imperial edicts would have been read and studied, and festivities of a sombre kind, the emperor's birthday for example, celebrated. Beyond is the Hall for Viewing the Grand Rockery, with its magnificent roof and eaves. As the name suggests, it looks across at the rockery, which is supposed to be one of the finest of its kind in China. Typically Ming, it is an example of the open type, where ravines are hewn out of the hills, to give an effect of grandeur and massiveness. At the time of its construction, this rockery was one of the highest points in the city, allowing an uninterrupted view across the Huangpu River. If you want to climb the rockery now, it will mean a small extra payment.

Between the Hall for viewing the Rockery and the rockery itself is a pretty pond, again replete with seething shoals of goldfish. Follow the path around the pond, past the guardian lions cast in the Yuan dynasty, walk along the corridor, bear right, and immediately right again. Here is a little arbour overlooking another pool, variously known as the 'Pavilion for Viewing Frolicking Fish', the 'Water Pavilion' and the 'Mirror Pavilion'. In front of you is a view of a creek, or the Yangtse Gorges, or whatever the imagination likes. Just by the arbour, on the right, is the serpentine trunk of a 300 year old wistaria. Reversing your steps from the Mirror Pavilion, turn right at the junction into the double corridor with its windows of various shapes which frame each vista differently, emerging in front of the Ten Thousand Flower Pavilion which looks upon another rockery. Note the 400-year-old ginko tree. Carry on through the wall, noting the dragon on top that surrounds much of the garden. Once through the wall you will see the Hall for Heralding Spring ahead. The Small Sword Society was based here during the rebellion of 1853, and there is a small exhibition commemorating the fact. Opposite this pavilion is another that was used for operatic performances (not dissimilar to the Great Stage in the Summer Palace in Peking). Turning back on yourself, but bearing slightly left, go through another arch into a bamboo grove. Here is another area of pavilions, pools, and fish. In one of the pavilions is a display of traditional Chinese musical instruments, and sometimes there are performances of folk music given here. Another pavilion has by now become a shop, selling Wuxi pottery, guidebooks, teapots, and Nanking coloured pebbles. Continuing southwards towards the exit in the 'inner garden', you will not fail to notice a large cratered rock, standing solitary. This is the 'Exquisite Jade Rock' and is typical of the ornamental rock found in most imperial gardens such as the Summer Palace in Peking. Such rocks come from Taihu Lake in Jiangsu Province; they are submerged beneath the waters and left for as long as it takes to produce the desired effect. Subsequently, they were placed in strategic places and incense smoke would waft up and out through the pits and holes, creating an effect mysterious and majestic. To the right of this, in one of the former pavilions, is an antique shop. The gate sometimes appears to be closed, but will usually be opened upon request. Behind the jade rock is the entrance to the 'inner garden' where there is often a display of traditional lanterns. Lavatories are available here, and the exit takes you back out into the bazaar.

Out of the old town

The street names are not clearly marked here, but since the area is small it is hard to avoid stumbling on anything of interest. Back in the bazaar you will pass the Lubolang Restaurant again, and at 124 there is a snuff shop that also sells pipes. Follow the lake around to the right, past the zig-zag bridge, to find another pair of restaurants on its banks. Just across the way from them is the Huaxian Pottery Store and, just to the north of that, the Wanli Walking Stick Store. At 6 Yinghui Lu, to the west of the pottery store, is a shop selling teas, and close to that a vegetarian restaurant. Going north from here, passing the umbrella shop, will bring you into the old square, where you cannot miss Tong Han Chun Ting on the left which has served as an apothecary since 1783. Old medicine pots are prominently displayed. Looking across the square from the shop, in the right hand corner is a chop stick shop.

Go north from the square to leave the old town. You will emerge on Fuyou Lu; to your right is a rather magnificent old cinema, and to your left the famous 'Shanghai Lao Fandian' (Old Shanghai Restaurant). Continuing westward along Fuyou Lu will bring you to the functioning mosque, but the first right, Lishui Lu, takes you northwards, past Nanshi District Traditional Medicine Clinic at number 9, and eventually to Sichuan Lu, crossing Renmin Lu and the site of the old wall. There is no trace of the wall, although to the west, at the Renmin Lu junction with Fujian Lu, is an ancient stone arch that looks as if it might have had some connection. The wall was first built in 1554 as protection against Japanese pirates, permission having first been sought from the Ming Emperor. It was surrounded by a moat, and had enough space atop its ten metre ramparts to accommodate men and wheelbarrows. The circumference was about five kilometres, and thirty towers stood at intervals along it to be defended by archers. Ten gates gave access to the countryside and river. Four of them were water gates, linking the canals inside with those outside beyond the moat.

Once on Sichuan Lu (see Chapter 16, 'The vicinity of Nanking Road') you are about 30 minutes' walk from Nanking Road.

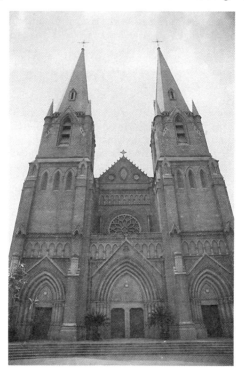

St Ignatius, Xujiahui. Badly damaged during the Cultural Revolution, the twin spires have been rebuilt and the cathedral is functioning once again.

EIGHTEEN

Visits and excursions

The Jade Buddha Temple

There are at least three functioning Buddhist temples in Shanghai, all of which have reopened following the disaster of the Cultural Revolution, and appear to be flourishing. Two of them are mentioned elsewhere — the Jing An in Chapter 16 and Longhua below under 'Parks'. The most famous, and perhaps the most spectacular, is the Jade Buddha Temple in the north west of the city, on Anyuan Lu. (Tel:537083)

It is not, by Buddhist standards, an old temple, and in fact has a history of only just over one hundred years. During the last century a local abbot, Wei Ken, went on a pilgrimage to Tibet and thence to Burma, where he was presented with two jade Buddhas. When he returned to Shanghai, he raised money for the purchase of land where a temple could be built to house them. It was completed in 1882, in the Jiangwan district, and moved to its present site in 1918 following a fire. Despite its recent construction, the temple buildings are in Song Dynasty style, with sharply raised eaves, roofs decorated with charming figurines, and heavily varnished woodwork, since it is an active place of worship, and despite the casual visitors, there is a genuine atmosphere of devotion.

The temple consists of three main buildings connected by two courts. The first, on the right as you enter, is the Heavenly King Hall. Along its sides are the four heavenly kings, defenders of the heavenly kingdom and protectors of the living. The first on the left is the Eastern King, who praises Buddha and assuages evil with the music of his pipa. The next is the Southern King, so called 'king of developing merit', whose aim is to persuade people of the virtue of a benevolent life, and who smites evil with his sword. The first on the right is the Western King, the king of far-sightedness — his eyes penetrate any falsehood or deceit. Next to him, the Northern King, the king of virtue, who holds a streamer with Buddhist inscriptions written on it. These four are supposed to inspire the believer, or non-believer, with fear, but the four weapons in their hands constitute a sort of incantation 'good omen of favourable weather for agriculture'. In one of the cabinets in the middle sits Maitreya, or the 'laughing Buddha', the successor to the Buddha himself, Sakyamuni. He offers welcome, and is suggestive of prosperity and well being in the future. Behind him, the Chief Guardian and Defender of Buddhist Law, the austere Skanda Bodhisattva.

Across the courtyard is the Grand Hall of Magnificence and, before it, an incence burner donated by believers anxious for their dead relatives. The names of the donors and their relatives are inscribed on the tripod. In the hall itself, you are confronted by the large statues of three Buddhas, under a glorious spiral ceiling. The statue in the centre is of Sakyamuni, founder of Buddhism; to the left is the Medicine Buddha, able to relieve worshippers of all pain and suffering; and to the right the Amitabha Buddha, able to guide true believers to paradise. Behind these three is a colourful vision of Guanyin, Goddess of Mercy.

Services normally take place here at 0830 and at 1430.

By leaving the Grand Hall of Magnificence through the back, bearing left, right, and then right again, you will arrive at the Jade Buddha Chamber. You then climb the stairs and, exchanging your shoes for slippers, may proceed to the chamber itself. The statue of Sakyamuni is 1.9 metres high, and carved out of a solid piece of white jade. The library to the left and right houses 7,200 volumes of Buddhist scripture. Photography is not permitted here, and there is usually a monk in attendance to ensure that this rule is observed. Offerings may be made, and incense sticks burnt.

There are two corridors along the east and west sides of the temple. On the west side is a chapel with a smaller jade statue of Sakyamuni in recumbant pose, as he was at the moment of his death. Pictures describe important moments in his life, and cabinets contain religious carvings that date back to the Tang Dynasty. The chapels at the northern end of the west corridor are used for offering prayers for dead friends and relatives. You will find the lavatories at this end too. Back along the corridor are small shops selling religious paraphernalia and postcards (including the Jade Buddha). The vegetarian restaurant is here too (cognac and whisky are available!), and the guest house for visiting believers.

The eastern corridor has a chapel with a black Buddha, and a bell, shaped something akin to an axehead, and a large drum stick in the form of a dragon and a fish. Note on the roof of the chapels here carvings that illustrate the classic Chinese legend 'Journey to the west'.

The temple now supports 160 Buddhist monks, of whom almost half are novices. The temple is also the home of the Sangha Buddhist Institute.

The entrance fee is one yuan. Guides are sometimes available. Opening Hours are from 0800 until 1700, with services at 0830 and 1430. The temple is particularly interesting on the first and fifth days of the lunar month, when hordes of worshippers come to pay their respects.

Parks

Shanghai boasts a number of attractive parks. They provide pleasant refuges from the crowds and noise of the downtown areas, as well as being open hides for watching something of Shanghai life. In the parks you can observe to your heart's content parents walking their children, grandparents playing chess or airing their pet birds, aficionados practising 'tai qi' (Chinese keep-fit) in the early morning, and students practising their English. You may have to pay a small entrance fee, usually a few fen only. Many of the parks have already been mentioned in passing through the former concessions (Chapter 16) — in that case they are here merely repeated by name.

Central
Renmin Park (People's Park) The old racecourse: see under 'Nanking Road'.
Huangpu Park The oldest and most infamous park: see under 'The Bund'.
Jing An Park See under 'Bubbling Well Road' and 'Jing An Temple'.

Central (south)
Fuxing Park The former 'French Park': see the French Concession under 'Fuxing Park'.
Shan Yang Park Charming park off the Huaihai Lu: see French Concession under 'Huaihai Lu'.

Southwest
Guilin Park Tucked away amidst the industries of Shanghai, not far from the carpet factory, is this attractive park built in Suzhou style,

with pavilions, rockeries, pools and bushes, in the grounds of what was a house belonging to Huang Jinrong, the gangster. The entrance fee is five fen, and it is open from 0700 until 1700.

Longhua Park, and Longhua Pagoda and Temple 2853 Longhua Lu. Tel:388104. This park has a long and confused history. The pagoda and temple were, according to a stone inscription dating from the Ming dynasty, constructed in the third century A.D., but it seems that this is no more than the following legend. A certain Hui, son of the minister of Kangju State in the Western regions of the Kingdom of Wu, left home to become a monk. His wanderings took him to the Longhua marshes, where he found that 'the water and sky were of one colour' and 'there were no traces of people or tracks of vehicles'. It thus seemed a good place for meditation and he built a house there. The Dragon King, in whose realm he was living, proposed that a temple be built there; and when the monk went to Nanking to see Sun Quan, the King of Wu, it was decreed tat 13 pagodas would be built to house 13 fragments of the bones of the Buddha. Longhua was one of them.

Modern scholarship has declared that both temple and pagoda date from the tenth century, during the Song dynasty. There is, however, a poem extant by the Tang poet Pi Rixie that indicates the presence of something earlier:

'The ancient temple, except the name, is lost,

People still walk on the bridge, slipping with frost,

The crescent moon with its dim light hangs low

On the creek is no more the pagoda's shadow'.

At any event, the style of the pagoda is most certainly Song, although it has been damaged and repaired so many times over the centuries that only the design can be said to be original. The temple was almost completely destroyed during the Taiping Heavenly Kingdom, but a monk, Guan Zhu, was able to garner enough money to have most of it reconstructed. This century it has been variously used as a warehouse and a barracks. The pagoda is an octagonal, seven-storey structure some 40 metres high. It is made of brick and wood, and is adorned with bells to prevent birds from nesting on it.

Now the whole has been restored to its proper use, and there are some 90 monks in residence. The present abbot is vice-president of the China Buddhist Association, and there is an attached seminary for 30 aspiring monks. There is also a hotel and vegetarian restaurant.

The park is famous for its peach blossom. When horses and carriages were first introduced to Shanghai by foreigners during the nineteenth century, it was a sign of status to be able to bring back a sprig of fresh blossom. Before, the journey had been too long.

The park is on the site of a Guomindang Garrison Headquarters prison where, between 1928 and the anti-Japanese War, more than 800 communists were put to death. During the Japanese occupation, the area around the pagoda became an airfield and internment camp.

Every April the surrounding streets become a market. It is immense and traders travel miles to take part. The merchandise is mostly domestic but the atmosphere is of a carnival.

Botanical Gardens 1110 Long Wu Lu. Tel: 389413. They lie to the southwest of the Longhua Park, (about 15 minutes by bus number 56 from Xujiawui) covering about 1,000 mu (about 25 acres) and were built in 1954. Famous for its potted landscapes, there are a hundred or so kinds of miniature trees, a rockery and 9,000 pots of flowers and trees on exhibition. Some of the miniature trees are several hundred years old. About one hundred species of orchid are on display according to the season.

West

Zhongshan Park Built in 1914, this park was known as Jessfield Park before 1949. Part of it was the campus of St John's American University, now the East China Institute of Health. This was one of those institutions, founded by the American Episcopal Church, that introduced generations of Chinese to Western ideas. Its values were Christian, but it also allowed young Chinese to examine their own society with a more critical eye. The park contains a peony garden and a rose garden.

North

Hongkou Park This park lies to the north of Suzhou Creek in that part of the International Settlement that was dominated by the Japanese ('Little Tokyo'). The park contains a large lake and there are rowing boats for hire (crowded in the summer); exhibitions are held on occasion, for example the autumnal chrysanthemum show. As always, the park is filled with citizens trying to do those things that crowded conditions render difficult; and so there are painters, fishermen, and opera singers. Shrubs abound and so do butterflies.

Above all the park is well known for its tributes to Lu Xun, the progressive writer of the early part of this century, who lived in Shanghai from 1927 until his death in 1936. His most famous work is *The true story of Ah Q* in which he lampoons the Chinese national character, with its contradictory elements of servility and swagger. He was one of the products of the May 4th movement, that literary protest at the cavalier manner in which China was treated by the Great Powers at the end of the First World War. One of the achievements of the movement — one with which Lu Xun was heavily involved — was the simplification of Chinese script. In Hong Kong and in Taiwan the older, more complex calligraphy is still in use, but the mainland has benefited from the work of Lu Xun and his colleagues.

In the park, to the right as you enter, is a museum devoted to his life and works. The museum shop sells modern paintings and some attractive 'ex libris' leaves. The tomb of Lu Xun, and a bronze image, are to the left as you enter. His remains were transferred here in 1956, on the twentieth anniversary of his death.

Lu Xun's former home is open to the public, and is located at 9, Dalu Xinchun, Sanyin Lu, just to the south of the park. The rooms are supposed to be arranged as they were when he died.

Shanghai Zoo

The zoo is on the Hongqiao Road, in the west of the city, not far from the airport. It was built in 1954 on the site of a golf club used by 'foreign adventurers in old days' as one guidebook has it. There are over 3,000 animals from more than 350 species. Some of the animals are rarities native to China (giant panda, golden monkey, Yangtze crocodile, Asian elephant, white-lipped deer, and the Manchurian tiger), and of course there are plenty of representatives from around the world. Some of these animals are extremely rare indeed (of the famous panda there are fewer than a thousand left in the wild, and frantic conservation efforts notwithstanding, numbers continue to decline), so it may be worth having a look whilst it is still possible.

Museums

Shanghai Museum of Art and History 16 Henan Nan Lu. The museum is housed in the former premises of the Zhong Hui Bank — the Chinese characters are still visible in the windows. The bank in question was connected with that ubiquitous character of pre-war Shanghai, the gangster Du Yuesheng, or 'Big-eared Du'. Exerting almost total control over the opium trade of Shanghai in the 1920s, Du was in constant search for respectability that would act as a cover and enable him to make more money. Hence the bank, sponsored by him and two others, Du becoming president of the board. The Zhong Hui was not among the largest of Shanghai banks — but that was not the point. Its purpose was to issue loans on security in opium trafficking and in gambling, the very businesses in which Du was so heavily involved. The chief accountant of the largest of the Shanghai gambling houses was none other than Jin Tingsun, who was a director of the bank.

The present building housing the museum was not the first Zhong Hui headquarters. This was the second, built in 1934 at a cost of 1½ million dollars. The bank itself occupied only the ground floor, whose northern part was the business department, and the northern part of the first floor, which housed the general administration offices and the office of the president, Du himself. Other parts were rented to companies like the Gong Mo yarn store, or insurance companies and the like.

Museums were not really in Du's line but this is now one of the finest in China. The first floor, recently completely redesigned, is devoted to the display of bronzes. This is not just a show of spear heads, but a magnificent collection of all manner of food containers, bells, wine containers and mirrors from the land where the use of bronze probably reached its apogee. Ancient methods of casting and mining are explained (in English too), and the work of the minority peoples of China is given an airing.

The second floor is an exhibition of ceramics. There are some explanations in English, but the beauty of the exhibits speaks for itself. Most periods are represented, from the earliest claywork to the distinctive Tang tri-coloured pottery to the perfection of white Ding ware and eighteenth century Jingde ware. The souvenir shop, specialising in reproductions, is on this floor.

The third floor is sculpture and painting. Again, the collection is excellent: religious work is represented by material in bronze, stone, wood, and clay. There are examples from the celebrated grottoes at Dunhuang.

Very few of the exhibited paintings have English explanations but nevertheless the collection is magnificent. There are polo scenes and pictures of horse and carriage from the Han dynasty; Tang dynasty women offering gifts to Princess Yong Tai; and paintings from the great schools of the Song dynasty. Here one can see the originals of so much that is sold in the shops, and follow the subtle changes that have occurred in Chinese painting over the centuries.

The museum is open from 0900 until 1645 (last admission 1530), and the cost is one yuan FEC.

Shanghai Natural History Museum 260 Yanan Dong Lu. Some of the exhibits have explanations in English. The first floor has a remarkable display of embalmed corpses up to 3200 years old, and of dinosaur skeletons. The second floor is mainly marine life, such as worms, shells, enormous crabs and fish.

The third displays snakes, birds and mammals. Some of the items on the upper floors look a bit mangy, but on the whole this is a fine, comprehensive collection.

It is open from 0900 until 1530, and closed on Monday afternoons. Admission costs two yuan.

Arts and Crafts Research Institute

The Institute at 79 Fenyang Lu (former Rue Pichow), is worth visiting if only to see the interior of a grand villa in the French style. On the other hand it also provides an opportunity to see members of the Institute at work. This Institute, the first in China, opened in 1956, specialises in dough figurine modelling, lacquerware, woollen embroidery, paper cutting, and boxwood carving. The purpose of such institutes is to create new ideas, to perfect old ones, and to act as adviser to the workshops and factories in the area. There are frequent demonstrations of the more mercurial arts (dough modelling and paper cutting), and opportunities to watch other artists and artisans at their more laborious acts of creation. Finally, there is the inevitable shop.

Touring the Huangpu River

A pleasant half day can be spent by taking a cruise down the Huangpu to the mouth of the Yangtse. The round trip lasts about three and a half hours, and begins from the wharf on the Bund, opposite Beijing Lu.

Since 1852 Shanghai has been the largest port in China, and has grown to be one of the largest in the world — by 1985 the port was handling a record 112.9 million tons, a third of the total handled at China's main ports (despite the setback of the Cultural Revolution which meant that the volume of 1960 was only exceeded in 1972). In all, there are some 14 kilometres of wharfs, 98 berths and 3,500 handling machines. Two modernised container berths of 10 metres were completed in 1985. Many other enterprises and factories have their own facilities along the river — the power plant, the iron and steel works, the chemical works and the oil refinery. About two thirds of inbound and outbound cargo for Shanghai is handled by the port and as much as 99 per cent of foreign trade. In 1985 over 3,600 vessels called at the port. There are about 300 warehouses with a floor space of 410,000 sq.m for storage and an open area of some 950,000 sq.m for storage outside. More than one hundred 10,000-ton vessels can be handled at any one time, and high tide will allow vessels of up to 50,000 tons to enter and unload. Yet because of the recent boom in the Chinese economy, the port facilities are inadequate and new cargo areas are being built.

The Huangpu is about 110 kms in length, and empties into the Yangtse 28 kms downstream. Its average width through the city is 400 metres, and its average depth eight metres.

The excursion ships are very comfortable in first class, with sun deck, bar, and shop. There is often a performance given on the return journey, perhaps a magic show, or acrobatics. On your way downstream, you will pass Suzhou Creek on your left, then Shanghai Mansions Hotel, the International Passenger Terminal, the Yangshupu Power Plant, and Fuxing Island, the site of Chiang Kai Shek's last stand before making for Taiwan, and of Shanghai's earliest industrial estate. Finally, the lookout tower at Wusong Kou (scene of a great naval battle against the British in 1842); and the Yangtse, with its muddy, turbulent waters. Directly in front of the boat is the dim outline of the island of Chongming, sitting in the middle of the great river. Here the boat will turn around and return to Shanghai.

The number of departures is variable, but there is certainly at least one a day in the afternoon, departing at about 1300. Tickets cost upwards of 15 yuan, and are available from the point of embarkation, about a quarter of a mile north of the Peace Hotel, at 28, Zhongshan Dong Lu.

Pudong

Pudong is the industrial area across the Huangpu from the Bund. There is not much to see (there is a park), but few foreigners go there, and it offers the best view of the Bund. The ferryboat leaves every few minutes from a jetty on the Bund, at the point where it meets Yanan Dong Lu, just after the footbridge, by the old signal tower from which used to be displayed the weather forecasts for the China coast as they were relayed from the Jesuit-run Observatory at Siccawei (now Xujiawei). The ticket can only be purchased on the Shanghai side, and costs six fen return — single tickets cannot be purchased. The journey takes five minutes and bicycles may be taken aboard.

Ziccawei Catholic Cathedral

Variously spelt in the past as above, or with one 'c', or Siccawei, this area in the southwest corner of the city, not far from the Sheraton and the Longhua Pagoda, is now known as Xujiawei. This corner of Shanghai had long associations with the Jesuits. An early resident, a certain Xu Guang Qi (1562-1633), was converted to Catholicism by the great Italian Jesuit, Mateo Ricci, and yet rose to become Grand Secretary to the Ming Court. Unlike other foreigners, the Jesuits succeeded in striking up a sort of relationship with the Chinese by the simple method of actually involving themselves in things Chinese — they learnt the language, made efforts to understand Chinese philosophy, and came to terms with Chinese manners and ways. They tried, too, to introduce elements of Western inventiveness to China, like watches, and geography and map-making. Xu, who met Ricci in 1600, translated European classics into Chinese, and amongst other things, invited the Jesuits to settle in Shanghai. There was a church, therefore, as early as 1608 within the city walls. French priests came too, and it was their presence that gave the French Government particular leverage when they demanded land in the late 1840s. As a result the French Jesuits occupied the area from 1848, making it an important base for their missionary work in the Yangtse Valley.

They established a museum (many of the exhibits are now housed in the Natural History Museum), schools, orphanages, and the Meteorological Observatory. This last achieved worldwide fame. It was linked to a network of seventy other stations from Irkutsk in Siberia to Viet-Nam. Its findings, as far as the weather was concerned, were relayed to the signal tower on the old French Bund.

Today's Cathedral of St Ignatius (158 Puxi Lu. Tel: 371328) was built between 1906 and 1911. Its red brickwork and gothic features, and its twin spires (rebuilt after their desecration, not to say dismantling, during the Cultural Revolution), are rather impressive. The interior, uncharacteristically austere for a Catholic church, has a couple of interesting features. Oriental fruits figure in the stained glass windows, and the pulpit is a remarkable Sino-European hybrid. There are services every day at 0500, 0600, and 0700.

Names and addresses of other places of worship are listed in Chapter 10.

NINETEEN

Farther afield

Shanghai is well located for visiting other sights and other cities. Some can easily be reached by bus or bicycle, whilst others would be more easily reached by train. Although Shanghai is well used to foreigners, you do not have to go very far out of the city to meet people for whom they are still something of a curiosity. It is also an opportunity to see the Chinese countryside and farming methods that in some cases have hardly changed in hundreds of years.

Most of the following places are in fact still in the municipality of Shanghai, which, it will be remembered, is divided into the city proper and nine metropolitan counties. The whole municipality is administered directly from Peking, despite its geographical location in Jiangsu Province.

Wherever possible, you are advised to go by taxi, unless you have a bicycle, and/or patience, and/or a lot of time. It is possible to reach most of the places in the area by bus, but it is something of a performance (see under Qingpu).

Jiading

Jiading is one of the counties, and the county seat of the same name boasts a Confucian temple, dating back to the Song Dynasty, and completed in 1252. It now houses the county museum. In the same town is the Fahua Pagoda, which was originally constructed during the same dynasty and restored in the early part of this century.

Nanxiang, famous for its dumplings, is also known for its Guyi Garden. There has been an ornamental garden on this site since the Ming Dynasty (1368-1644), and over the years it has been enlarged until it now covers an area of over fifteen acres.

In Zhenru Town the Zhenru Buddhist Temple is an excellent example of fourteenth century architecture.

Jinshan

This is another of the counties, to the south of the city. Huayan Pagoda is a well preserved example of Ming architecture in the town of Songwen. A bus can be taken at the Western Bus Station at 240 Caoxi Bei Lu. The county is also famous for its painters, country women who produce brightly coloured pictures of rural life in the 'naif' style.

Qingpu

Qingpu county lies to the west of Shanghai. The capital, Qingpu town, is well known for its Qushui Yuan (Meandering Stream Garden) on the shores of Da Ying Hu. This is a scenic Chinese garden built in the eighteenth century. Dianshan Hu is the huge lake that supplies Shanghai with its water. On its shores a sort of resort has been built, part of which is a recreation of the garden that figures in the classic novel *Dream of Red Mansions.* It could be rather attractive, but is spoilt by the fact that rubbish left by visitors has been allowed to accumulate. A journey out there is worthwhile, however, if only to get into the country and enjoy the lake. Getting there by public transport is not easy, however, and a taxi is recommended. If you want to test the difficulties involved in travelling by bus, this is how you would get there.

● Leave from the Western Bus Station at 240 Cao Xi Bei Lu for Qingpu town. Buses leave every 15 minutes, and the cost is 55 fen (at least it is cheap). There are no seat reservations, so try to get to the head of the queue. (It is possible to pay extra for unnumbered seat tickets, which theoretically entitle you to get on the bus before the others — this is only a theory.) The journey to Qingpu takes about an hour and a half.

● At Qingpu bus station buy another ticket for the lake area. You need to get off at a stop near Yangshe village, but it will be easier if you have everything written down in advance (CITS should be able to do this, or anyone you can find in your hotel). To the stop from Qingpu is a further one and a quarter hours.

● Then you follow the side road on foot to the resort. This takes about a half hour.

All that for about forty kilometres! The area around the resort is pretty — parkland, the lake itself and, if you are here late April, plenty of gorgeous blossom. There are a number of restaurants too. The buildings themselves look pretty authentic, even if faked

SHANGHAI REGION

Scale 1:4 500 000

deliberately. There is a fine pagoda, and a large array of pavilions, gardens, bamboo groves, rockeries and pools. The pavilions have in many cases been furnished with the appropriate period pieces and ornamentation. Apparently period films are often made here.

Songjiang

This is a county to the southwest of Shanghai, on the railway line to Hangzhou. Here stands the Square Pagoda that dates back to the Song Dynasty, and beside it is a Ming screen wall decorated with a bas-relief about 15 feet high and 20 feet long. It shows amongst other representations of human frailty a legendary beast named Tan, a symbol of greed.

At Gangbanghang, to the west of Songjiang town, there is a mosque dating back no later than the beginning of the reign of the Ming Emperor Yong Le, built to cater for the needs of the people from 'the Western Regions to worship Heaven'. It is considered to be one of the oldest Islamic buidings in China, and there is some evidence to support the theory that at least part of the mosque was constructed in the Mongolian Yuan Dynasty (fourteenth century). It is still active.

And beyond . . . . .

If you are spending more than a few days in Shanghai, there are several cities in the neighbouring provinces that warrant a visit: to the northwest, Suzhou, Waxi, Changzhou and Nanking; to the south, Hangzhou and Ningbo. With the exception of Suzhou, which can be visited in a single day (two would be better), all of these places would require at least an overnight stay, although two nights would be perfect. They can all be reached by train. Tickets can be arranged through CITS, or other travel agents, as can hotel accommodation and transfers. This will make things more expensive but it might well be worth it in the long run, since it is, as yet, only possible to buy one-way rail tickets, and obtaining transportation and a hotel once you have arrived at your destination will prove time-consuming. If you book an excursion through a travel agent, remember to take telephone numbers and addresses of the hotels and local branch of the agent concerned, in the event that your transfer fails to show up.

The same 'soft' and 'hard' class distinctions apply for daytime travel on the trains as on the sleepers, except 'hard' really is what it implies, as well as being extremely crowded. On some of the services on the Shanghai-Nanking line there is an air-conditioned soft class carriage. Otherwise, both classes are cooled by banks of overhead electric fans during the summer months.

There are regular bus services to some of these places (much better than the bus service provided to more local destinations). The long-distance bus station is on Qiujiang Lu, not far from the former main North Railway Station. From here you can take buses to Hangzhou, Wuxi, and Changzhou. Tickets for buses to Suzhou are obtainable at the ticket office on Renmin Square close to the junction of Fuzhou Lu and Xizang Zhong Lu. Check from which point the bus leaves. Tickets are very cheap.

There are flights available to Hangzhou and Nanking.

Suzhou

Suzhuo is one of the prettiest cities in the country, retaining most completely the image of old China, with its canals and hump-back bridges. Traditionally, Suzhuo is the home of China's most beautiful women, although it is apparently the way they talk that is the main attraction. The city is officially twinned with Venice. The streets around the canals are narrow and shaded by plane trees, the houses whitewashed and brown-eaved, one side facing the street, the other facing the canal. It is a charming city for leisurely strolls, but Suzhuo has more to offer, for it is known as the city of gardens, of which more than a hundred still exist, in the Chinese miniature, ornamental style. The gardens, with their rockeries, lakes, and villas, were the homes of wealthy merchants and government functionaries, and the best examples are the 'Lingering Garden', 'The Humble Administrators Garden', and 'The Garden of the Master of the Fishing Nets'. Other things to see are:
— The Silk Embroidery Research Institute.
— Silk factories (reeling and weaving).
— Sandalwood fan factory.
— North Temple and Pagoda
— Suzhuo Bazaar and, in the same area, Xuanmiao Si (Taoist Temple of Mystery)
— Tiger Hill.
— Precious Belt Bridge (Baodai Qiao).
Both the last mentioned items are outside the city.

The journey from Shanghai by train takes just over an hour.

Wuxi

Wuxi was only an average trading town on the Grand Canal until this century, when money from Shanghai was invested in textiles and other industries; now it ranks somewhere in the top fifteen economic centres of China. The main attraction for the visitor is Taihu Lake (area: 2200 sq. kms), well known for its fishing and the rocks that are deliberately submerged in its waters. The movement of the water shapes the rocks so that they are suitable for placing in ornamental gardens. A pleasant day can be spent wandering in the vicinity of the lake, around its shores, or on one of the islands that can be reached by ferry. The main hotels are at the lakeside.

Apart from the lake, there is an interesting free market, a silk reeling factory (with shop), parks, and the Huishan Clay Figure Workshop.

Wuxi is a further half an hour beyond Suzhou by train. There are cheap centrally located hotels, but the best are by the lake: the Taihu, the Hubin, and the Shuixiu.

Changzhou

Another city on the Grand Canal, and another prosperous textile producer, sitting in the middle of thousands of acres of mulberry. Despite its industrial success, it is a city like Suzhou where everyday life is centred around the canals, and which has managed to retain much of its original charm. It doesn't have the ornamental gardens of Suzhou, and is further away from Shanghai, but it is likely to be far less crowded. The main attractions, apart from walking around the old streets, are:

— The Temple of Heavenly Tranquillity (Tianning Si), which is magnificent.

— A huge free market.

— Ornamental comb factory (boxwood combs painted with opera masks etc.)

— Red Plum Park.

The farms in this area are well worth a visit, if it can be organised; as is the Hospital of Traditional Medicine. Changzhou has a couple of acceptable hotels (airconditioned, etc) — the Changzhou, which is more central, and the Baidung, in the south of the town — and is about three hours by train from Shanghai.

Nanking

Nanking is the capital of Jiangsu Province, and has been the capital of China several times, notably during the rule of the first Ming Emperor, from whom the city derived its current character and dimensions, and during the short period of pre-eminence of the Guomindang from 1927 to 1949. It lies at the foot of the Purple Mountain, on the banks of the Yangtse, and is one of only two cities in China that still retain a complete city wall (the other is Xian), the longest of any city in the world. Many people find it the most appealing of China's big cities, perhaps because it exudes a sense of well-being, and because the people are unpretentiously friendly; or because old and new blend happily together, without the sense of upheaval or the violent contrast that one finds in other Chinese cities. As far as sightseeing is concerned, Nanking is noted for the Sun Yat Tsen Mausoleum, which is built into the Purple Mountain, a short drive outside the city walls, and:

— The Yangtse River Bridge (double-decker, for train and road vehicles)

— Ming Tomb, and its avenue of stone animals

— Nanking Museum (noted for its Jade Warrior)

— Ming Dynasty Drum Tower

— Zhonghua City Wall Gate, and fortifications

— Site of Ming Palace

— Purple Mountain Observatory (by prior arrangement only)

— A variety of parks (especially the Xuanwu with its zoo, bonzai exhibition, and lotus in the season).

The journey from Shanghai takes about six hours by train, and under an hour by aeroplane.

There are a number of good hotels — the best, the most central, and the most expensive is the Jinling, a joint venture skyscraper with revolving bar on the thirty-third floor, and a swimming pool (Xinjiekou Square; Tel: 44141, 41121); but the Nanjing (259, Zhongshan Bei Lu. Tel: 34121) is an older and more homely hotel set in a garden, is central enough, and is famed for its chocolate soufflé.

The Grand Canal

The Grand Canal, which links Peking with Hangzhou, was started 2400 years ago. By the time it was completed, it connected not only several major cities and ports, but also four major rivers — the Yangtse, the Yellow (Huang He), the Huai, and the Qiantang. At 1800 miles long, it remains the longest man-made waterway in the world, and is still an important means of local transportation, very much alive with strings of small barges loaded with anything from bales of silk to heaps of coal. To travel its whole length to Hangzhou, as newlyweds used to do once upon a time, is no longer possible, but excursions between Changzhou, Wuxi, and Suzhou can be arranged through travel agents.

Yangtse cruise

If you have a lot of time on your hands, a cruise up river to the Yangtse Gorges might be worthwhile. The boats start from Shanghai, but since the landscape between there and Wuhan is rather monotonous, you may be better off flying to Wuhan or Yichang, and going from there by boat to Chonqing through the famous gorges. Going upstream of course takes longer, so the alternative is to fly to Chonqing and come downstream. The boat journey to Wuhan takes about 60 hours. From Wuhan to Chonqing is about 4 days. The ordinary boats are acceptable if you land soft class, but a bit grim otherwise; and the cooking is definitely sub-standard. Better class touring ships, with airconditioning, are now plying the waters between Wuhan and Chonqing, but they are a long way from local life. Tickets for the first type are sold at 1, Jinling Lu. For the second type, contact CITS at their information desk in the Peace Hotel.

Hangzou

Hangzhou is considered to be one of China's most beautiful scenic wonders — 'in Heaven there is Paradise; on Earth there is Suzhou and Hangzhou' is a well known Chinese epigram. Such fulsome praise is, perhaps, a little misplaced these days, but Hangzhou does remain a lovely town to visit because of its famed West Lake, a tranquil stretch of water surrounded by hills and, in the season, covered in lotus. There are many beautiful walks to be had through the luxuriant foliage at the waters' edge, and of course there are cruises across the lake and to the islands at its centre, including the famous 'Three Pools Mirroring the Moon' (Santanyinyue).

The town itself does not have the exotic charm of Suzhou but is picturesque, nevertheless, and a pleasant, peaceful place around which to amble.

There are several other places worth visiting in the vicinity:

— Silk weaving and spinning factories

— West Lake Township (Communes no longer exist, having been replaced by townships). It is here that the exclusive 'Longjing' (Dragon Well) tea is grown.

— Lingyin Temple

— Six Harmonies pagoda.

There are a number of hotels in the area around the lake, including the Shangri La Hangzhou Hotel (78 Beishan Lu. Tel: 22921. Telex: 35005/6), and the newly completed Dragon Hotel. Both of these are of international standard, and therefore comparitively expensive, but there are several others at more conventional prices.

The journey by train from Shanghai takes over three hours, and by aeroplane, about half an hour. If you are staying at the Hangzhou Hotel, arrangements can be made directly with the hotel for a transfer either from the airport or the station.

There are ten flights a week from Hangzhou to Hong Kong, and vice versa. Flight time is about two hours. The airport is about 40 minutes from the city centre.

Ningbo

Ningbo is an ancient port city about ninety miles south of Shanghai. Inhabited for at least 7000 years, the port became important as an exporter of a local type of porcelain (Yueyao Qingci) during the Tang Dynasty (618-907 A.D.), some of which reached the east coast of Africa. From the fourteenth century Ningbo was an important trader in ceramics and silk, and the Portuguese established a commercial base there from the sixteenth century. After the signing of the Treaty of Nanking, Ningbo became one of the treaty ports, but was quickly eclipsed by Shanghai. Nevertheless, many of the financial skills that Shanghai adopted for itself originally came from Ningbo (after the Cantonese compradores had their time, they were succeeded by people from Ningbo), and some of the wealthiest men in Hong Kong have their origins in this old port.

Since 1949 the port has been revitalised, and the new dock at Beilun has a wharf of 100,000 ton capacity, the largest in China. It is anticipated that Ningbo will soon be connected to the Grand

Canal, once a major dredging project has been completed.

Things to see in Ningbo are:

— Tianyi Ge Library (the oldest in China)

— Moon Lake

— Tianfeng Ta (fourteenth century pagoda and the highest structure in the city)

— Putuoshan (an island off the coast of Ningbo, a sacred Buddhist site with a variety of temples and beauty spots).

The Ningbo hotel (65 Mayuan Lu Tel:2451, 2598) is acceptable, but the Asia Garden on Mayuan Lu (Tel: 66888) sounds a better bet.

The train journey from Shanghai to Ningbo is about 8 hours but many people go by boat. The booking office in Shanghai is at 1, Jinling Lu and there are daily departures.

INDEX

accommodation 47-58
acupuncture 161-3
agriculture 157-8
air travel 21-2, 36-7, 40
airline offices 87
American Chamber of
  Commerce 196
American Club 196
American Concession 109, 165,
  168
American Consulate 90, 168,
  198
American Marine Club 187
antiques 95-6, 196
arts and crafts 96-8
Arts & Crafts Research Inst
  228
Astor House 167
Avenue du Roi Albert 209
Avenue Edward VII 201
Avenue Joffre 203-5

Bank of China 87, 173, 211
banks 87
banks, former locations of
  Bank of Communications 176
  Banque de l'Indochine 173
  Banque Franco-Chinoise 200
  Chartered Bank of India,
    Australia & China 176
  Chase Bank 194
  Commercial Bank of China
    177
  Continental Bank 194
  Credit Foncier d'extreme
    Orient 176
  German & China Bank 194
  Hong Kong & Shanghai
    Banking
    Corporation 177
  Italian Bank in China 194
  Kiukiang Road 194
  Mercantile Bank of India 173
  P & O Banking Corp 177

  Quai de France 200
  Qi Ye Bank 197
  Women's Commercial &
    Savings Bank 181
  Yokohama Specie Bank 173
  Zhong Hui Bank 226
banquets 60-1
bathhouse 195
Beijing Lu 175
bicycles 45, 102, 197
'Blood Alley' 201
books on Shanghai 34
bookshops 103, 181, 195
Botanical Gardens 225
British, Canadian and General
  Chambers of Commerce 176
British Concession 165
British Consulate 90, 171
Broadway Mansions 167
Bubbling Well Road 184-91
Bund 166-7, 169-78
business addresses 88-9

cafes and bars 84
calligraphy 97, 197
Canton Road 196
carpets 99-100
Cathay Hotel 173-5
Cathay Theatre 208
Cathedral of St. Ignatius 230
Cercle Sportif Français 112,
  208
Changzhou 236
Chiang Kai Shek 122, 138,
  168, 198, 206
Children's Palace 191
Chinese Bund 213
Chinese Customs Service
  148-52
churches and places of
  worship 89, 230
cinemas 82-3,184
circuses 79-80

climate 18-20
cloisonne 96
clothing, for visit 27-8
commerce 154
Communist Party of China
  121, 205, 206
concerts 82
concessions and settlements
  108-9, 165-6
consulates 90
cruising 88, 228, 238
Cultural Revolution 129-30
Culture Square 209
currency 39
customs and duty free 33, 42
Customs House 176

discotheques 83-4
doctors 90
drinks 65-6, 211
Du Yuesheng (Big-Eared Du)
  142, 200, 202, 211, 226
duty free goods 33, 42

electricity 28
entertainment 79-86, 113-16
entry/departure formalities
  35-42
etiquette 75-8
exhibition centres 90

Fanbang Zhong Lu 214
fans 182
finance and trade 154-5
Foochow Road 195
food
  Chinese 62-5, 72, 102
  imported 102
  not easily obtainable 33
Foreign Correspondents' Club
  of China 167
French Chamber of Commerce
  201

French Concession 109,
  198-212
French Consulate 90, 202
French Municipal Offices 202
Friendship Stores 94
Fuxing Park 205
Fuyou Lu 219
Fuzhou Lu 195

Gaolan Lu 207
Grand Canal 237
Great World 202
greyhound racing 112, 209
Guangdong Lu 196
Guilin Park 223
Guomindang 122, 127

Hahn, Emily 176
hai-alai 209
Hankou Lu 195
Hangzhou 238
Hardoon, Silas 144-5, 147, 188
Hart, Sir Robert 150-2
health care 16-18
Henan Nan Lu 197
Henan Zhong Lu 197
historical background 105-36
Holy Trinity Cathedral 194
Hongkou 168
Hongkou Park 225
Hotel des Colonies 202
Hua Lian Commercial Building
  181
Huaihai Lu 203-5, 207-12
Huang Jinrong (Pockmarked
  Huang) 142, 202
Huangpi Lu 186
Huangpu Park 169
Huangpu River 228-9

industry 153-4
International Settlement 109,
  165, 168

International Settlement Municipal Council 194

jade 101
Jade Buddha Temple 221-3
January Revolution 130-2
Japanese in Shanghai 111, 123-5, 168, 173
Japanese Chamber of Commerce 173
Jardine, Matheson & Co 173
jazz 79
Jesuits 230
Jiading 231
Jiangxi Lu 198
Jing An Park 190
Jing An Temple 189
Jinjiang Hotel 50, 208
Jinling Lu 202
Jinshan 232
Jiujiang Lu 194
Journal de Shanghai 202

Kiessing Coffee Houses 187
Kiukiang Road 194
Kung, H.H. 138, 173
Kunshan Lu 198

lacquerware 97
lanes 192-3, 195
Laozha Police Station 121, 193
leatherware 102
library 91, 186
Longhua Park, Pagoda and Temple 224
luggage 28
Lyceum Theatre 208

McBain Building 178
Maoming Nan Lu 208
maps 34, 197
markets 186, 214
Masonic Club 196

Medhurst Mansions 187
medical services 90
medicine, Chinese 102, 161-3
Messageries Maritimes 200
Metropole Hotel 196
money 28-9, 39
Moslem quarter 195
moxibustion 163-4
museums 226-8

Nanjing Dong Lu 178-82
Nanjing Xi Lu 184-91
Nanking 237
Nanking Road 178-91
National State Lottery Administration 201
New World 182
Ningbo 239
Ningpo Guild 203
North-China Daily News 176
Number One Provision Store 181

opera 80-2, 103
opium trade 106, 107
opticians 103
Overseas Chinese Hotel 182

painting 97, 197
Palace Hotel 173
Park Hotel 49, 182
parks 169, 183, 190, 205, 210, 223-6
passports 13-14
Peace Hotel 48, 80, 166, 173, 179
pens 180
People's Park 183
People's Square 184
photography 29-32, 102-3, 180
police 91
port 228-9
post offices 91, 179, 187, 198

presents 32
prices 15-16
Pudong 229
Pujiang Hotel 50, 167

Quai de France 200
Qingpu 232

race course 182-3
rail services 24, 37-8, 41, 91
reservations 15
restaurants 67-74
rice 158-60
rickshaws 116
Rue Cardinal Mercier 208
Rue du Consulat 202
Ruijin Er Lu 207
Russian community 111, 115,
  203, 209
Russian Orthodox Church 207

Sassoon family 143-8
Sassoon, Victor 145-8, 173-4
Seagull Hotel 50, 168
seals 98
Seamen's Club 167, 177
secret societies 142, 202, 203
Seventh Heaven Hotel 49, 181
Shaanxi Lu 188, 209
Shaanxi Nan Lu 209, 210
Shandong Lu 202
Shanghai Acrobatic Troupe
  186
Shanghai Antique and Curio
  Store 196
Shanghai Art Gallery 186, 187
Shanghai Arts and Handicrafts
  Store 184
Shanghai Arts Theatre 208
Shanghai Club 112, 177
Shanghai Department of Light
  Industry 197
Shanghai Industrial Exhibition
  Centre 189

Shanghai lanes 192-3, 195
Shanghai Mansions 48, 167
Shanghai Municipal
  Meteorological Dept 200
Shanghai Museum of Art and
  History 226-7
Shanghai Natural History
  Museum 228
Shanghai Race Course 182-3
Shanghai Youth Palace 202
Shanghai Zoo 226
Shanyang Park 210
sheets and blankets 182
Shimen Lu 187
shipping services 25-6, 38, 41,
  addresses 88
shipping companies, former
  locations 172, 177, 196, 198
shops and shopping 93-104
  see also name of road
Siccawei Observatory 200
Sichuan Bei Lu 168
Sichuan Lu 197
silk 98-9, 155-7
'Sincere' Company 181
Slovo 204
Songjiang 234
Soong family 137-41
Soong Ching-Ling 211-12
Soviet Consulate 90, 167
sport 84, 113, 209
stamp collecting 180
'Sun' Company 181
'Sun Sun' Company 181
Sun Yat Sen 138, 206
Suzhou 235
Suzhou Creek 169
Suzhou Lu 175
Szechuan Road 197

tailoring 99
taxis 43-4, 91
tea 210, 216
telephones 91, 179

Temple of the City God 214-16
theatres 187, 208, 209
 costumiers 180
Tianmu Travel Service 175
tipping 32, 75-6
transport, local 43-6, 91
travel agents 11-13
 local 92
Treaty of Nanking 107

Union Building 197
universities 92

vaccinations 16-17
visas 13-15

Wai Xiang Gua Jie 214
Waibadu Bridge 169, 171
watches and clocks 180
water 18
Wen Hui Bao 175
'Wing On' 181
Wusong River 169
Wuxi 236

Xikou Lu 201
Xingshang Hotel 196

Yanan Dong Lu 201
Yanan Lu 197
Yangtse cruise 238
Yates Road 187
Yu Garden 214, 216-19
Yu Yuan Road 215
Yuan Ming Yuan Lu 175

Zaria 204
Zhabei 168
Zhejiang Lu 195
Zhongshan Dong Er Lu 200
Zhongshang Dong Lu 167
Zhongshan Park 225

Zhou En Lai 206
Ziccawei Catholic Cathedral
 230
zoo 226

KEY

1. Former residence of
   Sun Yat Tsen
2. Former residence of
   Zhou En Lai
3. Former residence of
   Soong Ching Ling
4. Site of First National Congress
   of the Communist Party

5. Shanghai Mansions
6. Shanghai Museum
7. No. 1 Department Store
8. Jade Buddha Temple
9. Jing'an Temple
10. Jingjiang Hotel
11. Park Hotel
12. Peace Hotel